Soul Food

JOYCE WHITE

SOUL FOOD

RECIPES AND REFLECTIONS FROM AFRICAN-AMERICAN CHURCHES

HarperCollins*Publishers*

Photograph credits appear on page 341.

SOUL FOOD: RECIPES AND REFLECTIONS FROM AFRICAN-AMERICAN CHURCHES.
Copyright © 1998 by Joyce White. All rights reserved. Printed in the United States of
America. No part of this book may be used or reproduced in any manner whatsoever
without written permission, except in the case of brief quotations embodied in
critical articles and reviews. For information address HarperCollins Publishers, Inc.,
10 East 53rd Street, New York, NY 10022.

HarperCollins books may be purchased for educational, business, or sales promotional
use. For information please write: Special Markets Department, HarperCollins Publishers,
Inc., 10 East 53rd Street, New York, NY 10022.

FIRST EDITION

Designed by Stephanie Tevonian

Library of Congress Cataloging-in-Publication Data

White, Joyce, 1942–
    Soul food : recipes and reflections from African-American churches
    by Joyce White. —1st ed.
       p. cm.
    Includes index.
    ISBN 0-06-018716-6
    1. Afro-American Cookery.   I. Title.
  TX715.W587   1998
  641.59'296073—dc21   97-22454

05 06 07 08 ❖/RRD 20 19 18 17 16 15 14 13 12

To the loving memory of Arthur "Bill" Hayes

CONTENTS

ACKNOWLEDGMENTS

When I started this book more than two years ago I called the Reverend W. Franklyn Richardson, pastor of the Grace Baptist Church in Mount Vernon, New York, who, upon hearing my plans, exclaimed, "Just let me know how I can help you."

That was the kind of proclamation I heard time after time as I went about collecting the recipes and stories for this book. And the help came from so many different people that I almost hesitate signaling out a few, with thoughts of inadvertently omitting others.

But protocol says that I must, and I head the list with special thanks to my brother, John, and my sister, Helen, who not only helped me recount family history, but shared with me their vast knowledge of Southern cooking, often taking time out of their busy lives to do so.

My longtime friend Ann Pratt Hairston, and my neighbor Ashton Spann, passed word about the book to numerous friends and relatives. And so did Angela Dodson, Velma Mosley, Lillie Sherfield, Dr. Rubye Taylor-Drake, Judith Price, the Reverend Sharon Keeling, Karen Hess, Dr. Arlene Churn, Terrie Williams, and Dawn Jackson.

Irene Thomas admonished me to call her at any time if I had questions about how a certain recipe should be prepared. Julius "Jay" Manigault, a native of Moncks Corner, South Carolina, rolled up his sleeves and cooked gumbo with me. My homegirl, Barbara Linder, not only read my manuscript, but also tested recipes. Jim Huffman at the Schomburg Center for Research in Black Culture in Harlem rewarded my persistence with patience and understanding. Roy, my beloved son, kept on being Roy. To all of you, my sincere thanks.

I thank the dynamic people who made this book possible from day one, as the expression goes: my literary agent, Barbara Lowenstein, and her able associate, Madeleine Morel.

I also thank my editor at HarperCollins, Susan Friedland, who during many toe-to-toe sessions never lost her fine touch. And last, but certainly not least, I thank Sharon Bowers, an associate editor at HarperCollins, who is the best diplomat I know.

And of course I thank again the wonderful contributors to this book, without whose words and presence it would have remained a dream deferred.

Love and Peace.
Joyce White

FOREWORD

As I leaf through this book I can't quite decide which is most captivating, the wonderful stories that the author has told, or the fine recipes she's collected.

That's because Joyce White has so capably captured two of our most sustaining forces, stories of our faith and food, and in doing so, her book resounds with the spirit and creativity of African-Americans, and most significantly, with the enduring force of our church.

African-American food is serious food; and like gospel, this book spreads the news. Finally! We have here a book that celebrates our tradition of cooking and eating and rejoicing at church, and I can only say that the endeavor is long overdue.

Joyce White is a master storyteller, a sophisticated traveler and culinary expert who knows how to describe a recipe in exacting detail. The recipes she's collected are prepared the way our mothers and grandmothers used to cook: with the freshest ingredients possible and no modern-day shortcuts. The stories, as well, are heartwarming and heartfelt.

I commend this book, with the full confidence that it sheds another light on our most enduring institution—the Church—most importantly, the African-American church.

—Reverend Andraé Crouch, Pastor,
Christ Memorial Church, Los Angeles, California

INTRODUCTION

The food vendor was seated on a street corner in the city of Rio de Janeiro in Brazil, and right at her feet were two cast-iron pots, one brimming with black beans and pork and the other filled with rice. To her left was a large white enamel pan with a red rim that held delicious fritters, dried shrimp, hot pepper sauce, and a bowl of greens that looked just like my mother's collards. I thought of home.

For as long as I could remember, Mama would use two or three enamel dishes to carry food to Shiloh Baptist Church on the Sunday when our week-long revival got underway. As I stood on that street corner far away from home, in my mind I could see her carefully placing a sweet potato pie into the blue-and-white speckled dish. She would then cut in half the caramel cake she had baked, wrap the pieces in wax paper, and place the cake around the pie. She would always find space for a dozen or so plump tea cakes, and she would nestle the cakelike biscuits in the pan, too. When the pan was full, she would spread out a colorful cloth that she had trimmed with rickrack bought at the dime store, set the pan in the middle of the fabric, gather up the ends, and tie a knot for a handle.

Mama's white-and-red pan, the one just like the dish the sister in Brazil was using to transport her food, was packed with fried chicken, a bowl of greens, a pan of crowder peas, wedges of cornbread, and perhaps a bowl of potato salad. With our church "dinner" in hand, we would begin our day, happy for the occasion.

Our church revival was always held on the first Sunday in July, and it was a time of spiritual renewal, family reunions, and fellowship for the community. The celebration would begin on Sunday, and church service was held every night during the week, ending with a rousing closing sermon on Friday night. The nightly service was conducted by guest preachers, and worshippers would come from far and near to hear their favorite ministers. Each church in the county had a specific Sunday for its revival, and many of the people who had left our county years before would mark their return home by the revival at such and such church. The revivals, which some churches called homecomings, were always held during the summer, and the gatherings added a dash of excitement to our hot, hot days.

In some years, the sisters would hold a fish fry the Saturday evening before the Sunday service, and we would venture to the church, eager to see who had returned home sporting new clothes, fancy hairdos, and long stories about faraway urban places. Even though we knew that glamour often hides disappointment and unfulfilled expectations, we tried our best not to let our feelings show, for we were happy to revel in their city lives.

The big day though was Sunday, and all the families in the Negro community who were active in the church would prepare an array of dishes for the afternoon dinner. And since food was in many ways the women's métier, the womenfolk would vie to outdo one another. During the week I would hear my mother say out loud, "I wonder what Daisy is going to fix for Sunday?"

As we crowded into the old white-frame church, which often resounded with the songs and music of a visiting choir from another congregation, our solemnity would rise to joyfulness. After a spirited sermon by a guest preacher, we would file out the church and linger about, talking as the men set up tables and stands in the yard, while the women removed their food from the anterooms. Friends, families, and visitors from far and near would gather about, and we would all share the results of our labor.

Plate in hand, bypassing a bounty of other dishes, I would veer to Mrs. Daisy's garden-fresh turnip greens. The skin on Mrs. Mary Earl's buttermilk-fried chicken was as crisp as crackling, and she always saved a couple of wings for me, for these were my favorite part. Then I would dip into my mother's succulent potato salad, which she spiced up with diced apples and pickles.

I would find a cool spot in the shade and wait for the rainbow of desserts that were served later in the day. There were always peach cobbler, blackberry pie, banana pudding, chocolate cake, pound cake, and sometimes even homemade ice cream, if my sister, Helen, felt like tackling the task.

We would pass the afternoon in the comfort and security of this soul-satisfying place: the church. Just for the day the harsh reality of our Jim Crow world was light-years away.

Years later I realized that those summer revivals and homecomings at various black churches in Choctaw County, Alabama, had kindled my passion for food. By that time I had moved to New York City, where in the late 1960s I landed a job as a food editor at a women's magazine. But often on the weekend I would find myself at a church in Harlem or Bedford-Stuyvesant, sometimes for a concert or a play, other times for service, and at other times simply to enjoy the food and the company. Food was always an integral part of these gatherings, and it was always cooked with thought and care—the two most important ingredients for a successful recipe. I felt at home.

When I started this cookbook I wanted to capture the wonderful food and experiences that not only shaped my childhood, but that still remain a vital part of African-American life today. Our culinary history in this country is profound and influential: Our forebears worked this nation's great kitchens, from the White House to the plantations of the South, and after slavery they cooked in the robber barons' dining cars as the Pullmans made their way across the country. And out of the abomination of slavery came the country's most unique and distinctive cuisine, and we were the masters.

We have always cooked: at our own homes, at other peoples' homes, at work, and most significantly, at church. Today there is a kitchen and fellowship hall or dining area at almost every black church in the nation, of every denomination. Food is a part of the spiritual life at black churches; those churchyard feasts of yesteryear have simply moved indoors. Not long ago, almost one hundred church members of the Hartford Memorial Baptist Church in Detroit ventured into the church's kitchen and cooked a New Year's dinner for seven hundred guests!

Canaan Baptist Church in Harlem has a dining room that seats three hundred, a busy catering service, and an executive chef, Deaconess Ernestine Bradley, who enthusiastically shared many of her recipes with me.

In fact, all of the recipes in this book came from church people. They came from those unsung women—and men, too—who work long and unpaid hours on church kitchen committees, cooking with their hearts and souls. They came from church sisters who—like my mother, during anniversary celebrations, homecomings, and revivals—carry their best culinary creations to the gatherings. They came from those legions of busy black women and men who after a long work week pitch in and help prepare meals at the church for the homeless and needy; from families who depend on the church as their primary social network; and from pastors who cook (yes, some of them do!). And I thank every one of you for your time, patience, spirit, and generosity.

The recipes are varied and imaginative, and they reflect a much wider world than the one we lived in years ago. Today we add mushrooms to Grandma's smothered chicken and proclaim the dish fancy. One day we cook peas and rice or rice and beans and call it West Indian, and the next time we call it Hoppin' John, a dish that originated during slavery in the kitchens of the Carolinas and Georgia.

When company comes we fix gumbo or jambalaya or West African Jollof. Or we maybe stir up a pot of beans and rice and pork with chopped collard greens on the side, like our Brazilian soul sisters and brothers, and enjoy feijoada, their homeland's national dish. And when we cook at church we take all these inventive recipes with us, and they all reflect the culinary genius of the people of the African diaspora.

We are also keeping our eye on the prize; we are not living in a time capsule. Many people who contributed recipes expressed health concerns. So my challenge in testing and modifying the recipes was to preserve our rich and savory cooking methods, but to do so with nutrition and good health in mind.

And oh the stories! Sisters and brothers who shared their food style

and expertise with me also shared stories that explained in part why the church remains such a vital part of our lives. The people profiled in this book are doers; their dedication, faith, and commitment reflect why the church has long championed our civil rights struggle, our educational opportunities, our future.

One poignant thought came from Elnora Dean, a retired registered nurse who is director of hospitality at the all-black Westminster Presbyterian Church in Los Angeles, where she and her husband, Owen, a retired engineer, have been active for years. Recently she told me that a fellowship hour is held every Sunday after service at the church, and food is always served.

"We don't just come to church service and leave," she said. "Many of us stay here half the day. That way we get a chance to rub shoulders and see what is going on or going wrong with each other."

This cookbook is a compendium of more than 150 recipes as well as numerous stories and reflections. It brings our most important institution, the African-American church, to your kitchen, dining table, reading space, your life.

OUR DAILY BREAD

Years ago in the South no food defined our daily routine as much as cornbread. In my family we ate biscuits mostly on Saturday and Sunday mornings before church, when Mama had time to mix and knead and pat the dough into perfect rounds before popping the pan into our old cast-iron stove. The batter for flapjacks was stirred together for

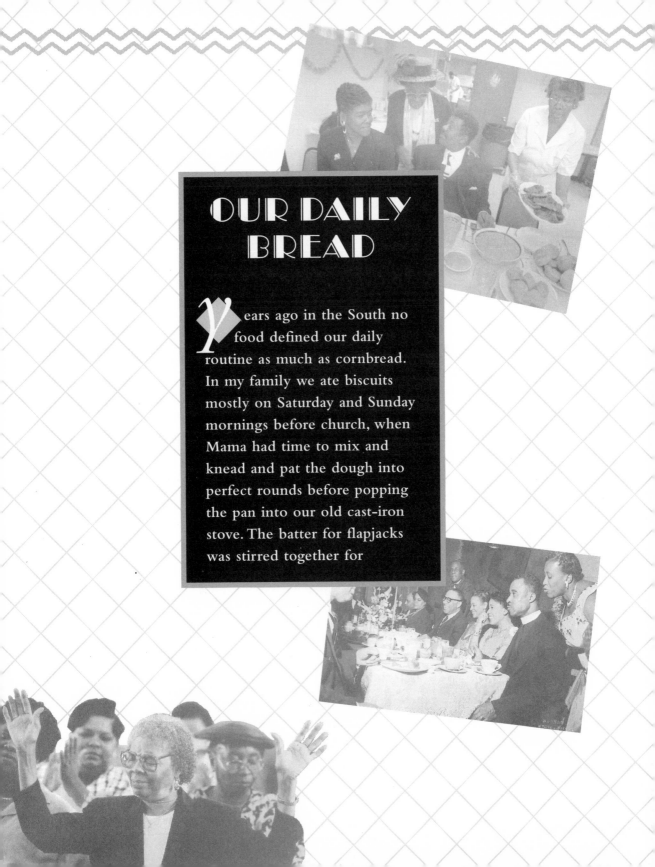

breakfast on most weekday mornings and grilled quickly in a heavy skillet. When we yearned for something a little sweeter, Mama would bake a pan of molasses or apple bread for evening supper. On special occasions my sister, Helen, would make yeast rolls, and to my young eyes the rising, kneading, and lusty aroma of this bread was almost magical.

Cornbread, though, was our "staff of life," for the batter could be quickly stirred up and the effort was minimal considering the reward: fragrant, grainy, moist bread that provided a filling meal in itself when eaten with a baked sweet potato and a glass of cold buttermilk. We baked and ate cornbread every day.

Although this bread was simple and easy to make, different families had their own way with cornbread. I can remember Helen at a church revival passing somebody with a plate full of food and mumbling, "That must be Snook's bread."

Some of the women added a little sugar to the batter, while others dismissed even a hint of sweetness as Northern and Yankee. Others used only white cornmeal, but Mama never, ever, baked a pan of cornbread from anything but yellow cornmeal.

Some families preferred thick cornbread, but I liked the thin, crunchy layer of cornbread that Aunt Agnes baked in a cast-iron skillet. Besides that, there was the matter of whether buttermilk, canned evaporated milk, or "sweet milk"—as whole milk was called—baked into the best bread. In addition, a half cup or so of white flour was always combined with the cornmeal for a pan of bread, but whether the best bread was baked with self-rising, cake, or all-purpose flour was also a matter of contention. (See "Flour Types" on page 15.)

Our love of cornbread goes way back. Food historian Charles Ritzberg, who is an expert on the food of Africa, says that when the local Native Americans greeted the Europeans and their slaves they offered a mashed corn seasoned with fat that was similar to the rice porridge and the pounded-yam dishes the slaves had eaten back home. Africans had long produced flour, mush, porridge, and dumplings from a variety of grains and roots, including millet and barley, and from tubers such as yams and cassava. So in a matter of time the newly enslaved Africans were using the same ingenuity with corn, producing both grits and the meal for a corn cake that evolved over the years into cornbread.

These memories flashed through my mind when a recipe for old-fashioned cornbread arrived from Esther Mae Archie, who now lives in Chicago but was born and raised in Port Gibson, Mississippi, which is near Natchez in the southwestern corner of the state. Mrs. Archie remembers that when she was growing up she milked the cows, churned the milk, and skimmed the butter, which was used to make the homemade bread her family ate daily. Work was hard in those days, and she remembers that the day started early with a sustaining breakfast that usually

Metropolitan Missionary Baptist Church, Chicago, Christmas holiday dinner, following a recital of "The Messiah."

Our Daily Bread

consisted of grits, sausages or ham, eggs, and buttermilk biscuits or flapjacks, which she began helping to prepare at an early age, since this was the simplest meal to learn to cook. Cornbread, corn muffins, or corn sticks were always baked for dinner, which was the midday meal.

Until a few years ago when she moved ten miles away to Broadview, Mrs. Archie and her late husband and five sons—now all grown—lived right down the block from the Metropolitan Missionary Baptist Church, a beautiful brick structure located on Chicago's West Washington Boulevard, which was built in the early 1900s according to the design theories of the world-famous Chicago School of Architects. For more than twenty-five years she has been a member of Metropolitan's Street Witness Team, an outreach ministry initiated by the Reverend Craig Melvin Smith, church pastor.

She also cooks all the time. And since she is quixotic and quirky, she often scurries about in her kitchen at 3 A.M. chopping nuts and fruits, rising breads and stirring batter, oblivious to the cover of darkness and the stony quietness outside. By 7 A.M. she is out on the streets, passing out her baked goods at prayer breakfasts, funeral repasts, and feeding programs for the homeless. Whenever she feels like it, in midafternoon she takes to the mean streets of Chicago again, and continues her work on behalf of her church and community.

"I was ordained by the Holy Spirit to do street witness," Mrs. Archie says forcefully. "You got to move beyond the sanctuary and go out into the wilderness and spread His word."

Mrs. Archie sends this recipe for basic cornbread, which she says, "is guided by the spirit." Sometimes she adds creamed corn to the batter; at other times she stirs in black pepper and hot pepper sauce:

Old=Fashioned Cornbread

Serves 4

2 cups yellow cornmeal
½ cup all-purpose flour
¼ teaspoon salt
2½ teaspoons baking powder

1 tablespoon sugar
1 large egg
¼ cup vegetable oil or shortening
1 to 1¼ cup milk

Preheat the oven to 425 degrees.

Oil a 9-inch square or round pan; place to warm in the oven for at least 5 minutes.

In the meantime, sift into a medium bowl the cornmeal, flour, salt, baking powder, and sugar. Add the egg, vegetable oil or shortening, and milk and beat vigorously for 30 seconds.

Carefully remove the hot pan from the oven. Pour in the cornmeal batter and shake the pan to level the batter. Set the pan in the oven on the lower shelf. Bake the bread about 25 minutes or until golden brown and puffy and a knife comes out clean when inserted into the center.

Remove the pan from the oven and let the cornbread rest for a few minutes before cutting into wedges. Serve hot.

Variation: Mrs. Archie uses this same batter for corn muffins. Preheat the oven to 425 degrees. Generously oil the muffin tin and warm in the oven for 5 minutes. Fill each muffin cup about ¾ full with batter. Pour water into any remaining empty cups so that they don't burn during the baking. Bake the muffins for about 20 minutes, or until they are golden brown and puffed.

Note: A cup of fresh fruit, such as blueberries, strawberries, or cranberries, can be tossed with ⅓ cup sugar and stirred into the batter for very special berry muffins.

PINEAPPLE CORNBREAD

Serves 4 to 6

rs. Archie sends this recipe for a fragrant pan of cornbread made with crushed pineapple, along with this cogent remark:

"I don't understand why women today think it is too much trouble to make up a batch of corn muffins or a pan of bread," she says wistfully. "Don't they know that good homecooked food is better for you than that mess they buy at those fast-food joints. Sometimes I get in here and cook a hundred muffins before daybreak. Sometime I even lose count."

This is Mrs. Archie's recipe:

1½ cups cornmeal
½ cup all-purpose flour
2 teaspoons baking powder
¼ teaspoon salt
1 large egg, lightly beaten

¼ to ⅓ cup sugar
¼ cup vegetable oil
½ cup milk
½ cup crushed pineapple, lightly
  drained

Preheat the oven to 425 degrees. Generously oil a 9-inch baking dish. Set the pan in the oven to warm for 5 minutes.

In a large bowl sift the cornmeal, flour, baking powder, and salt. Add the egg, sugar, vegetable oil, and milk. Beat vigorously for 30 seconds. Stir in the crushed pineapple and mix well.

Carefully remove the pan from the oven. Pour the batter into the pan and shake the pan to level the batter. Set the pan on the lower shelf in the hot oven. Bake for 20 to 25 minutes or until golden and puffed and a knife inserted in the center comes out clean.

Remove the pan from the oven. Let the bread rest for a few moments in a warm place. And then cut into wedges and serve warm.

Variation: Add ½ teaspoon ground nutmeg or mace to the batter.

Breads fall into two categories, depending on how they are made: either quick or yeast. Quick breads include biscuits; muffins; cornbread; waffles and pancakes; fritters; most fruit, vegetable, and nut loaves; and are so called because they are raised or leavened with baking powder or baking soda, sometimes with both. Quick breads require little or no kneading and can be stirred together in a matter of minutes.

Breads risen with yeast must be kneaded and allowed to rise, and therefore are more time-consuming than quick breads. Yeast is a living fungus that feeds on sugar in the dough and causes it to rise and expand. It also gives breads a unique flavor, chewy texture, and an incomparable aroma that make the time involved well worth the effort.

RED PEPPER CORNBREAD

Serves 4

Mary Cunningham lives in Choctaw County in Alabama, and she is a superb seamstress, a creative cook, and the mother of two grown daughters. She is also a loving woman and an active member of the C. J. Holiness Church, where during revivals and church functions she always arrives with a basket full of good food and memories.

She adds crushed red pepper to her cornbread, which gives it a piquant "bite" that perhaps reflects our love of hot, spicy food—an African tradition. Mary sends this message with her recipe:

"My mother, Mary Lee Whigham, taught me how to make Red Pepper Cornbread when I was ten years old. She was the mother of twelve children and a fine cook. When I make it today I think of her. My family loves this bread served with a good hearty Southern vegetable soup."

1½ cups yellow cornmeal
½ cup all-purpose flour
¼ teaspoon salt
½ teaspoon baking soda
2 teaspoons baking powder
½ to 1 teaspoon hot pepper flakes
¼ cup vegetable oil or bacon drippings
1 egg
1 cup buttermilk

Preheat the oven to 425 degrees.

Oil a 9 × 2-inch square or round baking pan with vegetable oil or shortening, or you can use a cast-iron skillet, which renders a crisper crust. Set the pan into the oven to warm for at least 5 minutes.

In the meantime, sift into a medium bowl the cornmeal, flour, salt, baking soda, and baking powder. Stir in the red pepper flakes and the vegetable oil or bacon drippings, mixing until well blended. Add the egg and buttermilk and beat vigorously with a wooden spoon for 30 seconds.

Carefully remove the hot pan from the oven. Pour the batter into the pan and shake gently to level. Place the pan on the lower shelf in the hot oven and bake the cornbread for 20 to 25 minutes or until golden brown and a knife inserted in center comes out clean.

Remove the pan from the oven and let the bread rest in the pan for a few minutes to settle; then cut into squares or wedges for serving.

FLOUR TYPES
(AND CORNMEAL, TOO)

Flour made from wheat is the best for baking because this grain contains a protein called gluten that causes the batter to expand when it is moistened or kneaded. However, bread can also be made from nonwheat flours such as rye, soy, rice, potato, buckwheat, and cornmeal, but the dough rises better and has a far superior texture when a small amount of wheat flour is added to a batter.

There are several types of wheat flour on the market, and they all have their place in a well-stocked kitchen pantry:

All-Purpose Flour is a white flour that is finely milled, bleached, and enriched with vitamins and minerals. It can be made from hard wheat, which has a lot of gluten, or from soft wheat, which has a lower gluten content, but usually it is a mixture of the two types of wheat. All-purpose flour is suitable for all baking, including breads, waffles, fritters, pastries, and cakes.

Unbleached All-Purpose Flour has risen in popularity over the past dozen years, and it is preferred by many bakers because it has a higher gluten content than bleached white flour, and therefore results in breads with a firmer texture. Although unbleached all-purpose flour can be used in recipes specifying all-purpose flour, it does absorb more moisture, and generally you have to increase the amount of water or milk called for in the recipe.

Cake Flour is used to make finely textured, crumbly, delicate cakes, and is made from soft wheats that are low in gluten. It is not suitable for yeast breads or pie crusts.

Self-Rising Flour is popular in the South, where baking is still a way of life for many home cooks. Basically it is either cake or all-purpose flour with added baking powder and salt. I prefer adding leavening as needed in a recipe and therefore never use self-rising flour.

Whole Wheat Flour, like unbleached flour, has grown in popularity over the past decade. The flour can be either coarsely or finely milled, but most significantly, it contains all the vitamins and minerals of the original wheat. Breads made only with whole wheat flour are heavy and dense. A couple of cups of all-purpose flour added to the dough bakes into a bread with a far better texture and taste.

Cornmeal is ground from corn and it varies in degrees of fineness, depending on milling methods. Some varieties are coarse and heavy in texture, while others are almost as finely ground as flour. And although it contains no gluten, cornmeal is as dearly beloved by African-Americans when baked into bread as bread made from wheat flour.

There is both a yellow and white cornmeal, and I have heard cornbread lovers express a strong preference for one or the other. I will join the fray and confess that I find no difference in the taste and texture of white and yellow cornbread made by the exact same recipe.

Basic Cornbread Dressing

Serves 6

mattie Hodges is just as soon to bake a turkey in July as at Thanksgiving. And she is just as quick to make the trimmings that go with the turkey.

Mrs. Hodges cooks with Martha Hemmans and a half dozen other fine cooks at the famed Ebenezer Baptist Church in Atlanta, located on Auburn Avenue, where visitors from around the world come to worship. This was the family church of the late Reverend Dr. Martin Luther King Jr.

Mrs. Hodges says that roast turkey is such a dollar stretcher that they often serve it to the church's numerous guests, paying no attention to the calendar.

She sends this recipe for old-fashioned cornbread dressing that she makes with homemade chicken stock, just like her mother used to do:

1 pan (9-inch) cornbread (see recipe on page 11)
1 onion
2 celery stalks
1 or 2 fresh sage leaves, or ½ teaspoon dried sage
3 tablespoons vegetable oil or bacon drippings
2 cups chicken broth or Homemade Chicken Stock (see recipe on page 234)
1 egg, well beaten
¼ teaspoon salt
½ teaspoon black pepper

Prepare the cornbread, let cool, crumble coarsely, and place in a large bowl. Set aside. Grease a 2-quart baking dish and set aside.

Preheat the oven to 350 degrees.

Finely chop the onion and celery. Chop the fresh sage or crush the dried herb.

Heat the oil or bacon drippings in a medium skillet. Stir in the onion, celery, and sage. Sauté over medium heat 4 or 5 minutes, stirring occasionally.

Remove from heat and mix with the cornbread. Stir in the chicken broth or stock, egg, salt, and black pepper. Using a fork, toss the mixture lightly until well blended.

Spoon the dressing into the prepared pan, spreading evenly with a metal spatula.

Place the pan on the middle shelf of the hot oven and bake for 30 to 35 minutes or until the stuffing is golden brown and the liquid is completely absorbed.

Serve with Perfect Roast Turkey (see recipe on page 257).

SAVING BREAD

All types of bread—muffins, cornbread, yeast bread, as well as fruit, vegetable, and nut breads—freeze very successfully and will keep several months if well wrapped. To freeze, cool the bread completely, wrap in plastic, and then wrap in foil and seal with tape. To keep track of what's what, label and date the package.

If the bread is to be eaten in a day or two, cool completely, place in a plastic bag, and close the bag with a wire twist. Or wrap the bread in foil. In any case, store the bread in a cool place or in the refrigerator. Reheat in a warm oven before serving.

SIZING UP: SPOON BY SPOON

Use this chart for measuring dry ingredients:

1 tablespoon = 3 teaspoons

4 tablespoons = 1/4 cup

5 1/3 tablespoons = 1/3 cup

8 tablespoons = 1/2 cup

10 2/3 tablespoons = 2/3 cup

12 tablespoons = 3/4 cup

16 tablespoons = 1 cup

BEST BISCUITS EVER

Over the years at homes and at church gatherings across the country, particularly in the South, I have eaten herb biscuits, biscuits made with molasses and sweet potatoes, biscuits with bacon bits, biscuits filled with bits of ham and sausage, jelly biscuits, as well as puffy and flaky Angel Biscuits, which are made with both baking powder and yeast. Mama, especially whenever she was having church company, used to stir a little finely minced onion into the batter and then scatter the top with several pinches of grated sharp Cheddar cheese.

Here are several variations:

BUTTERMILK BISCUITS

Makes 10 to 12 biscuits

Celestine Williams, a retired schoolteacher and octogenarian, is still hailed as the best cook at Mount Zion First Baptist Church in Baton Rouge, Louisiana. She writes:

"No matter how many of these biscuits I baked, the folks just couldn't seem to get enough of them. I don't know if it were my biscuits or they were just tired and hungry and fed up."

Mrs. Williams, at age eighty-eight, has been a member of Mount Zion First Baptist Church, which is located on Spain Street, since 1933, and she was referring to the tumultuous 1950s when the Reverend

Canaan Baptist Church, Harlem, New York, Black History Month celebration during gospel brunch. Celebrants help themselves at food-laden tables.

T. J. Jemison, church pastor, launched the country's first successful boycott

Our Daily Bread

by African-Americans against the local segregated city bus lines.

She was a fifth-grade teacher at the Clinton Elementary School at that time, and she remembers that on many evenings after walking and demonstrating all day, the boycott organizers would gather at her home for a hot meal. And I am positive that they devoured her biscuits because they are so flaky, crusty, and delicious.

Mrs. Williams's recipe:

2 cups all-purpose flour	*1 teaspoon sugar*
½ teaspoon salt	*3 tablespoons vegetable shortening*
½ teaspoon baking soda	*3 tablespoons butter, softened*
2 teaspoons baking powder	*¾ cup buttermilk milk*

Preheat the oven to 425 degrees.

Sift the flour, salt, baking soda, baking powder, and sugar into a large bowl. Add the shortening and butter. Using a pastry cutter or two knives, cut in the shortening and butter until the mixture resembles coarse cornmeal.

Add the milk and stir the batter lightly with a fork. Turn the dough onto a floured board or pastry cloth. (Mrs. Williams uses a large brown-paper bag.) Sprinkle a little more flour on the dough if it is sticky. Knead lightly 4 or 5 times. (See "Kneading Dough" on page 50.)

Roll out or pat the dough into an 8-inch circle, about ½-inch thick. Using a 2-inch biscuit or cookie cutter or glass rim dipped in flour, cut the dough into rounds. Gently reroll scraps and cut again into rounds.

Place the biscuits on a lightly greased baking sheet, allowing a little space between each. Place on the lower shelf of the hot oven and bake for 12 to 15 minutes or until golden brown.

Remove from the oven and serve hot.

SWEET POTATO BISCUITS

Makes 10 to 12 biscuits

*m*arlyn Banks remembers that years ago when the annual Homecoming Day was held in November at the Newman Memorial United Methodist Church in Brooklyn, her grandmother usually baked Sweet Potato Biscuits for the gathering, using a recipe that had been in the family for years.

Her grandparents had joined the church in the early 1930s, shortly after they moved from Atlantic City, New Jersey, to Bedford-Stuyvesant in Brooklyn. Today Marlyn lives in Long Island, in the town of Hempstead, but Newman Memorial, located on Macon Street in Brooklyn, is still her homechurch.

"Newman Memorial was my grandparents' lifeblood," says Marlyn. "That's the reason I make the trip and still go there."

Marlyn's recipe:

2 cups all-purpose flour
1 tablespoon baking powder
½ teaspoon salt

⅓ cup vegetable shortening
1 cup mashed sweet potato
¼ cup milk, or more if needed

Preheat the oven to 425 degrees.

Sift the flour onto a square of wax paper or onto a plate and then sift again with the baking powder and salt into a medium bowl.

Add the vegetable shortening, and using a pastry cutter or two knives, cut in the shortening until it resembles coarse cornmeal. Stir in the mashed sweet potato and milk, mixing lightly with a fork.

Spread flour on a pastry cloth or board. Sprinkle a little more flour on the dough if it is sticky. Turn out the dough onto the floured surface and knead quickly and lightly, 6 or 7 times. (See "Kneading Dough" on page 50.)

Using a floured 2-inch cookie cutter, cut dough into biscuit shapes. Place on an ungreased cookie sheet and set on the lower shelf of the hot oven. Bake 12 to 15 minutes or until the biscuits are lightly brown and puffed. Remove from the oven and serve hot.

SUGAR=CRUSTED BISCUITS

Makes 10 to 12 biscuits

We used to joke in my family that Aunt Mary was a sunshine Christian, which meant that she only went to church when the weather was absolutely splendid, and therefore couldn't use the cold or rain as an excuse to stay home. Aunt Mary lived on the Gulf Coast near Biloxi, Mississippi, and whenever she felt like it, she attended the Mercy Seat Baptist Church. The preachers though, enjoyed coming to her house for dinner, because not only was Aunt Mary a superb cook, she was a restless character and free spirit whose soul they were always trying to save.

I used to visit her during summer vacations from school, and often heard her neighbors say (and sometimes out of spite) that she "cooked fancy and talked proper." And sure enough, in the hours before the preacher came to dinner, Aunt Mary would begin to purse her lips and exaggerate the pronunciation of words, as though she was waiting for a theater curtain call.

She would sprinkle a little cinnamon, or grated orange or lemon rind, on the biscuits, and stick the pan into the oven. In a few minutes the kitchen would be perfumed by a toasty aroma that lingered until late into the Sunday afternoon.

Aunt Mary's recipe:

2 cups unbleached all-purpose flour	3 tablespoons butter
1 tablespoon baking powder	1 cup milk
½ teaspoon salt	1 egg white, well beaten
1 teaspoon sugar	1 tablespoon sugar
3 tablespoons vegetable shortening	¼ to ½ teaspoon ground cinnamon

Preheat the oven to 425 degrees.

Sift the flour, baking powder, salt, and sugar into a large bowl. Add the shortening and butter. Using a pastry cutter or two knives, cut in the vegetable shortening and butter until the mixture resembles coarse cornmeal.

Add the milk and stir the batter lightly with a fork. Turn the dough onto a well-floured board or pastry cloth. Add a little more flour if the dough is sticky. Knead lightly 4 or 5 times. (See "Kneading Dough" on page 50.)

Roll out or pat the dough into an 8-inch circle, about ½-inch thick. Using a 2-inch biscuit or cookie cutter or glass rim dipped in flour, cut the dough into rounds.

Gently reroll scraps and cut again into rounds. Place the biscuits on a lightly greased baking sheet, allowing a little space between each biscuit.

Brush the tops of the biscuits with a little of the beaten egg white. Mix together the sugar and cinnamon and sprinkle on the biscuit tops. Set on the lower shelf of the hot oven and bake for 12 to 15 minutes or until golden brown.

Remove from the oven and serve hot.

"Men's Day Dinner" at Emanuel African Methodist Episcopal Church, Harlem, circa 1952, with guests Bishop D. Ward Nichols (seated, fifth from left) and Rev. M. A. Hughes (seated, first from left).

Our Daily Bread

Cheese Straws

Makes about 4 dozen; serves 6 to 8

ometime during the throes of the late 1960s or early '70s during a visit to my hometown in Choctaw County, Alabama, either Aunt Agnes or Mama passed on to me an old bread board that must have been in the family for the past sixty or so years. I believe that the board had originally belonged to my grandmother, Addie, who was Aunt Agnes' sister, and since this was such a tumultuous time in our family–and in the lives of many other African-Americans—I think they wanted to make sure that I moved on to the future with a relic from the past. Political opinions in my family ranged from conservative to anarchistic.

The bread board passed on to me is made of wood and has sloping sides like a trough and a smooth patina from much use. Mama used it to mix biscuits and pie crusts and other breads and pastries, especially if company was coming.

When I look at the board today so many memories and scenes run through my mind, but none more vivid than those associated with Reverend Barlow's visit to our house for Sunday dinner.

I grew up in a large family and our food was fresh, mostly garden-grown, well-seasoned and basic. But Mama was extremely house proud, and she always wanted the Reverend Barlow to have something to nibble on while she hurried about pulling the Sunday dinner together.

Early that morning she would cut off a wedge of cheese from a chunk she kept in the kitchen, grate it, and weave together cheese, butter, and flour in the bread board. She would then roll out the golden-tinged dough, cut into strips, and then dust with paprika or cayenne or sesame seeds.

In a matter of moments the kitchen would be perfumed with a delightful aroma. I always purloined a couple of the cheese straws, glad that it was our turn to feed the preacher for dinner. This was Mama's recipe:

8 tablespoons (1 stick) butter or
   margarine, softened
3 cups finely grated extra sharp
   Cheddar cheese
2 cups all-purpose flour

¼ teaspoon salt
½ cup cold milk or light cream
1 egg white, lightly beaten
Paprika
Sesame seeds

Combine in a large bowl the butter or margarine and the cheese. Using fingertips, blend the cheese and shortening together until well mixed.

Sift into the bowl the flour and salt, and still using your fingers, blend in the flour with the cheese and shortening until the mixture resembles tiny peas or very coarse cornmeal.

Sprinkle over the cold milk or cream a tablespoon at a time, using a fork to lift up the dough so all portions can be moistened.

Quickly form the dough into a ball, squeezing firmly to make it hold a shape.

Wrap the dough in plastic wrap or wax paper or aluminum foil and chill for 15 minutes.

Preheat the oven to 400 degrees.

Scatter the work surface lightly with flour. Divide the dough in half.

Roll out one half of the dough into a 10 × 10-inch square. Using a sharp knife, cut the dough into strips about 5 inches long and ½ inch wide.

Twist the strips, like a candy stick, and pinch each end. Brush the tops with a little of the beaten egg white. Sprinkle generously with paprika or sesame seeds.

Roll out the remaining half of dough and cut and shape in the same way.

Place the cheese straws on a large ungreased baking dish. (You may have to bake two batches.)

Set the pan on the lower shelf of the hot oven and bake for 8 to 10 minutes or until golden brown and crisp, turning over at least once during the baking.

Our Daily Bread

HOT BREADS TO FLIP OVER

At black churches in New York City you are just as likely to be served waffles and fried chicken at a breakfast prayer meeting or Sunday gospel brunch as at a New Year's watch service supper, which shows the popularity of this hot bread. One plausible story says that the tradition began during the late 1940s when bebop jazz musicians such as Miles Davis and Thelonius Monk played at Harlem nightclubs until early Sunday morning, and then would stumble out for breakfast at a local restaurant called Wells. The legend goes that many of the musicians ordered waffles for breakfast, and since they had missed dinner on Saturday night because they were gigging, also ordered fried chicken to go with the hot bread.

Like so much lore about black food traditions, this story may be part fiction, but the fact remains that waffles, pancakes, griddle cakes, and fritters are served often at black church functions, and they provide a wonderful lift to a meal. Sometimes bits of ham or chicken, fruits such as blueberries, apple, and pineapple, as well as wheat germ, corn kernels, and oat bran are stirred into the batter, which is baked and topped with fruit sauces, preserves and jellies, or flavored syrups and honey.

These hot breads are quick and easy to make, and can be made as successfully in a simple cast-iron skillet as on a modern thermostat-controlled griddle. However, there are three elements to consider: Mix as quickly as possible and don't overbeat; ignore lumps because they will disappear during the baking; and make sure that the skillet or griddle has reached the right temperature before you pour on the batter.

If you are using a thermostat-controlled griddle, set the dial on medium-high heat, oil the cooking surface lightly, and allow the iron to heat for at least 5 minutes. (Oil the pan with vegetable oil, not butter or margarine, which burns too easily.) If you are using an iron skillet, oil the pan lightly, place on medium-high heat for a few minutes, and then test to see if the skillet is hot enough by sprinkling on a few drops of water.

If the water just sits and percolates, the skillet is not hot enough, and the cakes will absorb too much oil and end up heavy and greasy. On the other hand, if the water evaporates, the skillet is too hot and will cook the outside of the pancakes too quickly, leaving the inside runny and wet. If the water bounces and sputters, the griddle is ready to use and you can pour on the batter.

SATURDAY WAFFLES

Makes about 6 waffles

Karen Phillips is a founder and the chief executive officer of the Abyssinian Development Corporation, an independent, community-based, nonprofit organization that was initiated several years ago by the Abyssinian Baptist Church in Harlem. The Church is located on 138th Street.

Under her leadership the organization has created or managed over five hundred much-needed housing units, plus initiated funding for local businesses and developed several other programs. She is a Harvard graduate and is involved in so many community activities that she always seems just a little out of breath, as though she has too many things to do.

Actually, this is to be expected. Abyssinian is a beehive of activities. Events from fund-raising to political rallies are regularly held there. This was the family church of the late Reverend Adam Clayton Powell Jr., who was a congressman, and it has long been in the forefront of our civil rights struggle.

Whenever Karen can catch

Christian Hope Baptist Church, Philadelphia, Pa., church anniversary celebration. Jazzmin Wells, whose great-grandparents were among the founders of the church, sets the table.

27

Our Daily Bread

her breath—which isn't often—she prepares these waffles for church friends, which she, too, sometimes serves with fried chicken, even though this was not a tradition in Ocilla, Georgia, where she was born and raised.

Karen, who is in her forties, sends these memories:

"I am an only child. But when I was growing up I had nine cousins, all with an age span of four years older or younger than me, so I never felt alone. When I started to cook I would make four batches of waffles and invite all my cousins over for Saturday morning breakfast. We would have an eating good time.

"We couldn't have a feast like this on Sunday morning because it was understood that everyone would be up and out to Sunday school at the Pleasant Grove First Baptist Church. Sunday school in the morning, church service every fourth Sunday, Bible Training Union (BTU) once a month on Sunday afternoon, and various church programs on holidays provided the basis of my religious training.

"Those church experiences, which stressed organized activities, leadership roles, dealing respectfully with people, and public speaking, helped prepare me for my role in managing the Abyssinian Development Corporation. They were as valuable as the skills I learned at Harvard."

This is Karen's recipe:

2 eggs, at room temperature
2 cups all-purpose flour
2 teaspoons baking powder
½ teaspoon salt
⅓ cup vegetable oil
1¼ cup milk

1 tablespoon sugar
8 tablespoons (1 stick) butter or
  margarine, melted
½ cup hot syrup, fruit preserves,
  or jelly

About one hour before making the waffle batter, remove the eggs from the refrigerator so that the egg whites can warm to room temperature. If the eggs are icy cold they won't form stiff peaks when beaten.

Separate the eggs, placing the whites into a spotless-clean medium bowl. Place the yolks into a small cup.

At least an hour later, lightly grease the waffle iron with vegetable oil and preheat at medium-high heat.

Sift into a large bowl the flour, baking powder, and salt. Stir in the vegetable oil, egg yolks, and milk and mix lightly, just until batter is blended. Set aside.

Using an electric mixer, beat the egg whites until foamy. Gradually add the sugar and continue beating on high speed until the peaks are stiff and shiny. Don't overbeat.

Carefully fold the egg whites into the batter, mixing only until blended. Raise the waffle iron temperature to high. Pour about ½ cup batter for each waffle (or slightly more) onto the griddle.

Reduce the heat to medium and bake the waffle until well browned and the iron no longer throws off steam. This should take about 5 minutes. Remove the waffles and keep warm in an oven set at 250 degrees.

Pour the remaining batter onto the waffle iron and bake in the same way. Serve the waffles with melted butter or margarine, syrup, or fruit preserves or jelly.

Our Daily Bread

HOT CORN FRITTERS

Makes 16 to 18 fritters

ecently Marion Wells and another church sister, Juliette McCrary, collected a cache of favorite recipes from members of the West Hunter Street Baptist Church in Atlanta, Georgia, and compiled them into a booklet. Until his death in April 1990, the Reverend Ralph Abernathy, the civil rights leader and associate of the Reverend Dr. Martin Luther King Jr., was pastor of the church, which is located on Ralph Abernathy Boulevard.

Mrs. Wells, a retired schoolteacher who is involved in many church projects, says that much of the church's rich social life was put into motion by Reverend Abernathy, whom she said believed firmly in the theology of the table.

"He felt that you could ease a lot of hurts and soothe a lot of souls by sitting down and eating together," says Mrs. Wells. "I think that is one reason you see so much food here at the church today. I think that years ago we even did more cooking here at the church."

Mrs. Wells sends a recipe for corn fritters, a Southern delicacy that is similar to a pancake and can be either deep-fried or cooked on a griddle:

1 large ear fresh corn	*2 eggs*
3 cups vegetable oil for deep-frying	*½ cup milk*
(or more)	*1 tablespoon vegetable oil*
1 cup flour	**SAUCE**
½ teaspoon salt	*1 cup maple syrup*
1 teaspoon baking powder	*¼ teaspoon grated nutmeg*

Husk and silk the corn and then cut the kernels from the cobs, scraping the cobs well to extract the corn milk. Discard the cob. You should have 1 generous cup of corn kernels. Set aside.

Pour enough vegetable oil into a deep heavy kettle or pot to reach a depth of at least 3 inches. Place the pot on high heat and insert a deep-frying thermometer to gauge the oil temperature.

In the meantime, in a medium bowl sift together the flour, salt, and

baking powder. Add the eggs, milk, and oil. Mix only until blended and then stir in the corn, mixing lightly.

Check the thermometer to make sure the oil has reached 370 degrees. If so, using a tablespoon and a rubber spatula to scrape the batter out of the spoon, drop the batter by spoonfuls into the hot oil. Don't overcrowd the pan.

Turn the fritters over in the hot oil, and fry for 2 minutes or until they are puffed and golden brown.

Remove the fritters from the oil with a pair of long-handled tongs. Drain on paper towels and keep warm in an oven set at 250 degrees while frying the rest of the batter.

Meanwhile, in a small pan over low heat, stir together the maple syrup and nutmeg. Heat through and serve with the corn fritters.

Variation: This same batter can be used for griddle cakes. Lightly oil the griddle or a heavy skillet, and heat until a few drops of water sprinkled on the iron or pan sizzles. Pour on about ¼ cup of batter for each cake. Don't overcrowd the skillet or griddle iron. Cook until the underside is brown and the top is puffed and full of bubbles. Using a pancake turner or large metal spatula, flip the cake and cook on the other side until brown. When done, transfer to a warm platter and cook the remaining batter in the same way.

Our Daily Bread

SCENT-SATIONAL BREADS

Mr. Ras owned the sugarcane mill in the section of Choctaw County where my family lived, and in late fall when the cane was harvested and it was time to make the molasses, my father, like the men in many other families, would go and help out, for this was a hot and tedious and tiring all-day task. The work began at daybreak and lasted until nightfall. The stalks of cane were fed through a hand-operated press to extract the sugar-sweet juice, which was poured into large vats. A fire was set and the juice was boiled until the sugar caramelized and turned into molasses. Daddy would arrive home dead tired. In those days black families bartered services for goods and produces, and his earnings were several gallon cans of molasses, which Mama cooked with throughout the winter.

When Mary Cunningham's recipe for Molasses Bread arrived it not only brought back memories of that long-ago sugarcane harvest, but the tapestry of events that followed the harvest.

Mama was a member of the Home Mission Club at our church, Shiloh Baptist, and when it was her turn to have the members at our house, invariably she would bake a pan or two of molasses breads, or perhaps some tea cakes, which were like biscuits but were almost as sweet as cake. The meeting was held in midafternoon, and since people didn't eat much between meals in those days, the ladies only served each other a little something to hold them until supper.

I used to look forward to those club meetings with both apprehension and excitement, because despite the anxiety involved in all the work that Mama insisted upon doing, it did offer me a chance to mingle with the grownups.

This was before we built our new house in the mid-1950s, and at the time we lived in a small lime-washed frame house in the Negro quarters, not far from the interstate highway. Mama was a meticulous housekeeper and our humble dwelling was always kept neat and tidy. But she still had to "straighten up," as she called it, for the sisters, and that meant washing and ironing the crocheted and embroidered doilies and scarves that adorned every table and dresser top. We also polished the furniture, scrubbed the front porch, washed the windows, and swept the front yard with a broom made of twigs, and then

Sunday morning at the Macedonia Missionary Baptist Church in Eatonville, Florida—the birthplace of Zora Neale Hurston. Gladys Jenkins prays during a devotional service.

would drag the broom across the loamy soil to create pretty designs and patterns, which I later learned is an African tradition.

Around 2 or 3 P.M. the women would arrive: Mrs. Daisy; Mrs. Ada; Mrs. Bessie; Sister Charity; Aunt Agnes; Mrs. Mary Earl; Mrs. Doll, the church organist; and often my only sister and oldest sibling Helen, and her friend, Betty Busby, who represented the next generation. The sisters would report on who was sick, what family was out of work, who needed the assistance of a church collection, whose child was heading for trouble, what girl was going to end up pregnant if she didn't watch out, and what the white folks were up to.

Pretty soon the conversation would slip into aimless chatter. Some of the women would reach into their purse and pull out their crochet or embroidery, and I would settle back into a corner, sip lemonade or buttermilk, and eat a wedge of molasses bread, glad to be in their company.

This is Mary Cunningham's memorable recipe:

Our Daily Bread

Molasses Bread

Makes 1 loaf

½ cup melted butter or vegetable oil

2 eggs

¾ cup dark molasses or dark syrup

¼ cup sugar

1 teaspoon vanilla extract

2 cups unbleached flour

¼ teaspoon salt

½ teaspoon baking soda

2 teaspoons baking powder

1 cup buttermilk

Preheat the oven to 350 degrees.

Butter a 9 × 5 × 3-inch loaf pan, dust lightly with flour, and set aside.

In a large bowl, combine the butter or vegetable oil, eggs, molasses or syrup, sugar, and vanilla extract. Beat until well blended.

In another bowl or on a sheet of wax paper, sift together the flour, salt, baking soda, and baking powder. Stir in about ⅓ of the flour at a time to the molasses mixture, alternating with ⅓ of the buttermilk. Stir after each addition, beginning and ending with the flour. Mix the batter until well blended.

Pour the batter into the prepared pan. Set the pan on the lower shelf of the hot oven and bake for 1 hour or until the bread is golden brown and puffy and a knife inserted in the center comes out clean.

Remove the pan from the oven and cool on a wire rack for 10 minutes and then turn out the bread onto the rack and cool completely.

Pumpkin Bread

Makes 2 loaves

S aint Mary's Episcopal Church in Washington, D.C., is not only an historical landmark, but it also represents a landmark in our struggle for equal rights and human dignity. The picturesque late-Victorian-style structure was designed in the late 1800s by a leading nineteenth-century architect, James Renwick, but the valiant efforts of a group of twenty-eight black man and women opened its doors.

According to church annals, in 1865, the last year of the Civil War, these freed men and women gathered to establish an Episcopal church in Washington, D.C., so black people could worship without being subjected to the discriminatory rules of the white church. At that time the church's unwritten rules called for separate pews for black and white parishioners, no wedding celebrations or funeral services for people of color, and of course, segregated classes for schoolchildren. Saint Mary's became the first black Episcopal church in Washington.

This historic capsule comes from Thelma R. Campbell, a member of Saint Mary's Episcopal Church, which is located on 23rd Street. Mrs. Campbell reports that the beautiful structure, with its carved oak furniture, handsome bronze sanctuary railing, patterned tile-and-marble floor, and expansive altar windows, including one that is paneled in stained glass from the Tiffany studios, has changed little over the past 110 years.

She also sends along this message, which shows that our faith and food tradition transcend denominations.

Mrs. Campbell says: "Our church has a coffee hour every Sunday during which the parishioners who have a birthday serve food. About fifteen years ago I served this pumpkin bread for my birthday, which was made from a recipe developed by Norma J. Brown, one of our parishioners. It is fun to make and bake, and I always serve it with coffee and cream cheese. The parishioners love it.

"Whenever I make the bread, our minister, Father Darwin Price, always remarks, 'We stand on the shoulders of others who have gone before.

We thank you Norma Brown.' Norma was ninety-something when she went to glory."

Mrs. Campbell sends this recipe:

2 cups sugar

¾ cup vegetable oil

4 eggs

2 cups cooked pumpkin

3½ cups all-purpose flour

2 teaspoons baking powder

2 teaspoons baking soda

¼ teaspoon salt

½ teaspoon ground cloves

1 teaspoon ground nutmeg

1 teaspoon ground allspice

1 teaspoon ground cinnamon

⅔ cup water

¾ cup chopped pecans, walnuts,
    dates, or raisins

Preheat the oven to 350 degrees.

Butter and lightly dust with flour two 9 × 5 × 3-inch loaf pans and set aside.

In a large bowl beat the sugar and oil until well blended. Stir in the eggs and pumpkin and mix well.

In another bowl, sift together the flour, baking powder, baking soda, salt, cloves, nutmeg, allspice, and cinnamon.

Add a heaping cup of the flour and spices to the pumpkin mixture at a time, alternating with a little of the water, beginning and ending with the flour, mixing well after each addition.

Stir in either chopped nuts, dates, or raisins and mix thoroughly. Pour the batter into the prepared pans, dividing evenly between the two.
Shake the pans gently to level the batter. Place the loaves on the lower shelf of the oven, diagonally across from each other, making sure that the pans don't touch.

Bake for 1 hour and 15 minutes or until the loaves are golden brown and puffed and a knife inserted into the center comes out clean.

Remove from the oven and cool the loaves in the pan on a wire rack for 10 minutes. Remove from the pan and serve warm if desired.

LEVITY AND OTHER HEAVY MATTERS

Rich and sinfully delicious quick breads made with buttermilk, molasses, honey, spices, nuts, fruits, and vegetables must be leavened with both baking powder and baking soda. That's because the baking soda is needed to neutralize the acid in these ingredients. This helps the baking powder to raise the breads quickly, hence the name.

Since these are heavy-textured breads, they should be baked on the lower shelf of the oven, where the heat is the hottest. And don't be surprised if the top crust cracks. It often does because the crust browns before the center of the bread has finished rising, and as the center expands, it cracks.

ZUCCHINI BREAD

Makes 2 loaves

*i*t was hard to get this recipe out of Mary Louise Henderson, simply because the octogenarian was in the throes of working on a starter batter for a new bread recipe, and she didn't want to stop and turn her attention to her tried-and-true Zucchini Bread. She also had j338 her church commitments to think about.

That's the kind of schedule Mrs. Henderson keeps. She is a retired professor of home economics at Norfolk State College and the founding president of the Golden Heirs, a senior citizens club at the Banks Street Memorial Baptist Church in Norfolk, Virginia, which is located on Chesapeake Boulevard. She is also a member of the church's Missionary Society.

Mrs. Henderson bakes year round and gives breads and cakes, especially her Zucchini Bread, as gifts to church members, friends, and relatives.

This is one of her favorite gifts for giving:

3 eggs

1½ cups sugar

½ cup vegetable oil

1 teaspoon vanilla extract

2 cups grated unpeeled zucchini

3½ cups all-purpose flour

½ teaspoon salt

1 teaspoon baking soda

2½ teaspoons baking powder

1 tablespoon ground cinnamon

¾ cup chopped pecans or walnuts

Preheat the oven to 350 degrees.

Oil two 8½ × 4½ × 2½ loaf pans and set aside.

In a large bowl beat the eggs until they are frothy. Add the sugar, vegetable oil, and vanilla extract and beat until well blended. Add the zucchini and mix well.

Sift into the bowl the flour, salt, baking soda, baking powder, and cinnamon. Mix until well blended. Stir in the chopped nuts.

Pour the batter into the oiled loaf pans, dividing evenly between the two. Shake the pans gently to level the batter.

Place the pans on the lower shelf of the hot oven, diagonally across from each other. Don't allow the pans to touch.

Bake for 1 hour or until the breads are golden brown and puffy and a knife inserted into the center comes out clean.

Remove the breads from the oven and cool in the pans on a wire rack for 10 minutes. Turn the breads out of the pans and onto the wire rack and cool before serving.

JUNK MUFFINS

Makes 9 to 11 muffins

When Nora Hudson was growing up in Detroit, Michigan, she says she didn't personally know one lawyer. But she knew she wanted to be one. Nora is now a lawyer, and today she spends a lot of time sharing her knowledge about career paths and choices with others in her community and church.

Nora is co-founder of Project Bloom, a Detroit-based self-empowerment organization aimed at, she says, helping African-American students between the ages of eighteen and ninety to navigate the rough and bumpy road from high school to college to employment.

She is the mother of two young children, Chelsea and Johnathan, and also is a substitute Sunday school teacher at the Oak Grove African Methodist Episcopal Church in Detroit, located on Cherrylawn, where she serves as committee chairperson of the church's Boy Scouts Club.

On rainy days Nora bakes these healthy muffins for the Scouts:

⅓ to ½ cup brown sugar

1 egg

¼ cup melted butter or vegetable
   oil

½ teaspoon vanilla extract

¼ cup finely diced apple

¼ cup grated carrot

¼ cup raisins

¼ cup crushed pineapple, drained

½ cup milk

1½ cup unbleached flour

¼ teaspoon salt

1 teaspoon baking soda

2 teaspoons baking powder

Preheat oven to 400 degrees.

Oil lightly a 12-cup muffin pan and set aside.

In a large mixing bowl combine the brown sugar (use ⅓ cup sugar for less-sweet muffins), egg, butter or oil, and vanilla extract. Beat until well blended.

Stir in the apple, carrot, raisins, pineapple, and milk and mix well. Sift into the fruit mixture the flour, salt, baking soda, and baking powder. Using a large spoon, stir the batter together, mixing only until dry ingredients are blended in.

Spoon the batter into the prepared muffin tins, filling each cup about ¾ full. Fill any remaining cups with water to prevent the pan from burning.

Place the pan in the hot oven on the lower shelf and bake for 18 to 20 minutes, or until the muffins are golden brown and a knife inserted into the center comes out clean.

Place the pan on a wire rack and cool the muffins in the pan a few minutes before turning out onto the rack. Serve the muffins either warm or cool.

RISE AND SHINE: YEAST BREADS

Today Frances Jackson lives in a spacious home in Northwest Detroit, far away from Montgomery, Alabama, where so many of the people whom she loves were born and raised. Frances holds a Ph.D. and is a professor of nursing; her husband, Frank, is a lawyer, but in certain respects their lives have been frozen in time, replete with many of the traditions and living patterns that formed her early life.

On Sundays when the Reverend Hamilton comes to dinner after church service, Frances rises early and begins preparing the meal just as her grandma did years ago Down South. By 9:30 A.M. she is already admonishing Frank and their two children not to eat the freshly baked yeast rolls, and then she hurries them out and they head for the John Wesley African Methodist Episcopal Zion Church, which is located on Lower West Side Detroit on Beechwood. Frances has been a member of the church all of her life.

At times Frances and her family seem almost tethered to their church. Frances is an assistant choir director and also oversees an AIDS and cancer-screening health project. Frank is vice president of the trustee board, and besides that, twice monthly on Sundays drives a van throughout inner-city Detroit to pick up members and transport them to church. Their teenage daughter, Alaina, is a church usher, and their son, Frank III, is already an ordained minister at age twenty-three.

"John Wesley A.M.E. is our roots, our culture, our history," says Frances. "Somebody is always asking why don't we join a church closer to our home. I say never. We feel connected to the people there."

Church members, family, friends, and colleagues gather at their home often, and at such time the house rattles with good times and laughter. Guests go in and out of the kitchen, peeping into pots, tasting this dish, sharing cooking tips for another dish. Frances relishes these moments, and over the years she has equipped her kitchen with a fancy, high-tech Jenn-Air stove plus enough pots and pans and serving dishes

Our Daily Bread

Black History Month celebration during gospel brunch at the Canaan Baptist Church in Harlem, New York. Deaconess Ernestine Bradley, executive chef, gets ready for the crowd.

to rival a restaurant.

Frances tells this story: "When I was a teenager, my maternal grandmother, who lived in Montgomery, Alabama, could no longer live alone. My mother had eleven siblings, nine of whom lived to adulthood. Five of the nine children lived here in Detroit; two in Chicago, and two in Montgomery.

"Everyone in the family wanted to keep Grandma. And while she visited her other children for several weeks or months, she spent most of her time at our house. My mother was her daughter.

"My mother is a good cook but she doesn't like to. Cooking, though, was Grandma's life and the kitchen was her domain. My father worked midnight to morning and Grandma would get up early every day and cook Dad's breakfast. The rest of us would wake up when the wonderful smells drifted from the kitchen through the house.

"Whenever I went into the kitchen to cook it wouldn't take long for Grandma to saunter in. Physically, Grandma was in pretty good shape, but mentally she was forgetful, and often she couldn't remember names. Although I was named after her, from time to time she would call me girl.

"She would say with a warm smile, 'What are you doing girl, can Grandma help?' I would say yes, and sit down and watch her make whatever dish I had named.

"I remember watching Grandma making rolls. She never measured anything! And she never tasted anything. I also cook without tasting but I usually measure when I cook.

"The one thing I could never match was Grandma's ability to know just how hot the water should be for the yeast. If the water is too hot it will kill the yeast and the bread will not rise. On the other hand, if the water is not warm enough the yeast will not activate and the bread still won't rise properly. That's why I use a thermometer.

"Grandma would not only knead the dough, she would slam it against the counter several times. Sometimes I do that, but I can't tell if it makes any difference in the texture of the bread. But it sure helps when you're feeling frustrated!

"To this day I can remember the aromas in the house when homemade bread was baking. There's no other like it. I would brush the freshly baked bread with melted butter and then filch a hot roll when Grandma's back was turned. Grandma's breads were wonderful.

"Grandma died here in Detroit in 1966. I still miss her. I would encourage everybody who has living grandparents to spend time with them now. They know things about the family and about life that may disappear forever when their lives end.

"My father's mother, who was a Seventh Day Adventist, made the most exquisite whole wheat rolls. Nobody thought to get that recipe or have her teach us how to make them. I've made whole wheat rolls, but they're not as light or tasty as Grandma's. Luckily, my maternal grandmother lived with us, and I was able to learn many things about food and life from her. I learned that the 'bread of life' is not only food to sustain us, but these precious relationships feed our bodies and soul."

OLD=FASHIONED DINNER ROLLS

Makes 24 Parker House or 36 Cloverleaf rolls

2 packages active dry yeast
½ cup warm water (105 to 115 degrees)
⅓ cup sugar
½ cup butter or margarine
½ cup milk

2 teaspoons salt
5 to 6 cups all-purpose flour
3 eggs
2 tablespoons butter or margarine, melted

Place the yeast in a small bowl and pour over the warm water. Stir to dissolve. Set aside.

Combine in a small saucepan the sugar, butter or margarine, milk, and salt. Place over low heat and heat for 4 or 5 minutes, stirring to dissolve the ingredients. Remove from the heat and pour the milk mixture into a large mixing bowl and allow it to cool to lukewarm, between 105 and 115 degrees.

Stir in 2 cups of the flour to the cooled milk mixture. Using an electric mixer, beat the batter until well blended. Add the dissolved yeast and the eggs and beat again. Stir in 1 cup more of flour and beat until smooth.

You may have to put aside the mixer at this point and beat the batter with a wooden spoon. Add another cup of the flour and beat the batter until smooth. Add the 5th cup of flour and mix again. (You can also mix in the flour with your fingers.) The dough will still be wet but it should pull away from the sides of the bowl.

Turn the dough out onto a well-floured board or work surface. Flour your hands. Measure out another cup of flour and sprinkle the dough with a little more of that flour and form into a ball. Use the additional flour during the kneading but use it as sparingly as possible. Too much flour results in a heavy, streaked dough that won't rise properly.

Knead the dough for 8 to 10 minutes or until it is soft and shiny and satiny and no longer sticky. (See "Kneading Dough" on page 50.)

Lightly butter or oil a large bowl. Place the ball of dough into the bowl

and turn over once or twice so that the top of the dough is buttered, which keeps it from drying out.

Cover the bowl with plastic wrap or a towel and allow it to rise in a warm, draft-free place for about 1½ hours or until the dough doubles in size. (See "Rising High" on page 46.) If you stick your finger into the dough and the dent remains, it has risen sufficiently.

Punch down the risen dough with your fist and then remove it from the bowl. Place the dough on a lightly floured surface and knead it for a minute or so to smooth out any bubbles. Now cover the dough with a towel and allow it to rest for 10 minutes.

Shape the dough into either Parker House or Cloverleaf rolls:

For Parker House rolls: Dust the work surface lightly with flour. Divide the dough in half. Roll out one half of the dough into a circle about ¼-inch thick.

Using a 2-inch cookie or biscuit cutter, cut the dough into rounds. Dip the handle of a dinner knife into flour and use it to make a deep crease just off center in each round.

Fold over the round, overlapping the smaller half. Press the edges of the two halves firmly together. Brush the tops with melted butter or margarine, but not the edges. If the edges are buttered they are more likely to pop open during the rising or baking. However, if this does happen don't consider it a catastrophe since this shape is pretty, too.

Place the rolls on the greased baking sheet, about 1 inch apart. Repeat with the remainder of the dough and place the shaped rolls on the other baking sheet.

For Cloverleaf rolls: For each roll pinch off a 1-inch piece of dough and roll it between the palms of your hands until it is smooth, shaping into a ball.

Place three balls in each muffin cup, pressing to make sure that the balls are touching.

Brush the tops of the Parker House- or Cloverleaf-shaped rolls with a little melted butter or margarine.

Cover the rolls and let rise again until doubled in bulk. This should

Our Daily Bread

take from 30 minutes to an hour, depending on the size and shape of the rolls.

Preheat the oven to 400 degrees.

Place the pans on the lower oven shelf. Bake the Parker House rolls for 10 to 12 minutes; the Cloverleaf rolls for 12 to 14 minutes; or until they are golden brown and puffy.

RISING HIGH

Breads should be raised in a draft-free area with a temperature between 80 to 85 degrees, so that the dough can double in size in an hour or so. If the kitchen is around 70 degrees, then usually a dark pantry, kitchen cabinet, hall closet, or an unheated oven will provide all the extra warmth needed.

However, if the kitchen is moderately cold, you will need to set the dough near—but not on—a warm oven or radiator. And if the kitchen is real cold, place the dough in an unheated oven on the top rack and then place a pan of very warm water on the floor of the oven. Don't place the bowl into the water; this may kill the yeast.

If you decide to bake bread and the weather is extremely hot, remember that if the kitchen temperature is above 85 degrees this will cause the dough to rise too quickly. Slow-raised breads have a better texture and are more flavorful than breads that are fast-risen.

So consider setting the bowl of dough over a pan of cool water to rise, and keep the dough out of direct sunlight. Or wait for the fall of the year, which is actually a better time of year to bake yeast bread.

EATING TO LIVE

My first apartment in New York City was in the Bronx, right off the Grand Concourse, which was the main thoroughfare of a neighborhood that I later learned was "changing," the Up North euphemism for "white fright and flight." The apartment was in a once-elegant prewar building with high ceilings and wood floors and had a large lobby rimmed with slate gray marble. And it seems that virtually overnight all the white tenants moved out.

In the late 1960s, two neatly dressed, dashingly handsome young black men who wore bowties used to go up and down the stairways in the cavernous building, knocking on doors, selling a newspaper called *Muhammad Speaks*. The newspaper was the official voice of a group in those days referred to as the Black Muslims. I would banter with the brothers and then buy and read the paper with the eager appetite of the young, particularly attracted to the articles on food and healthy living, which had long been two of my passions.

Sister Wanda Muhammad and I were reflecting on those halcyon days recently, and not surprisingly the conversation turned to food and health. She is on the administrative staff at the Muhammad University of Islam in Chicago, and a few years ago when she was teaching a cooking class at the school and mosque, she contacted Muslim sisters across the country and compiled more than one hundred recipes that stress eating for good health and longevity. The collection was sold to raise funds for the university, which is located on South Stony Island Avenue.

Sister Wanda sends a recipe for a delicious and nutritious Whole Wheat Bread that is made with honey, whole wheat, and unbleached flour, and leavened with yeast. She also says that in Muslim tradition the bread should not be eaten for at least twenty-four hours after it is baked.

"I know that is going to be hard to do because of all those wonderful aromas," she says jovially, "but yeast is a living fungus, and although the heat from the baking kills the yeast, we want to make sure that it isn't alive when we eat the bread. That can cause digestive problems. So we let the bread rest twenty-four hours after it comes out of the oven to make sure that yeast is not alive. We don't want to resurrect anything in this bread."

WHOLE WHEAT BREAD

Makes 2 loaves

4 tablespoons butter or vegetable oil
⅓ to ½ cup honey
1 cup milk
1 cup water
2 packages active dry yeast
½ cup warm water (105 to 115 degrees)

2½ cups whole wheat flour
3½ cups unbleached all-purpose flour, about
2½ to 3 teaspoons salt

In a medium saucepan combine 3 tablespoons of the butter or oil, honey, milk and water. Heat, stirring, over low heat for 4 or 5 minutes, or until the mixture dissolves.

Remove from the heat and pour the mixture into a large mixing bowl and allow to cool to lukewarm, between 105 and 115 degrees.

In the meantime, dissolve the yeast in the lukewarm water. Check again to make sure that the milk mixture has cooled to lukewarm. If so, stir the dissolved yeast into the bowl.

Sift into the yeast-milk mixture 1 cup of the whole wheat flour, 2 cups of the unbleached flour and the salt. Using an electric beater, beat the batter for about 2 to 3 minutes or until it is well-blended.

Sift in the remaining 1½ cups whole wheat flour into the bowl. Using a wooden spoon, beat the dough until it begins to pull away from the edges of the bowl.

Sift in the remaining 1½ cups unbleached flour. Using your hands, mix in the flour well and then form the batter into a smooth ball. If necessary, sprinkle on a little more flour if the dough sticks. Turn the dough out onto a floured board, cover with a towel, and let it rest for 10 minutes.

At the end of the resting period knead the dough for 8 to 10 minutes (See "Kneading Dough" on page 50.) or until it is smooth and elastic, sprinkling with flour as needed.

Place the dough in a large greased warm bowl, turning it over so that it is oiled all over. Cover the bowl with a towel and let rise in a warm, draft free place for about 1½ hours or until it doubles in size. (See "Rising High" on page 46.)

Punch down the risen dough with your fist and turn out on to a work surface. Knead the dough lightly for 1 minute. Divide the dough in half and shape into 2 loaves.

Oil two 8½ by 4½ by 2½ inch loaf pans. Place the dough into the pans, turning in the pan to oil all over. Cover with a towel and let rise again for about 45 minutes to 1 hour, or until the loaves double again in size.

Preheat the oven to 350.

Melt the remaining tablespoon of butter (or use vegetable oil) and lightly brush on top of each loaf. Place the loaves on the lower shelf of the hot oven, diagonally across from each other. Bake for 50 minutes to an hour, or until the bread is crusty and brown and shrinks from the sides of the pans, and sounds hollow when tapped.

Remove from the oven and cool the bread in the pans on a wire rack for 10 minutes. Turn out of the pans onto the rack and cool completely.

Wrap the cooled bread in plastic wrap or aluminum foil, and serve 24 hours later. (The bread will keep in the refrigerator for 2 or 3 days or can be wrapped in plastic and then in foil and frozen for several months.)

Slice the bread and toast it before serving, if desired.

KNEADING DOUGH

Kneading actually looks more complicated than it really is, and when push comes to shove, you really can just massage the dough and push it around and get good results. The purpose of kneading is to develop and stretch a protein substance in wheat flour called gluten so that it can expand the dough and help the yeast to rise the bread.

The process is relatively simple: First dust the hands and the work surface lightly with flour. Form the dough into a ball and place on the work surface.

Flatten the dough slightly and then pick up the edge farthest from you and fold over to the edge nearest you. Using the heels of your hands, press down gently but firmly on the dough and push the dough away from you.

Now turn the dough one quarter of the way around on the board and repeat the folding and pushing. Continue to fold, push, and turn the dough this way for 8 to 10 minutes or until it is smooth, satiny, and elastic.

If the dough sticks as you work, sprinkle your hands and the work surface lightly with flour. Add extra flour sparingly; working in too much dough can make the dough heavy.

Angel Biscuits

Makes 24 to 28 biscuits

t's a wonder that Velma Mosley ever has time to cook, considering the wide array of church activities and community projects that she is involved in. Her volunteer efforts range from canvassing for local African-American political candidates to collecting and compiling recipes for her church and social clubs. A few years ago in recognition of her many, many services, the mayor of Tyler, Texas, her hometown, proclaimed in her honor "Velma Mosley Day."

True to form, a few days later Mrs. Mosley baked up a batch of Angel Biscuits and carried them out to a fellowship hour in her honor at her church, the Greater Hopewell Baptist Church in nearby Swan, Texas.

These "light as a feather" biscuits are heavenly. They are similar to yeast rolls, but also have the crunchy, flaky texture of kneaded biscuits, plus a wonderful aroma.

Mrs. Mosley's recipe:

1 package active dry yeast
¼ cup warm water (between 105 and 115 degrees)
1½ cups buttermilk
4 to 4½ cups all-purpose flour
1 teaspoon baking soda

1 tablespoon baking powder
½ teaspoon salt
1 tablespoon sugar
⅔ cup vegetable shortening
2 tablespoons melted butter or margarine

Dissolve the yeast in the warm water and set aside.

Place the buttermilk in a small saucepan and heat over low heat for 4 or 5 minutes, just until lukewarm, no more than 110 degrees. Remove from the heat and mix with the dissolved yeast, stirring to combine well. Set aside.

Sift into a large bowl 4 cups of the flour, the baking soda, baking powder, salt, and sugar. Add the shortening. Using two knives or a pastry cutter, cut the mixture until it resembles coarse cornmeal.

Add the buttermilk-yeast mixture to the flour mixture, sprinkling over a little of the liquid at a time while stirring with a fork to moisten. Turn the dough out onto a floured cloth or board and form into a ball. Sprinkle with a little more of the remaining ½ cup of flour if the dough is sticky.

Place the dough on a floured board or cloth and knead lightly for about 2 minutes, sprinkling with a little more flour if necessary. (See "Kneading Dough" on page 50.)

Roll out the dough into a large ½-inch thick circle. Using a 2-inch cookie or biscuit cutter or a glass rim, cut into rounds.

Place the biscuits on two ungreased baking sheets, at least 1 inch apart. Brush the tops lightly with a little melted butter or margarine. Cover with a towel and allow the biscuits to rise in a warm place for 1½ hours, or until they have doubled in size.

Preheat the oven to 425 degrees.

Bake one pan of biscuits at a time, setting the pan on the lower shelf in the hot stove. Bake for 10 to 12 minutes or until they are golden brown.

Remove immediately from the baking sheet and serve hot.

Note: Leftover biscuits can be cooled, placed in a plastic container, and frozen for later use. To serve, reheat in an oven set to 300 degrees for about 10 minutes.

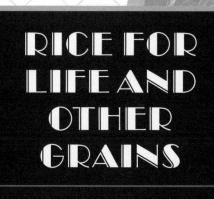

RICE FOR LIFE AND OTHER GRAINS

Many African-Americans from South Carolina and the coastal region of Georgia eat rice three times a day, and although I hail from Alabama, I could eat it daily, too. We African-Americans have a long, glorious but pained history

with this grain, and it stamps our culinary landscape as much as cornbread.

It is generally conceded that rice was introduced to the United States in the 1680s via Charleston, South Carolina, probably by a ship captain who brought in a few handfuls of seeds from the island of Madagascar, off the coast of East Africa. The arrival of the rice seeds in the New World set in motion an industry that remained for two hundred years, until it was ravaged by the Civil War.

Rice growing in Carolina and Georgia was once a booming industry, and exactly who did what where is a matter of debate, like most issues concerning food. But most food historians and experts agree that rice was cultivated by slaves who had tended rice in West Africa, where the grain had been grown for more than five thousand years, or as long as or longer than in Asia.

Culinary historian Karen Hess notes in her excellent book, *The Carolina Rice Kitchen: The African Connection,* that the labor-intensive efforts and skills of African slaves amassed great fortunes for rice plantation owners in the low country coastal region of South Carolina and Savannah, Georgia. A local variety of rice known as Carolina Gold, which was named for the beautiful golden grains that cooked to a pristine white color, became world famous and fetched "gold" on the international market. (A very limited quantity of Carolina Gold rice is now made in South Carolina, available locally at the price of ten dollars for a two-pound bag.)

However, the mass production of rice gradually halted in South Carolina after the Civil War, primarily because many of the slave families that had the expertise to cultivate the crops left the plantations. Rice cultivation was back-breaking work, and as time went on many ex-slaves left the rice fields for better-paying jobs in phosphate mines and sawmills while others moved North. With the labor force gone, the industry lost most of its glory and never recovered. And even as significant, by the late 1880s the Carolina rice industry was facing competition from a growing number of new rice fields in Louisiana, where many African-

American slaves had long tended a little patch of rice for their own use. A new commercial rice industry cropped up in that state, and eventually the planting of rice moved on westward to Texas and Arkansas, where it thrives today.

But the efforts of African slaves in the Carolina rice industry remain indelible. Since the African slaves had been growing rice for millennia in Africa, they also knew how to cook it. This is why today rice is a staple food for people who were torn from Mother Africa and scattered around the world, whether in Latin America, the Caribbean, or the United States.

Sometimes the rice is colored with saffron or turmeric; or in Latin America, with tiny red seeds called achiote; or in Mexico and Cuba, with chili peppers and cumin. Or it is cooked plain and serves as a bed for a variety of peas and beans, as in the Caribbean, or as a perfect foil for smothered chicken and gravy, or ham with red-eye gravy, which is favored in the Deep South, even for breakfast. In some African-American families a bowl of leftover rice stirred with hot milk, sugar, and a dash of cinnamon is as popular for breakfast as grits. Red rice reigns supreme on the southern coastal regions of the United States, and food lore says the dish harks from the rice kitchens of South Carolina and Georgia.

Marion Wells, who is a member of the West Hunter Street Baptist Church in Atlanta, often makes such a dish, called Savannah Red Rice, which has been in

Pot luck at Our Lady Queen of Peace Catholic Church in Arlington, Virginia, a Catholic church established by African-Americans in 1945. The meal celebrated the Feast of the Epiphany, also known as Three Kings Day.

Rice for Life and Other Grains

her family for at least one hundred years. Mrs. Wells is a member of the church's Alice M. Ogletree Service Guild, a missionary club, and every first Saturday the members prepare food at their homes and donate it to a local shelter for battered women.

Mrs. Wells is usually among the twenty or so women who set aside their day and provide food and companionship for their troubled sisters, and she finds the tomato-rice dish easy to prepare and savory. She learned how to make the dish years ago when she was a child living in Waycross, Georgia, and it's one of the mainstays of her extensive collection of recipes.

"It was my mother's recipe," says Mrs. Wells, a retired schoolteacher and a fine cook. "And don't ask me how long I've had the recipe because I'm not ready to tell my age."

SAVANNAH RED RICE

Serves 4

4 or 5 bacon strips	*2 cups finely chopped tomatoes*
1 onion	*½ cup water*
1 green or red pepper	*¾ teaspoon salt*
2 tablespoons vegetable oil	*¼ teaspoon black pepper*
1 cup long-grain white rice	*½ teaspoon hot pepper sauce*

Preheat the oven to 350 degrees. Oil a 2-quart ovenproof baking dish and set aside.

In a medium skillet, fry the bacon until brown and crisp and then remove from the pan and set aside.

Chop the onion and core and dice the green or red pepper.

Drain off the bacon fat in the pan and discard. Add the oil to the pan. Stir in the onion and pepper and sauté over medium-low heat for 4 or 5 minutes, or until the vegetables are translucent and tender.

Remove the pan from the heat and stir in the rice, tomatoes, water, salt, black pepper, and hot pepper sauce. Spoon the rice mixture into the

IN A STEAM OVER RICE

The right way to cook a pot of plain rice is often a source of good-natured debate, with starchy, sticky rice considered a bane. The ultimate goal is fluffy, dry rice with every grain separate.

In this quest I have seen church sisters steam white rice with a kitchen towel wrapped around the lid of the pot so that the moisture collecting on the lid doesn't fall back onto the rice and make it mushy.

My Aunt Mary would boil the rice for about five minutes, quickly drain in a colander, and then rinse with cold water "to remove the starch," she said. She would then return the rice to the pot, add enough water to barely cover, and place it back on the stove and let it cook over a very low heat for another ten minutes or so.

Mama, on the other hand, would add a pinch of salt to a quart of water, add a little butter, bring the water to a boil, and then add two cups of rice. The pan was covered tightly and the rice was cooked for exactly fifteen minutes. The heat was turned off and the rice left on the same burner for exactly ten minutes.

Both of these methods produced fluffy rice, with each grain separate—and I will not get between the memories of these two women by choosing one method over the other.

baking dish. Crumble the bacon and sprinkle on top of the rice. Cover the pan tightly with a lid or aluminum foil, sealing the edges.

Place the dish on the lower shelf of the oven and bake for 45 to 50 minutes or until the rice is tender, stirring two or three times during the baking.

SO MANY GRAINS OF RICE

It seems that every few months there is a new variety of rice in supermarkets and specialty shops, and this undoubtedly reflects the increasing popularity of a grain that has long been cherished in African-American households. Actually there are hundreds of varieties of rice, as the grain is grown on every continent except frigid Antarctica.

When I was growing up we just cooked plain white rice, and most times it was the long-grain variety, which is so called because it is four to five times longer than it is wide. My family didn't care much for plump, round, short-grain rice, since we found it often ended up sticky and gummy, despite our best cooking efforts.

But today a world of rice has opened up to consumers and cooks. Familiar varieties include basmati, the aromatic, long-grain rice of India and Pakistan; jasmine, the perfumed and silken grain of Thailand; characteristic black rice; and a bounty of domestic aromatic types, such as wild pecan rice of Louisiana; texmati, of Texas, which is akin to basmati; and Wehani, a domestic rice that is similar to wild rice but with a distinct earthy color.

There is also a bevy of medium-grain rices, which are shorter than long-grain rice but longer than short-grains. These include the rice grown for the most part in Italy and Spain. The plump Italian rice, arborio, sells for about $2.50 per pound.

Brown rice, which requires longer cooking than white rice, has also risen in popularity, and this is due primarily to its health benefits. The bran layer is left clinging to brown rice, resulting in a chewy texture that provides more fiber, vitamin E, and magnesium than white rice. However, white rice is enriched with the B vitamin thiamin and with iron. Brown rice also comes in short-, medium-, and long-grain varieties. The short-grain brown rice of Japan is particularly popular.

A POT OF RICE AND A MEAL

Harriet Rakiatu Campbell remembers that whenever there was a grand celebration in her West African village of Freetown, Sierra Leone, the host family would set out three large rocks in the backyard, put a few planks across the rocks, place a sheet of metal over the planks, then light a fire and the cooking would get underway, sometimes for as many as two hundred guests.

Then the ingredients for the Jollof were gathered: cabbage, yams, tomatoes, onions, hot peppers, garlic, herbs such as thyme and bay leaf, followed by chicken, salted fish, pork for Christians, beef for Muslims, and always rice—the staple ingredient.

Pots were assembled. A tomato sauce for simmering the chicken, fish, and meat was made in one pot; the vegetables were cooked in another; and the rice in a third. Once done, the food was placed in large brightly colored bowls, basins, or gourds, and the feast was on, following a centuries-old tradition.

"Every family made Jollof—for weddings, for Christmas, for Muslim holidays—and every family made it a little different," says Harriet, who now lives in Annapolis, Maryland. "The one thing we all used was rice. Rice is our staple; it is grown in Sierra Leone. We ate rice with everything. We ate rice with salted fish, with meat, with vegetable sauces made with okra, tomatoes, or with a green leaf that looks like spinach which actually is the leaf of the cassava root.

"We also made a ground nut sauce out of what you call peanuts. We roasted the peanuts and ground them to a paste, and then mixed it with onions and peppers to make a sauce to serve with the rice. When I was growing up in Freetown we ate rice twice a day, every day."

Nine years ago, shortly after arriving in this country, Harriet joined the Mount Moriah African Methodist Episcopal Church in Annapolis, and has felt right at home ever since. She laughs and says that some of the sisters at Mount Moriah fuss at her just as the sisters did at her church in Freetown, the Baughman United Methodist Church.

Harriet's welcome is not surprising. Mount Moriah has an illustrious history of community outreach and involvement dating back to the nineteenth century. Records show that when the church was dedicated in 1874, the great emancipator Frederick Douglass attended the ceremony. At that time Mount Moriah was located in downtown Annapolis on Franklin Street, in a beautiful Victorian Gothic building that now houses the Banneker–Douglass Museum, operated by the state.

The church has since relocated to Bay Ridge Avenue to meet its growing needs, and today it seems that something is always going on at Mount Moriah. And in black church tradition, much of the fund-raising and fellowship involve food.

Recently the ushers had a fish fry, and during the church's annual Women's Day and Men's Day programs, members vie to get into the kitchen to cook for the events. The Women's Ministry Choir was formed a few years ago and is composed of fifty dedicated members, including Harriet, who travel from church to church, spreading the gospel.

Most of the choir members are accomplished cooks, and when they decided that money had to be raised to buy new robes and to defray travel and other expenses, someone hit upon the idea of a cookbook. The choir members submitted their favorite recipes to Cherie Whyms, a public relations expert and church member, who compiled them for publication and sale.

A celebration followed, Harriet made Jollof, and the choir had something else to sing about. This is Harriet's recipe:

JOLLOF

*h*arriet says that when this dish was cooked back home in West Africa, there were generally more than one set of hands stirring the pots. In other words, the preparation is quite involved, so set aside a day for the cooking and invite a friend or two or a family member to help you cook. That way, they will have a head start on the party.

Jollof takes it name from the ancient West African kingdom, Wolof.

1 broiler-fryer chicken, 3¼ to
   3½ pounds
¼ cup vegetable oil
¼ cup lemon or lime juice
1 teaspoon salt
½ teaspoon freshly ground
   black pepper
1 pound lean boneless beef sirloin
1 onion
1 green or red pepper
2 to 3 cloves garlic
1 to 2 hot cayenne or Jamaican
   chili peppers
3 or 4 sprigs fresh thyme, or
   1 teaspoon dried thyme
3 cups chopped canned or fresh
   tomatoes

3 cups chicken broth or Homemade
   Chicken Stock (see recipe on
   page 234)
3 tablespoons tomato paste
1 teaspoon salt
½ teaspoon black pepper
2 bay leaves
2 tablespoons chopped parsley
4 Baked Sweet Potatoes or yams
   (see recipe on page 160)
1 head green cabbage
4 cups water
1 teaspoon salt
2 cups uncooked long-grain
   white rice

Cut the chicken into serving pieces: the breast into halves, and the legs, thighs, and wings separated, for a total of eight pieces. Trim off as much visible fat as possible.

Rinse the chicken with cold water and then dry well with paper towels.

Heat 2 tablespoons of the oil in a large heavy pot, at least 6-quart size. Place three or four chicken pieces at a time in the pot and brown quickly over medium-high heat, turning often.

Remove the chicken from the pan when browned and transfer to a platter or bowl. When all the chicken is browned, pour over the lemon or lime juice and then sprinkle with the salt and pepper. Set aside.

Cut the beef into 1-inch chunks. Place the beef in the pot and brown quickly on all sides, adding another tablespoon of oil if necessary. Remove the meat from the pot when browned and set aside.

Slice the onion; core and dice the pepper; mince the garlic and the chili peppers. Chop the fresh thyme or crush the dried herb. Add the remaining tablespoon of oil to the pot, and stir in the vegetables and herb. Sauté over medium-low heat for 4 or 5 minutes.

Stir into the pot the tomatoes, chicken broth or stock, tomato paste, salt, black pepper, bay leaves, and the parsley.

Bring the sauce to a boil, reduce the heat to low, cover, and simmer for 30 minutes, stirring occasionally.

Meanwhile, preheat the oven and prepare the Baked Sweet Potatoes or yams.

When the tomato sauce is done, return the chicken to the pot and simmer, covered, for about 50 minutes, or until the chicken is tender and done, turning occasionally.

Meanwhile, cut the cabbage head into eighths. Rinse well. Place the cabbage in the top of a large steamer over hot water and steam for 20 minutes or until the vegetable is tender.

In the kitchen at the Hartford Memorial Baptist Church, Detroit. Left to right: Lula Cunningham, Audrey Coleman, Delores Brandon, Carolyn Drake.

In another large pot or saucepan, bring the water to a boil. Add the salt and then stir in the rice. Reduce the heat to medium-low and cook the rice only until it is no longer hard but not quite tender, for about 10 minutes. Watch carefully and don't cook the rice until done.

Drain the rice and return it to the pot it was cooked in. Stir into the rice about 2½ cups of the tomato sauce from the chicken.

Place the pot with the rice back on the heat, cover, and simmer for about 15 minutes or until the rice is tender and all the sauce is absorbed. If the rice sticks, add a little more sauce to the pot.

Add the beef to the pot with the chicken, submerging the pieces into the tomato sauce. Cover and cook for 15 to 20 minutes or until the meat is heated thoroughy. Remove the bay leaves and discard.

At serving, transfer the chicken and beef to a large warm bowl, basin, or platter. Surround with steamed cabbage and pour over some of the tomato sauce.

Place the remaining tomato sauce into another bowl or platter. Cut the baked sweet potatoes or yams into halves and serve on another platter.

Transfer the rice to a warm bowl or platter, and let the feast begin.

Variation: Brown rice is also delicious in this recipe. Cook the rice for 20 minutes, drain and combine with the tomato sauce.

JAMBALAYA

Serves 4

i have eaten jambalaya in African-American homes all the way from Charleston, South Carolina, to Houston, Texas, and I find this dish as exciting as Jollof, (and, actually, not quite as complicated to make).

There are many versions of jambalaya, and its history, origin, and name, in true food-lore tradition, is steeped in debate. Some food historians, noting its striking similarity to the pot rice meals of Africa, believe that the dish was created in the rice kitchens of South Carolina by slaves and then moved on to Louisiana, traveling as recipes do, with the tide of events and the movement of people.

Mount Moriah African Methodist Episcopal Church, Annapolis, Maryland. Fundraising pot-luck dinner held for the women's choir. Jacqueline Evans, the church's minister of music (second from right) with (left to right) daughter Torria Evans, granddaughter Ashley Stocks, and daughter Lakeesa Evans.

Whatever the origin, the main ingredient is rice, and the dish can be made with either a brown sauce or with a tomato sauce. And along with the rice, there can be shrimp, chicken, sausage, ham, or—as in authentic, one-pot African cooking—whatever is available.

Curtis Moore, owner of the Praline Connection Restaurant in New Orleans, sends a recipe for jambalaya that has been in his family for generations. Mr. Moore hails from Verret, Louisiana, in the parish of Saint Bernard, where his mother was one of the reigning cooks at the First Baptist Church.

The church has many social functions, and whenever Mr. Moore is asked to cook or bring out a dish, his spicy jambalaya is a favorite offering. Mr. Moore's recipe is made with a brown sauce, which is just as delicious as the tomato sauce variation.

2 or 3 smoked link sausages, about
   ½ pound
1 boneless chicken breast
½ pound smoked ham
2 tablespoons vegetable oil
1 onion
1 small red or green pepper
2 to 3 cloves garlic
2 green onions
1 teaspoon dried thyme
1 tablespoon chopped parsley

3 cups chicken broth or Homemade
   Chicken Stock (see recipe on
   page 234)
¼ to ½ teaspoon hot pepper flakes
1 teaspoon paprika
1 teaspoon salt
½ teaspoon freshly ground
   black pepper
1 bay leaf
1½ cups long-grain white rice

Cut the sausage crosswise into ½-inch slices. Cut the chicken into 2-inch pieces. Dice the ham.

Heat the oil in a large heavy saucepan or pot. Add the sausage and ham and cook, turning, over medium heat for 4 or 5 minutes, or until lightly brown. Remove from the skillet and set aside.

Raise the temperature a bit. Add the chicken strips, a few pieces at a time, and quickly brown for 2 or 3 minutes, turning to brown evenly. Remove from the pan and set aside.

Chop the onion; core and dice the pepper; mince the garlic; and chop the green onions. Crush the thyme. Stir the vegetables, herb, and the parsley into the pot and sauté 5 minutes, stirring.

Add the chicken broth, hot pepper flakes, paprika, salt, black pepper, and bay leaf and bring to a boil. Stir in the rice, sausage, chicken, and the ham. Reduce the heat to low. Cover and cook 25 to 30 minutes or until the rice is tender and the liquid is absorbed.

The dish is especially delicious if made a day in advance and served the next day, which allows the flavors to meld.

Shrimp Jambalaya

Serves 4 to 5

ecently a friend at the Mount Zion United Methodist Church in New Orleans sent a booklet of recipes that had been compiled by the church's "great cooks and friends."

Next to Emily Moran's jambalaya recipe, she scribbled: "Real down-home gourmet cook; excellent in every way."

This accolade came from Azalea Stevenson, the administrative assistant at Mount Zion, who along with Mrs. Moran is involved in many of the church's activities.

She sends another recipe for the famous local dish, which has so many variations. Mrs. Moran's recipe is made with a spicy tomato sauce.

2 pounds fresh shrimp
½ pound spicy sausage
2 cloves garlic
1 red or green pepper
3 or 4 fresh thyme sprigs, or
   1 teaspoon dried thyme
2 tablespoons vegetable oil
¼ cup chopped parsley
½ cup chopped green onions

1½ cup chopped tomatoes
1 bay leaf
¼ teaspoon cayenne
1 teaspoon salt
½ teaspoon freshly ground black
   pepper
1½ cup water or Fish Stock (recipe
   follows)
1 cup long-grain white rice

Peel and devein the shrimp (see "Not in Vein" on page 198). Rinse the shrimp well with cold water, drain, and pat dry with paper towels. Cut the sausage into bite-size chunks. Mince the garlic, core and dice the pepper. Chop the fresh thyme or crush the dried herb. Set aside.

Heat the oil in a large saucepan or pot. Add the sausage and sauté 4 or 5 minutes or until lightly browned. Add the garlic, pepper, thyme, parsley, and green onions. Sauté, stirring, 3 or 4 minutes longer.

Stir in the chopped tomatoes, bay leaf, cayenne, salt, and black pepper. Add the water or fish stock and bring to a boil. Reduce the heat to low, cover, and simmer for 30 minutes.

Stir in the rice and simmer for 20 minutes or until just tender. Add the

CRUSH ON HERBS

When using dried herbs, measure the amount needed and then rub between your fingers to crush, or pulverize with a mortar and pestle. This action releases both wonderful aroma and flavor.

shrimp and cook over low heat for 20 to 25 minutes, or until the shrimp turn pink and the rice is soft and tender. The jambalaya should be creamy.

FISH STOCK

Makes about 2 1/2 cups

Shells from 2 pounds raw shrimp and/or large fish head and fish bones
1 onion
1 stalk celery

1 clove garlic
½ teaspoon dried herb, such as thyme, marjoram, or basil
1 or 2 whole cloves
3 cups cold water

Rinse the shrimp shells or fish head and bones well with cold water. Slice the onion, cut the celery in half, mince the garlic. Crush the dried herb.

Combine the vegetables and herb in a large saucepan with the shells or head and bones, cloves, and water. Bring to a boil. Cover and reduce heat to simmer.

Cook for 1 hour or until the stock is flavorful. Strain and use in jambalaya or in fish soups and stews.

Note: The stock will keep for two days in the refrigerator or for three or so months in the freezer. To store or freeze, cool completely and pour into a plastic container that has a tight-fitting lid.

Rice Chicken Pilau

Serves 6

*e*very third Sunday in December, 125 senior citizens at the Antioch Baptist Church in Rochester, New York, are served a multi-course menu: roast Cornish hens, cornbread dressing, roast beef, fried chicken, steamed cabbage with red and green peppers, rice chicken pilau, butternut squash with brown sugar and walnut topping, black-eyed peas and baby lima beans, hot dinner rolls, plus ice cream and sherbet for dessert, courtesy of Flora Chaney and the church's Kitchen Committee.

Mrs. Chaney is chairwoman of the committee, and she brings to this volunteer post years of experience as a food service supervisor at a restaurant chain. She also has the commitment and skills of some fifteen church members who spend hours preparing for the feast.

"I don't understand people who say that they don't know how or like to cook," says Mrs. Chaney, who for thirty years has been a member of the church, located on Baden Street. "We have a wonderful time in the kitchen at Antioch. The church is known for its generous kitchen and hospitality."

Mrs. Chaney was born and raised in Albany, Georgia, and she sends a delectable recipe for a rice pilau that has a long culinary history. Author Karen Hess notes in her book, *The Carolina Rice Kitchen: The African Connection,* that this country's rice pilau, or pilaf, came out of the rice kitchens of Carolina and Georgia, developed by African slaves, who in their native land had been influenced by Arabs, who had taken the dish from ancient Persia, which is now called Iran.

Despite the dish's circuitous route, Mrs. Chaney says that this delightful pilau has been in her family for generations:

*¾ to 1 pound chicken parts, such
   as necks, backs, gizzards, wings*
2½ cups water
*½ cup chopped celery stalk and
   leaves*
1 chopped onion
½ to ¾ teaspoon salt

*½ teaspoon freshly ground
   black pepper*
1 bay leaf
*2 tablespoons soy sauce, or
   1 chicken bouillon cube*
1¼ cup long-grain white rice

Rinse the chicken parts well with cold water. In a large saucepan combine the chicken, water, celery, onion, salt, black pepper, bay leaf, and soy sauce or bouillon cube.

Cover and bring to a boil. Reduce the heat to simmer and cook 30 to 40 minutes or until the chicken parts are tender and the broth is flavorful.

Stir in the rice. Cover and cook over low heat for 20 minutes or until the rice is fluffy and the broth is absorbed. Turn off the heat and let the rice pilau remain on the same burner for 5 minutes, and then serve.

Variation: This pilau dish is especially delicious made with the white basmati rice of India.

WILD RICE PILAF

Serves 6

*d*uring one six-week period recently, the Reverend Dr. Arlene Churn conducted revivals, seminars, workshops, and conferences in Detroit, Michigan; Orlando, Florida; Atlanta, Georgia; Durham and Greensboro, North Carolina; Stratford, Connecticut; and Brooklyn, New York.

She then returned to the church she pastors, the Cathedral of Faith Baptist Church, which is located on Grand Avenue in Camden, New Jersey, and conducted Sunday service.

Dr. Churn is a consummate hostess, so when she finally had time to unwind, she invited over a few friends for a gourmet dinner. She served this delicious wild rice dish with baked Cornish hens.

1 cup wild rice
1 clove garlic
½ red or yellow pepper
2 tablespoons olive oil
1 cup chopped green onions
3 cups chicken broth or Homemade
* Chicken Stock (see recipe on*
* page 234)*

½ teaspoon salt
¼ teaspoon freshly ground
* black pepper*
½ cup long-grain white rice

Rinse the wild rice several times under cold running water. This helps get rid of a "woody" flavor and removes any hull that sometimes clings to the rice after processing. Drain and set aside.

Mince the garlic, and core and dice the red or yellow pepper. Heat the oil in a large saucepan. Stir in the garlic, red or yellow pepper, and green onions. Sauté for 3 or 4 minutes over medium-low heat.

Add the wild rice, chicken broth, salt, and black pepper. Bring to a boil and reduce to low heat. Cook, covered, for 25 minutes or until the rice is almost tender. Stir in the white rice and cook 20 to 25 minutes longer or until all of the grains are fluffy and tender. Let the rice set for 10 minutes in a warm place before serving.

SOUL FOOD   70

WILD ABOUT RICE

Botanically speaking, wild rice is actually not rice but an aquatic grass that also flourishes in water and marshes. Its name, like so much of food lore, is not really known, but is attributed to seventeenth-century French explorers and trappers who stumbled upon the grass in the Great Lakes region of Minnesota and Michigan and called it *"folle avione,"* or "crazy oats." This name eventually evolved to wild rice, so the story goes, because of the grass's similarity in texture to rice.

Anyway, wild rice is full of vitamins and minerals, and its nutty flavor lends an earthy but elegant tone to holiday dining and to the rice family. Since it has an assertive flavor, it mixes well with either white or brown rice.

FOR A HAPPY MARRIAGE

One cup of love
One cup of understanding
One half-cup of no nagging
One and one-half cups of patience
One and one-third cups of tolerance
Two cups of forgiveness
One cup of no fault-finding

Stir all ingredients together and mix well.
Let stand for eighty years.

—A Black Church "Recipe"

CHILI RICE

*t*he busiest woman in Tyler, Texas, may just be Velma Mosley, a septuagenarian who is a member of the Greater Hopewell Baptist Church, located in nearby Swan, Texas. Mrs. Mosley has produced three cookbooks for civic groups, and her church and community activities are boundless. A few years back she was chairwoman of the Kitchen Committee of the Greater Hopewell Baptist Church.

She sends this recipe for a delicious rice dish made with ground beef and chili powder, which she says is the perfect way to stretch a meal at a church potluck dinner:

1 onion
2 cloves garlic
½ teaspoon dried thyme or oregano
2 tablespoons vegetable oil
2 tablespoons chopped parsley
½ pound lean ground beef
1 tablespoon chili powder

¾ teaspoon salt
½ teaspoon freshly ground
* black pepper*
1 cup long-grain white rice
1 cup water
1 cup tomato or V-8 juice

Chop the onion and finely mince the garlic. Crush the thyme or oregano. Heat the oil in a large saucepan. Stir in the onion, garlic, the oregano or thyme, parsley, and the beef. Sauté over low heat for about 10 minutes, stirring to break up the meat into small pieces.

Add the chili powder, salt, black pepper, and the rice and stir well. Add the water and tomato or V-8 juice and bring to a gentle boil.

Reduce the heat to medium-low, cover, and cook for about 20 minutes or until the rice is tender and the liquid is absorbed. Serve with a green salad and rolls.

RICE=VEGETABLE SOUP

Serves 4 to 6

*d*uring my childhood my sister, Helen, was a cook at a local café, and her culinary skills were well-known in our community. Whenever choir rehearsal, prayer meeting, or members of the Home Mission Club gathered at her home, the food was as sustaining as the service.

Helen often seasoned this hearty soup with a ham bone instead of chicken, and served it with buttery, moist cornbread.

1 onion
1 green or red pepper
1 stalk celery
2 to 3 cloves garlic
1 cayenne pepper, more if desired
2 tablespoons olive or corn oil
5 cups water
½ pound chicken parts, such as
    wings, necks, gizzards, backs, or
    meaty smoked ham bone or
    turkey thigh

¾ cup uncooked brown rice
1 cup lima beans or butter beans
2 cups green peas or green beans
1 cup coarsely chopped fresh
    tomatoes
1 teaspoon salt
½ teaspoon freshly ground
    black pepper
½ pound small whole okra pods

Slice the onion; core and dice the green or red pepper; chop the celery. Finely mince the garlic and the cayenne. Heat the oil in a large heavy pot. Add the onion, red or green pepper, celery, garlic, and cayenne pepper.

Sauté over medium-low heat for 4 or 5 minutes. Add the water and chicken parts or ham or turkey and bring to a boil. Reduce the heat to low, cover, and simmer for 30 minutes.

Stir in the rice, lima or butter beans, green peas or green beans, tomatoes, salt, and black pepper. Bring to a boil, reduce the heat to simmer, and cook for 30 minutes or until the rice and vegetables are tender.

Add the okra and simmer for 20 minutes longer or until the okra is done.

Serve the soup with crusty bread or corn muffins.

CURRIED RICE AND CHICKEN

Serves 4

*t*his is one of my favorite ways to prepare rice for church company. Sometimes I substitute shrimp for the chicken, and both dishes draw rave reviews.

1 pound boneless chicken breast
3 tablespoons olive oil
1 cup uncooked long-grain
 white rice
2 to 3 teaspoons curry powder
2 tablespoons chopped parsley or
 cilantro
½ cup chopped green onions

1 teaspoon salt
¼ teaspoon freshly ground
 black pepper
1 cup chicken broth or Homemade
 Chicken Stock (see recipe on
 page 234)
1 cup water

Cut the chicken into 2-inch pieces and set aside.

Heat 2 tablespoons of the oil in a medium saucepan until quite hot. Add a few of the chicken strips at a time and sauté quickly, until lightly browned. This should take 2 to 3 minutes. Remove the chicken when browned and continue sautéing the remaining chicken in the same way and remove from the pan.

Stir the remaining tablespoon of oil into the pan. Add the rice, curry, parsley or cilantro, green onions, salt, and black pepper. Cook over low heat, stirring, for 3 or 4 minutes.

Stir in the chicken broth and water. Cover and bring to a boil, stir again, and then reduce heat to medium-low.

Cook the rice for 12 minutes or until it is almost tender. Stir in the chicken and cook for 5 minutes longer, or until the chicken is done and the rice is fluffy and all the liquid is absorbed. Turn the heat off and let the dish sit on the same burner for 5 minutes.

LOVE OF LIFE

Chip said later that the moment he laid eyes upon Mabel he decided he wanted to spend the rest of his life with her. She remembers thinking that he was terribly attractive, but since she was already involved with someone else, she decided she would introduce Chip to one of her girlfriends.

It was a cold day in February 1989, and Mabel was having a small cocktail party at her home in Manassas, Virginia, in honor of a friend who was visiting from California. In walked Chip, a cousin of the friend.

As they stood facing each other in the living room, neither Chip nor Mabel had the slightest idea what the other was thinking. But nature and circumstances intervened and soon the telephone line was on fire from Greenbelt, Maryland, where Chip lived at the time, to Mabel's home in Manassas.

Mabel and Chip found out they had a lot to share. Both had been married and divorced; Mabel had two grown sons. Chip was nearing forty and Mabel was already in her forties. They weren't exactly pining for instant love.

"At first we didn't click," recalls Mabel. "But we started talking and became good friends. After a while I was telling him all of my business and he was telling me all of his."

Then this idyllic friendship began to change ever so slightly. Dates followed. Passions bloomed. They went on a loveboat cruise together to Nova Scotia in August of that same year, and somewhere out in the yonder, Chip proposed and Mabel accepted.

A little more than a year later, on September 3, 1990, Mabel James and William "Chip" Kinzer were married in a small service at the Little Union Baptist Church in Dumfries, Virginia. In keeping with an ancient ceremony, a handful of rice was thrown at the newlyweds, wishing them prosperity and abundance.

"Both of us had been married before," says Chip, "and although we had both been brought up in the church, as adults we moved away. We have God in our life now, and that is our common bond and nothing

Rice for Life and Other Grains

can separate that bond. We decided we were going to get married in the church and stay in the church. We love our church; we love the camaraderie, the fellowship."

The Little Union Baptist Church was founded in 1903 by a prominent local family, the Bates, who are still leaders of the church, which has some three hundred members. The original church is a small dwelling with aluminum siding and a brick front and sits in a picture-pretty, quiet, wooded area in the small town of Dumfries, which according to Chip, who has done thorough research on the county, was an important mining town during the nineteenth century. It now adjoins a new million-dollar structure that opened last year, in part with a $100,000 donation from David Robinson, a basketball superstar with the San Antonio Spurs, whose mother, Freda Robinson, is a member of the church.

Like many other black church members across the country, Chip and Mabel put their career skills to use for the good of the church and the community. A few years ago Mabel retired from the Department of the Navy, where she had worked as a program analyst. Recently she began her own travel business, specializing in booking cruises. Chip is a facilitator for the United States Postal System, and he produces a postal newsletter and video that are used as employee-training tools.

Four times a year Chip and Mabel write, edit, and produce the church's newsletter, *The Gazette*, which covers a wide range of events, including profiles, church and community history, wedding and anniversary announcements, testimonials, interviews with politicians, health and other currents issues, in addition to a children's and youth corner. Mabel is also the church's official photographer.

"This is our gift to the church," says Mabel, referring to their volunteer work. "We love our church. It keeps the community connected; it keeps us connected."

And with that said, the couple turned to the kitchen to prepare the baked rice that they served at their reception and which Mabel cooks all the time.

BAKED RICE

2 cloves garlic

½ onion

2 stalks celery

½ green or red pepper

2 tablespoons butter or margarine

7 or 8 chopped basil leaves
  (optional)

1½ cups long-grain white rice

¾ teaspoon salt

Pinch each of ground red, white,
  and black pepper

3 cups chicken broth or Homemade
  Chicken Stock (see recipe on
  page 234)

Preheat the oven to 350 degrees. Butter a 9 × 5 × 3-inch loaf pan or a 2-quart baking dish and set aside.

Mince the garlic; finely chop the onion; dice the celery; core and dice the green or red pepper. Heat the butter or margarine in a large skillet. Stir in the garlic, onion, celery, and green or red pepper, and the basil if desired. Sauté over medium heat for 5 minutes. Stir in the rice, salt, and the red, white, and black pepper. Remove from heat.

Spoon the rice mixture into the loaf pan or baking dish. Pour in the chicken broth or stock. Cover the pan with a layer of aluminum foil and seal the edges tightly.

Place the pan on the lower shelf of the oven. Bake for 50 minutes or until the rice is tender but not mushy, stirring once or twice.

Spoon the rice onto a warm platter.

Variation: For a nice fragrant touch, substitute imported jasmine rice from Thailand for the long-grain variety. Jasmine rice is similar in length to long-grain rice, but yields a creamy cooked texture like short-grain rice. (See "So Many Grains of Rice" on page 58.)

TRUE GRITS: GROUNDING CORN

During slavery African-Americans dried ears of corn, pounded the kernels in a mortar, and then sifted, creating two or three different grain sizes. The finest grain was cornmeal, which was used for cornbread. And since nothing went to waste on the plantations–certainly as far as the slaves were concerned–the coarser grain was simmered with bits of pork fat and cooked pretty much the same way many people cook grits today.

When I was growing up we ate our grits plain, with a dab of butter, a sprinkling of salt, plenty of black pepper, and occasionally with a dusting of grated cheddar cheese. Nowadays grits take all kind of guises, from soufflés to casseroles, and they have moved from the breakfast table to brunch, lunch, and dinner fare.

Recently Ouida Evans prepared grits the old-fashioned way for her church's annual tea, which is held in late morning at the First Missionary Baptist Church in Handsboro, Mississippi, on the Gulf Coast.

Ouida's family history dates back more than one hundred years at the church, and she seems duty bound to tradition by her genes. Her great-grandfather, Henry Barnes, was a church pastor during the 1800s; a generation later her grandfather, Earl Barnes, was a head deacon; and her grandfather's sister, Agnes Perry, who is ninety-two and for years was the church's pianist, still cringes at the sound of a faulty struck V7-chord.

"This is a family church in every sense of the word," says Ouida, who is in her early forties. "Everybody here is kin to each other. My whole family was raised in this church."

The historic 138-year-old red-brick church is located on the Pass Road, a main thoroughfare in Handsboro, and it has a membership of eight hundred or so, including a dazzling children's choir of eighty-eight strong voices. On Sundays, the Reverend S. V. Adolph Jr. preaches to a standing-room crowd, including many visitors attached to nearby military bases.

Ouida works nights as a nurse's assistant so she has days free to devote to the church. She sings in the choir, attends service regularly, and is a member of the Ever Ready Club, which, as the name implies, doesn't stand on ceremony.

"We take our name from that battery commercial," says Ouida, by way of explanation. She laughs and adds, "Whenever somebody needs something done we try to do it."

The club, which has some thirty-five members with an active core of half that number, assists the infirm with day-to-day living, raises money for scholarships, delivers gift baskets to senior citizens during the holidays, and sponsors teenage girls in local beauty pageants and coming-out events.

One of Ever Ready's biggest affairs is the church's annual tea, which offers a glorious Southern breakfast prepared by club members: sweet rolls, toast, bacon, eggs, spicy sausages, hot breads with jellies and preserves, quiche, mixed fruits, a variety of teas, and of course, grits.

Ouida prepares the grits. And she uses a recipe that has been in her family for years.

Down=South Grits

Serves 4 to 6

he key to cooking good grits, says Ouida, is to keep stirring and stirring, so that they end up fluffy and light, in true Southern style. A wooden spoon works best for the stirring, and don't even think of using quick cooking or instant grits.

3 cups water
1 cup regular hominy grits
½ teaspoon salt
2 tablespoons butter or margarine

1 to 1½ cups milk
¼ teaspoon freshly ground
black pepper

Pour the water into a large heavy pot and bring to a boil. Gradually stir in the grits. Add the salt. Reduce the heat to low, and cook, uncovered, stirring occasionally with a large spoon, for 10 minutes, or until the water is almost absorbed.

Stir in the butter or margarine and reduce the heat to low. Pour in a couple of tablespoons of the milk and stir until it is absorbed.

Continue adding the milk this way for about 20 minutes, making sure to stir from the bottom of the pot so that the grits don't burn.

The total amount of milk you add will depend on whether you prefer creamy or stiff grits. When fluffy and done, stir in the black pepper and serve on warm plates.

Maya Moore, age 6, resorts to her fingers during the Christmas holiday dinner at the Metropolitan Missionary Baptist Church in Chicago.

CORN MATTERS

The corn that we enjoy today is a culinary blessing that descended from the wild corn that Native Americans cultivated hundreds of years ago. Their corn was a grain for life, and it was deified and used for celebrations and ceremonies, as well as eaten for sustenance.

Numerous varieties of corn are cultivated today and at the height of the summer corn season this grain is absolutely delicious, requiring a very brief cooking.

For best results and to appreciate this grain for all of its magnificence, plunge the ears into a big pot of boiling water, cook for 2 minutes, remove the pot from the heat, and allow to stand for 7 to 10 minutes. Now devour the corn, either plain or with a slathering of olive oil or butter and a sprinkling of freshly ground pepper or spices such as chili powder or cumin.

However, there are a couple of caveats to remember about corn: Overcooking makes it starchy and tough, and you should use corn as quickly as you can after buying it (refrigerate corn immediately if you're not going to use right away). Corn is loaded with sugar and the longer it lingers, the better the chance for the sugar to turn to starch.

Remember, too, that pulling back the husk and peeking at the corn kernels is a waste of time: It only exposes the kernels to the air and speeds the sugar-starch conversion. Learn to choose corn with your eyes and by touch. Look for plump, heavy ears that are shiny and glistening, with tightly wound, moist silks. Avoid ears with mealy, withered husks and dried silks.

Rice for Life and Other Grains

CREOLE CORN

Serves 6

*i*n one way it could be said that Phyllis Harris goes to church every day. Actually, she is the program director for a drug and alcohol facility sponsored by a nationwide Christian prison ministry. And she is also a trustee and member of the Finance Commission at the New Bethel African Methodist Episcopal Church in Orlando, Florida.

Mrs. Harris is involved in numerous activities at New Bethel, which is located on West Columbia Street.

She sends a delectable recipe for a corn dish that is perfect summer fare, when the corn season is in full splendor. She writes: "This recipe is ideal for outdoor activities, such as church fish fries, barbecues, and picnics.

Her suggested menu: pan-fried fish or fried chicken, steamed rice, collard or mustard greens, hush puppies or corn muffins, lemonade, and of course, the Creole Corn.

4 or 5 large ears yellow or bicolored corn kernels
1 onion
1 red or green pepper
1 chili pepper, jalapeño or cayenne
2 to 3 cloves garlic

¼ to ⅓ cup corn oil
2 firm ripe tomatoes, chopped, or 4 plum tomatoes, chopped
1½ teaspoons chili powder
1 teaspoon salt
½ teaspoon black pepper

Husk the corn, remove the silk, and then cut the kernels from the cobs, scraping to extract as much corn milk as possible. Set the corn aside. Discard the cobs.

Peel and chop the onion; core and dice the red or green pepper. Finely mince the jalapeño or cayenne and the garlic.

Heat the oil in a large heavy skillet. Add the onion, red or green pepper, chili pepper, and garlic to the pan and sauté for 5 minutes or until the onions are soft. Stir in the tomatoes, chili powder, salt, and black pepper; sauté 5 minutes longer. Stir in the corn and cook over low heat for 15 to 20 minutes, stirring occasionally, or until the corn is tender. Serve hot or at room temperature as a relish.

CREAMED FRESH CORN

Serves 3 to 4

eborah Sherow and Velma Mosley have known each other for years, and both are tirelessly involved in civic and church activities in Tyler, Texas. They are members of the Rosebud Civitan Club, which assists the mentally and physically disabled, and they also cook a lot.

Mrs. Sherow sends this recipe for a corn casserole—which she often carries out to the Greater Saint Mary Baptist Church, located on Texas College Road—along with good news about her church. She writes:

"The Reverend M. K. Mast has served as pastor of the Greater Saint Mary Baptist Church for twelve years. Under his leadership the church has converted many souls and added many members to its congregation.

"We started a bus ministry, organized the monthly prayer breakfast, added a vestibule to the entrance, added a covered shed to the side of the church, purchased and paved an additional parking lot, purchased new pews and carpeting, expanded kitchen facilities, added a fully equipped office, and employed a secretary. All praise go to God for our prosperity!"

Mrs. Sherow's recipe:

4 or 5 large ears fresh corn
1 teaspoon sugar
2 tablespoons butter or margarine
   or vegetable oil
½ teaspoon salt
¼ teaspoon freshly ground
   black pepper
½ to ¾ cup light cream or
   undiluted evaporated milk

Husk the corn, remove the silk, and cut the kernels from the cobs, scraping to remove as much of the corn cream and pulp as possible. Combine the corn with the sugar, place in a bowl, cover, and chill for 1 hour.

When ready to cook, heat the butter, margarine, or oil in a large skillet. Stir in the corn and cook over low heat for 10 minutes or until tender, stirring occasionally.

Add the salt, black pepper, and light cream or evaporated milk, mixing well. Cook for 10 to 15 minutes longer over low heat, stirring, or until the corn is tender, hot, and bubbly.

CORN PUDDING

Serves 4 or more

a commitment to social change runs deep with Dr. Ruth Wells, whose family members were among the founders of the Christian Hope Baptist Church in Philadelphia, Pennsylvania, established in 1925 by migrants from in and around Abbeville, South Carolina.

"As soon as a couple of people got on their feet," recalls Dr. Wells, reflecting on her family's migration pattern, "others would come. We all have a responsibility to give back. I come from that tradition."

Dr. Wells, who is a retired policewoman and safety educator at the University of Pennsylvania, is involved in numerous programs at Christian Hope Baptist Church, which is located on North 26th Street. At least once a month the church prepares dinner for the homeless. A van is sent to pick up the visitors, the table is set, and the guests are served baked or fried chicken, collard greens, a green salad, corn pudding, macaroni and cheese or potato salad, followed by ice cream for dessert.

"We try to make people feel comfortable, regardless of how they are attired or their station in life," says Dr. Wells, who is president of the Women's Division of the Pennsylvania Baptist State Convention. "When we feed the homeless we are sharing our bounty. We want them to eat just as we do. We don't have the homeless standing in line here. We have to do more to reaffirm our people."

Dr. Wells sends this recipe for corn pudding, which she says has been in her family for generations:

2½ cups fresh corn kernels

2 tablespoons flour

2 tablespoons sugar, more if desired

½ teaspoon salt

¼ teaspoon freshly ground black pepper

⅛ teaspoon cayenne pepper

2 tablespoons butter or margarine

2 eggs, room temperature

1 cup milk

¼ teaspoon ground nutmeg

Preheat the oven to 325 degrees.

Generously butter a 2-quart baking dish and set aside.

Place ½ cup of the corn in the blender and whirl until puréed.

In a large bowl, combine the puréed corn, remaining corn kernels, flour, sugar, salt, black pepper, and cayenne pepper and mix well. Cut the butter or margarine into small pieces and stir into the corn mixture.

Anniversary celebration at the Christian Hope Baptist Church in Philadelphia. Dr. Ruth Wells and the church's pastor, Reverend Boyce Jordan, serve guests.

Place the eggs into a medium bowl and beat vigorously until they are light and foamy. Add the beaten eggs and the milk to the corn mixture, stirring well.

Pour the pudding into the baking dish. Sprinkle the top with the nutmeg.

Set the dish into a large roasting pan and pour enough water into the roasting pan to reach about one-quarter of the way up the sides of the baking dish.

Carefully set the roasting pan (with the baking dish inside) in the hot oven on the middle shelf.

Bake the pudding for 40 to 45 minutes or until a knife inserted in the center comes out clean.

Remove from the oven, let set a few minutes, and serve hot.

MACARONI AND CHEESE

Serves 4

ust how and why African-Americans developed a love for this dish is lost with history, but one thing is known for sure, macaroni and cheese is family eating. It is a part of our ceremony, and this steaming-hot, creamy casserole is usually served at backyard barbecues, church picnics, funeral repasts, and holiday celebrations.

I have been served many versions of the dish over the years, but none was more delicious than this classic recipe sent by Mary Godfrey, who carries out food all the time to Shiloh Baptist Church in Choctaw County, Alabama. And although her family says she cooks "way too much" food, Mary always returns home from church empty-handed.

3 tablespoons vegetable oil
½ pound uncooked elbow
    macaroni
1 finely chopped onion
¼ teaspoon ground nutmeg
⅛ teaspoon cayenne
¼ teaspoon freshly ground
    black pepper

½ teaspoon salt
2 teaspoons spicy mustard
1½ tablespoons flour
2 cups milk
2 cups grated sharp Cheddar cheese

Preheat the oven to 375 degrees. Oil a 1½-quart ovenproof casserole and set aside.

Fill a large stockpot with a least 6 quarts of water. Add one tablespoon of the vegetable oil to the water, so as to keep the macaroni from sticking together during cooking. Place the pot on high heat and bring to a rolling boil.

Add the macaroni and cook for the length of time specified on the package, making sure not to overcook the pasta. Drain immediately, and rinse the pasta with cold, running water. Set aside.

Heat the remaining oil in a large skillet. Add the onion and sauté

over medium-low heat for 4 or 5 minutes or until tender and translucent. Stir in the nutmeg, cayenne, black pepper, salt, mustard, and flour and sauté 3 or 4 minutes longer.

Add the milk and 1 cup of the cheese. Increase the heat to medium-high, and bring the sauce to a gentle boil. Reduce the heat to low and cook, stirring, for about 10 minutes longer or until the sauce thickens.

Remove the sauce from the heat and stir in the well-drained macaroni. Pour the mixture into the oiled baking dish. Sprinkle the macaroni with the remaining cheese.

Place the dish on the middle shelf of the hot oven and bake for 18 to 20 minutes or until hot and bubbly and the cheese is melted.

A BOUNTY OF PEAS AND BEANS

i was grown and living in New York before I realized that everybody didn't eat peas or beans two or three times per week. Back home during the summer we ate garden-fresh crowder peas, black-eyed peas, and green lima beans, which were also called butter beans. In the winter we moved on

to Mama's canned jars, and when that supply ran out in late winter or early spring, we ate a variety of dried peas and beans, such as navy, kidney, limas, split pea, and a little red chili bean that we cooked with tomato rice.

Regardless of the time of year, there was always a pot of savory peas or beans simmering on the stove, which we would ladle over a wedge of cornbread or spoon over a mound of rice or macaroni or white potatoes. We would quickly forget the meat that we didn't have—or by that time—really want, since the peas or beans were so downright delicious.

People have been eating peas and beans since Biblical days. In the book of Genesis, Jacob gave Esau bread and pottage of lentils. In the book of Ezekiel, bread was made of "wheat and barley, and beans and lentils and millet, and fitches" ("fitches" is a Middle English word of Latin origin for "*vetch*," which means "legume"). Archaeological traces show that prehistoric, nomadic tribes subsisted on berries, seeds, and wild peas, beans, and grains. There is also evidence that the early Egyptians actually worshipped dried beans.

However, for some reason, through the passage of time, peas and beans fell out of favor and became known as the "poor man's meat." But what a substitute! Dried peas and beans are a fine source of nonmeat protein, as well as a good boost of bone-building calcium, a fair amount of iron, and a healthy dose of the B vitamins, and all this in a "meat" that's virtually fat- and cholesterol-free.

A bowl of beans or peas served with grains, such as unpolished rice or barley or millet, is a staple diet in many parts of the world, and provides as much protein as meat.

There are hundreds of varieties of peas and beans grown around the world, available in a rainbow of colors and an array of shapes and flavors. The color range is dazzling: white, beige, pink, red, purple, lavender, tan, yellow, green, brown, black, mottled, speckled, dotted, and splashed. The legumes, as this family of plants is called, can be round, oval, tiny or fat, flat or kidney shape. And the flavors vary, from the subtle delicacy of the red lentil to the earthy robustness of the black bean.

The most commonly seen dried legumes are (in alphabetical order):

baby lima bean, black bean,
black-eyed pea, cannellini bean,
chick-pea, cow pea, cranberry
bean, crowder pea, fava bean,
Great Northern bean, kidney
bean, lentil, navy bean, pigeon
pea, pink bean, pinto bean,
red bean, soybean, and split pea,
which can be either green or
yellow, the latter possessing
the more distinctive flavor of
the two.

Peas and beans can be used
in soups, puréed and used as
a velvety spread for bread and
crackers; prepared and ladled
over rice and potatoes, or

Pot-luck feast at Our Lady Queen of Peace Catholic Church in Arlington, Virginia.

tossed with herbs and a little bit of olive oil and
garlic for a delightful salad. But for many African- and Caribbean-
Americans, no New Year's celebration is complete without a big
pot of black-eyed peas, crowder, or red beans or peas, which brings
prosperity and good luck for the rest of the year.

Over the years I have heard many African-Americans express their
love for peas and beans, but few can match the zeal shown by the
great trumpet player and favorite son of New Orleans, Louis Armstrong,
who signed autographs, "Red beans and ricely yours."

That is, unless you discount the praise songs of Albert Stevenson, who
like Satchmo, was born and raised in the Crescent City, or the Big Easy,
as he calls New Orleans.

Mr. Stevenson remembers that when he was growing up his family
ate peas and beans several times a week, beginning with red beans on
Mondays, which is still a New Orleans tradition. The story goes that this
custom harks back to the days when black cooks put on a pot of beans

to cook on Mondays while doing the laundry by hand all day.

During the rest of the week, he recalls, the family ate white beans or perhaps a bowl of fresh butter beans simmered with a chunk of pickled pork. Fried chicken was served on Sundays, to go with the beans and rice, and during the week there was a slice or two of boiled beef brisket or roast pork.

"We ate those red beans and rice out of necessity," recalls Mr. Stevenson. "It was a way to stretch a meal. But now that I think about it, we ate pretty well. My father was a seaman, a merchant marine, and he traveled around the world. But there was nothing he loved more than red beans and rice."

Mr. Stevenson and his wife, Azalea, are members of the Mount Zion United Methodist Church, which is located on Louisiana Avenue in New Orleans. Mr. Stevenson is the church's treasurer.

A while back Mount Zion launched a drive to raise funds for renovations and then set in motion a series of events, including a fish fry contest, cake sales, a flea market, and a series of breakfasts and banquets. Mr. Stevenson often cooked beans and rice.

He sends this recipe:

LOUISIANA RED BEANS

Serves 8

1 pound dried small red beans, soaked (see "Getting Soaked" on page 98)
1 onion
1 green pepper
8 cloves garlic
2 tablespoons vegetable oil
¼ cup chopped parsley

5 to 6 cups water
½ teaspoon freshly ground black pepper
1 bay leaf
½ pound smoked ham, preferably with bone
1 teaspoon salt

Rinse the soaked beans well with cold water and set aside. Slice the onion; core and dice the green pepper; mince the garlic.

Heat the oil in a large heavy pot. Add the onion, green pepper, garlic, and parsley. Sauté over low heat for 4 or 5 minutes. Add 5 cups of water, soaked beans, black pepper, bay leaf, and ham. Bring to a boil. Reduce the heat to simmer, cover, and cook for 1½ to 2 hours stirring occasionally, or until the beans are tender and creamy. (If the beans become too dry, heat the remaining 1 cup of water and add as needed.)

When the beans are tender, remove a cup or so from the pot. Place in a bowl and mash with a fork. Stir the mashed beans back into the pot. Remove the ham from the pot, cut the meat into small pieces and stir back into the pot. Discard the bone.

Stir in the salt, if needed, and simmer the beans for 15 minutes more. Serve the beans over hot rice.

NEW YEAR'S BLACK=EYED PEAS

Serves 6 to 8

sther Hurd remembers that her family ate red beans and rice several times a week when she was growing up in Wiggins, Mississippi, but come New Year's Day, her mother would put on a pot of traditional Southern black-eyed peas, which were supposed to bring prosperity and good luck for the rest of the year.

Mrs. Hurd has lived in Chicago since 1944, but her cooking still reflects her roots. And so does her celebrations and her faith. She is an active member of the Saint Ethelreda Roman Catholic Church, located on South Paulina Street, where she is involved in a range of activities.

She is a fine cook, favoring spicy dishes with lots of herbs and hot peppers, and she often carries out a dish or two to the church senior citizen hall. On New Year's Day, following that old Southern tradition, she always serves black-eyed peas to church friends and family, and everybody present is blessed by her presence and beneficence.

Mrs. Hurd sends this recipe:

1 pound dried black-eyed peas, soaked (see "Getting Soaked" on page 98)
2 celery stalks
2 onions
4 cloves garlic
3 tablespoons vegetable oil

¼ to ½ teaspoon dried thyme
½ teaspoon freshly ground black pepper
¼ teaspoon cayenne
1 meaty ham bone, about ½ pound
4 cups water
1 teaspoon salt, if needed

Rinse the soaked beans and set aside. Dice the celery, chop the onions, and mince the garlic.

Heat the oil in a large heavy pot. Add the celery, onion, and garlic and sauté over medium heat for 4 or 5 minutes. Crush the thyme and add to the pot.

Stir in the black pepper, cayenne, ham bone, water and the soaked peas.

COUNTING PEAS AND BEANS

We know from our foremothers that dried peas and beans go a long way. One cup of dried peas or beans will yield from 2½ to 3 cups of cooked legumes, or enough for 4 servings. And similarly, 2 cups of dried peas and beans weigh approximately 1 pound and yield 5 to 6 cups of cooked legumes, which should serve 8.

The cooking time of peas and beans varies, depending on the variety. Lentils and split peas have thin skins and require no soaking and therefore cook in 30 minutes or so. Dried black-eyed peas and baby limas can be cooked in 40 minutes or so. On the other hand, tough-skinned legumes, such as the pinto or navy bean, are best soaked for at least 8 hours and require 3 or more hours' cooking.

Bring to a boil. Cover, reduce heat to low, and cook for 45 minutes or until the peas are tender but not mushy.

Remove the ham from the broth and shred coarsely, or cut the meat from the ham bone and stir back into the pot. Stir in the salt, if desired.

If the peas become too dry during the cooking, heat a little water and add as needed.

Butter Beans with Sausage

Serves 4 or 5

ovie Williams doesn't like to get into any hassles in the kitchen at the Mount Calvary Christian Center in Jackson, Mississippi, so when the younger women come in with their clipboards and notepads and talk about planning menus and assigning duties, she goes along with the program, as the saying goes. Often they would ask her whether she would like to do the chicken and dumplings, sweet potatoes, greens, baked ham, fried chicken, fish, dinner rolls, cake or pies, or butter beans.

Actually, Mrs. Williams could cook for a roomful of people without giving much thought to it. She is the mother of fifteen children, and she knows a lot about cooking for a crowd.

This valiant, spunky, indomitable, God-fearing woman is the mother of the church at Mount Calvary Christian Center, a Baptist church, located on Yarbrough Street, and every time I talk with her I feel her energy and courage.

At age seventy-two she works twelve hours weekly as a home attendant, explaining, "I like to remain active, and I like to be independent with my own money."

She sends this recipe for fresh butter beans, or as Northerners say, lima beans, which during the height of the summer growing season can be nutty and sweet and almost ethereal in flavor. In the old days, Mrs. Williams simmered the beans with ham hocks, but now she often uses turkey sausage.

3 pounds fresh butter beans in pods (limas)	*1½ to 2 cups water*
½ green or red pepper	*½ teaspoon salt*
2 links turkey sausage	*¼ teaspoon freshly ground black pepper*
3 tablespoons bacon drippings or vegetable oil	*¼ teaspoon cayenne or hot pepper flakes*

Shell the beans, rinse well with cold water, and set aside.

Finely mince the green or red pepper and cut the sausage crosswise into ½-inch-thick slices.

Heat the bacon drippings or vegetable oil in a large saucepan. Add the green or red pepper and the sausage and sauté, turning, for 5 or 6 minutes, or until the sausage is lightly browned.

Stir in the water, salt, black pepper, and cayenne or hot pepper flakes, and the beans. Bring to a boil. Reduce the heat to low, cover, and simmer for 40 to 50 minutes or until the beans are tender.

Variation: If fresh limas aren't available, substitute frozen baby lima beans, using two 10-ounce packages. Proceed as directed above, reducing the cooking time to 10 to 12 minutes and the water to 1 cup.

GETTING SOAKED

The purpose of soaking is to remove some of the gas-causing sugars in dried legumes and to soften the skin to cut the cooking time. Years ago Mama always soaked her dried peas or beans overnight in a big bowl of water. But the processing and cultivation of beans have changed in recent years and dried legumes no longer have to be soaked overnight. Most dried beans and peas can be used after 3 or 4 hours of soaking. But if it is more convenient to soak overnight, then do so.

Unfortunately, there are few absolutes in cooking. I have found that dried navy beans are particularly tough-skinned and should be soaked at least eight hours or overnight, while black-eyed peas and dried limas cook quicker and require only a few hours soaking. On the other hand, lentils and split peas are "thin-skinned," and don't have to be soaked at all.

The soaking procedure is simple: Pick over the dried peas and beans and remove any stones or debris or clumps of dirt. Rinse with cold water and then place the dried legumes in a large pot, cover with enough cold water to rise at least 3 inches above the peas or beans, and let stand for 4 hours. (If you cover with boiling water you can cut the soaking to 2 hours.) At the end of the soaking, rinse the peas or beans well with cold running water.

However, if you are really pressed for time, there is a popular quick way to "soak" dried peas and beans: Pick over the legumes and rinse well with cold water. Place the peas or beans in a large pot, cover with at least 3 inches of water, and place on medium-high heat. Bring to a boil and cook for 2 minutes. Remove immediately from heat and let set for 1 hour. At the end of the soaking, rinse the beans or peas again under cold running water.

Word of caution: I am not so keen on the quick-soak method since it seems to cause the beans or peas to split during cooking and become mushy. But if you must, you must.

BAKED LIMA BEANS

Serves 8

every Saturday Vera Edwards gives piano lessons to a half-dozen youngsters at the Newman Memorial United Methodist Church in Brooklyn, continuing a cycle that began more than sixty-five years ago when she was a child studying music at the church.

This was the 1930s, and fleeing the crippling effects of the Great Depression, her mother and father, Celestia and James Ralph, who originally were from Baltimore, left their home in Atlantic City and moved again, this time to Bedford-Stuyvesant in Brooklyn, to seek a better life.

Her family quickly joined Newman Memorial Church, and soon Vera was studying piano with a renown pianist and church member, Maude B. Cummings Taylor, whose tutelage she remained under for twelve years.

Mrs. Edwards's life has revolved around music ever since. She has taught piano to hundreds of neighborhood youths, many of whom came to the studio she operated on President Street in Crown Heights, Brooklyn, from late 1973 to 1986.

In later life she developed a passion for writing, and with the encouragement of her daughter, Marlyn Banks, she enrolled in a writers course. In 1993 a children's story by Mrs. Edwards, "Oops, Poor Baby," was selected and published by the American Literary Press as one of the top ten stories of the year.

Today Mrs. Edwards lives in Hempstead, New York, with her daughter, Marlyn, but Newman Memorial remains their homechurch.

"I can't see myself going to another church," says Mrs. Edwards. "We have so many memories there. I grew up in Bedford-Stuyvesant and that church was my family's lifeblood."

She sends up this recipe for lima beans that she bakes during the holidays in memory of her mother, who carried the dish to Newman Memorial during its annual homecoming celebration, held in November.

1 pound dried lima beans, soaked
  (see "Getting Soaked" on
  page 98)
4 cups cold water
1 or 2 whole cloves
3 tablespoons olive oil
¼ cup dark brown sugar, or more,
  if desired

2 tablespoons dark molasses
1 teaspoon cinnamon
1 teaspoon ground nutmeg
½ teaspoon salt
¼ teaspoon freshly ground
  black pepper
1 cup tomato sauce, canned or
  homemade (recipe follows)

Rinse the soaked beans well under cold running water. Place the beans in a large pan and cover with the water. Add the cloves. Bring to a boil, reduce the heat to low, and cook the beans for about 50 minutes or until they are just tender.

Drain the beans, reserving 2 cups of their cooking liquid.

Preheat the oven to 325 degrees.

Oil a 2-quart baking dish with a little of the olive oil. Place the beans in the baking dish. Drizzle over the remaining oil and mix well. Set aside.

Combine in a medium saucepan the reserved water, sugar, molasses, cinnamon, nutmeg, salt, black pepper, and tomato sauce. Place on low heat and cook 3 or 4 minutes, stirring. Pour the sauce over the beans, mixing well.

Set the pan in the middle shelf of the hot oven and bake for 1 hour and 15 minutes, stirring occasionally, or until the beans are brown and glazed.

QUICK TOMATO SAUCE

Makes about 2 cups

*6 or 7 fresh basil leaves, or
  ½ teaspoon dried basil or
  oregano leaves*
½ onion
2 cloves garlic
*2 tablespoons olive oil or
  vegetable oil*

¼ teaspoon salt
*⅛ teaspoon freshly ground
  black pepper*
⅛ teaspoon cayenne
1 tablespoon soy sauce
*2 cups chopped fresh or canned
  tomatoes*

Chop the fresh basil or crush the dried herb. Chop the onion and mince the garlic.

Heat the oil in a medium saucepan. Stir into the pan the herb, onion, and garlic. Sauté over medium-low heat for 5 minutes or until the onions are soft and translucent.

Add the salt, black pepper, cayenne, soy sauce, and tomatoes. Bring to a boil, and then reduce heat immediately. Cover and simmer the sauce for 15 to 20 minutes.

If desired, whirl the sauce in the blender to purée, and reheat again if serving warm.

IN REMEMBRANCE

Ivora Peazant is quick to say that the success of the bereavement program at the Downs Memorial United Methodist Church in Oakland, California, is owed more to her organizational skills than to her culinary expertise. She is a retired analyst for the Department of Health and Human Services in Berkeley, and has had years of experience executing plans. But she is also an accomplished cook who has carried out many covered dishes to Downs Memorial over the years, even while she was fine-tuning the church's system for providing a funeral repast for families of the deceased.

The church has designed its congregation into a unique system of geographical units based on zip codes, so as to connect its members to the pastor, the Reverend Douglass Fitch, and to one another. Many of the church's six hundred or so members live from thirty to forty miles away in the cities of San Jose, Richmond, Vallejo, and Freemont, as well as in nearby Berkeley. Each unit has a leader, and each unit generally covers twelve to fifteen households. For several years Mrs. Peazant served as chairwoman of this system.

When a church member passed, Mrs. Peazant would notify the unit leader, who in turn would meet with the family to find out if assistance was needed with burial arrangements, buying flowers, contacting family members, and whether the family desired a benevolence meal at the church after the interment. This system is still in operation today.

Downs Memorial offers families of the deceased a standard menu, which consists of baked turkey, mashed potatoes or rice, a steamed vegetable, tossed salad, cake, punch, and coffee. The church uses its funds to buy the turkey, but the members of the unit prepare and donate the rest of the food.

"Often during a death the family has so much to do that the members don't have a chance to sit down and have a decent meal," says Mrs. Peazant. "The whole purpose of this repast is to allow the family to sit down after a traumatic experience, and for the church and the community to show and express their sympathy. Sometimes the family members linger at the church until late afternoon, and the gathering becomes a family reunion."

Mrs. Peazant, a native of New Orleans, sends this recipe for navy beans, which she has carried out to Downs Memorial, located on Idaho Street, on many occasions.

HOME=STYLE NAVY BEANS

Serves 8

1 pound dried navy beans, soaked overnight or at least 8 hours (see "Getting Soaked" on page 98)
½ pound smoked ham or meaty ham bone
6 cups water
2 cloves garlic
1 large onion

1 red or green pepper
2 tablespoons chopped parsley
1 bay leaf
½ teaspoon cayenne
½ teaspoon freshly ground black pepper
1 teaspoon salt

Rinse the soaked beans and set aside.

Combine the ham and water in a large pot. Bring to a boil, cover, reduce the heat to simmer, and cook for 30 minutes.

Remove the meat and the bone from the cooking liquid. Reserve the liquid in the pot, shred the meat, and save the bone. Set the meat and bone aside.

Mince the garlic, chop the onion, core and dice the red or green pepper. Add to the pot the soaked navy beans, garlic, onion, red or green pepper, parsley, bay leaf, cayenne, and black pepper.

Bring to a boil. Return the shredded ham and the bone back to the pot. Reduce the heat to simmer. Cover and cook for 3 hours or until the beans are tender and creamy. If the beans become a little dry during the cooking, heat a little water and add to the pot as needed.

Stir in the salt and cook 15 minutes longer.

Variation: Mrs. Peazant sometimes substitutes a chunk of smoked turkey, either the neck, wing, or thigh, for the ham.

Glorious Crowder Peas

Serves 4 or 5

When I was growing up every family was expected to feed the preacher at least once during the year, so we always tried our best to save a couple jars of crowder peas for the Reverend Barlow, who especially liked the way Mama prepared them. Mama kept her canned fruits and vegetables in an old massive Empire mahogany sideboard that sat at the end of the dining room. As the fall moved quickly into winter, we would watch her pull jar after jar from the sideboard, and our summer harvest would appear on our tables as inviting as sparkling jewels.

When the pastor came to dinner Mama would make fried chicken or roast pork, rice with gravy, stewed tomatoes and corn, macaroni and cheese, cornbread, one or two fruit pies, and always crowder peas with okra, which Reverend Barlow and I ate more of than anybody else.

We grew the vegetables in our garden in a patch that sloped gently toward a wooded area flanked by tall majestic pine trees. This was the mid–1950s, and by that time we had built our new house and now lived in the Negro section of town with the Methodists, some of whom came out of Reconstruction with a mule and an acre or two—if not the promised forty—of land.

The house was located on the top of a grass-covered red-dirt hill, separated from the garden by several heavy-bearing plum and fig trees that stood on the north side of the garden, within arms' distance of the back porch. This wasn't an extraordinarily big lot, and Mama apparently planted what she liked best. I remember greens; scallions or green onions;

Gloria Ransom, a member of Ben Hill United Methodist Church in Atlanta, Georgia, prepares a savory bean dish for a family-church gathering.

sweet potatoes; tomatoes; okra; hot peppers; squash; corn; beets; white potatoes; and three or four kinds of peas and beans—usually crowder peas, lima or butter beans as they were sometimes called; black-eyed peas; and snap beans. Whatever else we wanted for canning we gathered from neighbors, who usually gave away more than they sold.

As I reflect on those days it seems that Mama never ceased working, and since I was the only girl at home and was her constant companion (I have four brothers; my sister, Helen, was married by then). I guess I did my share, too. In late August, when it was time to pick the peas and beans for canning, Mama and I would rise early, grab a foot tub, and head for the garden, wearing floppy straw hats and long-sleeve shirts to shield us from the hot Alabama sun. By 10 A.M. we were drenched with perspiration, which we wiped at with our shirttails, and taking this as a cue, we would pick up our tub of vegetables and call it quits for the day.

We would pack the peas and beans in large burlap bags and store them in a shed in the backyard, and then we'd pick again the next day. When we had picked enough peas and beans to can, Aunt Agnes—actually my great-aunt, for she was my maternal grandmother's sister—would come over in late afternoon, after the midday sun cooled, and help with the shelling.

This was more or less our leisure time. We always drank iced tea, ate a tea cake or two, and exchanged news and gossip as our fingers skillfully scaled the peas and beans and split open the pods.

The next morning Mama would rise early and start canning, for again, we had to be out of the hot kitchen before midday. For years we had an old wood-burning cast-iron stove that Mama kept in the kitchen as a relic, but during the canning season she would put it to work, although I am sure now that the stove threw off so much heat that it was anything *but* charming.

It was my job to sterilize the canning jars, which were put in a big pot and placed on the old stove. Mama would work on the gas range, processing the peas and beans as I passed on the jars to her.

When the jars were packed, cooked, and cooled, Mama would place

NAME CALLING

Crowder peas are grown in many home gardens in the South, and in true Southern tradition, there is no general agreement on their name. Some people call them cow peas and others call them field peas. Regardless, crowder peas have a nuttier flavor than black-eyed peas, although the two can be used interchangeably in most recipes.

Fresh crowder peas are sold during the summer and fall at vegetables stands, farmers' markets, and African-American specialty stores across the country. In the winter, the frozen variety is found in supermarkets and is a good substitute for the fresh legume.

them in the sideboard that was already gleaming with row after row of our harvest. I would take a deep breath, glad that we had finished canning one lot of the vegetables, and even happier that we would have crowder peas and okra during the winter, which the Reverend Barlow liked a lot.

This was Mama's recipe:

3 pounds fresh crowder peas
  in pods
1 onion
1 hot chili pepper
3 tablespoons vegetable oil
½ pound smoked ham or smoked
  turkey, preferably with bone
1 small bay leaf

¼ teaspoon freshly ground
  black pepper
½ teaspoon salt
2 cups water, or chicken broth
  or Homemade Chicken Stock
  (see recipe on page 234)
1 cup fresh okra pods

Shell the pods, pick over the peas, and discard any with wormy holes. If any of the peas are too tiny to shell, snap in half. Rinse well with cold water and set aside.

Chop the onion. Finely mince the chili pepper. Heat the oil in a large pot. Add the onion and pepper and sauté for 4 or 5 minutes or until the onions are soft.

Add the ham or turkey, bay leaf, black pepper, salt, and water or chicken broth or stock. Bring to a boil, cover, and cook over low heat for 30 minutes.

Stir the peas into the pot, bring the pot to a boil. Reduce to a simmer, cover and cook for 30 to 40 minutes or until the peas are just tender.

Add the okra and cook 20 minutes longer, or until all the vegetables are tender.

Baccalaureate Day, held in honor of all graduating church youngsters, from kindergarten to college, at Hartford Memorial Baptist Church, Detroit. Visiting that day were some 80 members from the First African Baptist Church in Savannah, Georgia. Left to right: Reverend Thurmond Tillman, pastor of the First African Baptist Church, at table with the Reverend Charles Adams, pastor of Hartford Memorial Baptist Church, and his wife, Mrs. Agnes Adams. Delores Brandon, the church's kitchen manager-administrator, serves the guests.

A Bounty of Peas and Beans

Hoppin' John

Serves 6 to 8

here has been much speculation about the name of this dish, but the true origin still remains a mystery. Some say that the man who created the dish walked with a limp. Others suggest that the name could be an Arabic derivation used by slaves in the rice kitchens of Carolina, who had been exposed to a considerable Muslim presence in Africa before the Middle Passage to the Americas.

The only thing known for sure about Hoppin' John is that the dish came out of South Carolina, and it is made with black-eyed peas and rice, although I have heard my Southern relatives say that it really should be made with crowder peas. Whatever.

Al Bridges, the owner of Chanterelle's, a "gourmet soul food" restaurant in Atlanta, makes the dish with black-eyed peas, rice, and a handful of corn, which he says is the right way to him.

Al is a member of the Big Bethel African Methodist Episcopal Church in Atlanta, located on Auburn Avenue, and until recently, every other Sunday he and his staff cooked and served 125 worshippers after service.

In the quixotic way of some black churchfolks, Mr. Bridges himself is a vegetarian, and therefore his "meat" is actually peas and beans. And yes, Mr. Bridges serves beef and lamb at his restaurant, but no pork.

"I've been catering food at Big Bethel since the mid–1980s," says Mr. Bridges, "and the people there have gotten used to my cooking style. They know when I cook Hoppin' John or black-eyed peas for New Year's I am not going to

Executive chef, Deaconess Ernestine Bradley, prepares her popular vegetable fritters at Canaan Baptist Church in Harlem, New York, for the Black History Month celebration.

SOUL FOOD 108

add any ham hocks. I season so well with herbs and spices that I don't think they notice the difference anymore."

This is Al's Hoppin' John recipe:

4 cups cooked New Year's Black-
  Eyed Peas (see recipe on
  page 94)
2 cups water
½ teaspoon salt
½ teaspoon freshly ground
  black pepper

¼ teaspoon ground mace or nutmeg
  (optional)
2 tablespoons vegetable oil
1 cup long-grain white rice
½ cup corn kernels

Cook the black-eyed peas, using ½ pound smoked turkey for seasoning instead of ham. Drain when done.

About 20 minutes before the peas are done, combine in another large pot the water, salt, black pepper, mace or nutmeg (if desired), and the vegetable oil.

Bring to a boil. Add the rice, cover, and cook over medium-low heat for 15 minutes, or until the rice is almost tender.

Stir the cooked and drained black-eyed peas and the corn into the pot with the rice. Cover and simmer over low heat until all the liquid is absorbed and the rice and corn are tender.

SAVORY BLACK BEANS

Serves 4

*a*l also sends a recipe for a creamy bowl of black beans, which he says is just as popular at Big Bethel A.M.E. Church as his black-eyed peas.

1 cup dried black beans, soaked
    (see "Getting Soaked" on
    page 98)
1 onion
1 hot chili pepper (or less), such as
    cayenne or Jamaican hot pepper
2 carrots
2 cloves garlic
2 tablespoons corn or peanut oil

2 tablespoons chopped parsley
1 teaspoon ground cumin
3 cups chicken broth or Homemade
    Chicken Stock (see recipe on
    page 234)
½ teaspoon salt, or more if desired
½ teaspoon freshly ground
    black pepper

Rinse the soaked beans with cold water and set aside. Slice the onion, finely mince the chili pepper, scrape the carrots and dice finely. Mince the garlic.

Heat the oil in a large saucepan or Dutch oven. Stir in the onion, chili pepper, carrots, garlic, parsley, and cumin. Sauté over medium-low heat for 5 or 6 minutes, or until the onions are soft.

Add the chicken broth, the soaked beans, salt, and black pepper. Bring to a boil. Reduce the heat to low, cover, and simmer for 1 hour or until the beans are tender but not mushy.

Serve over rice or with a wedge of crusty cornbread.

Beans and Corn Chili

Ouida Evans's roots go way back at the First Missionary Baptist Church in Handsboro, Mississippi. Her great-grandfather was church pastor during the 1800s, and Ouida herself is involved in many activities at the historical 138-year-old church.

She is a member of the Ever Ready Club, an organization that assists the young and aged alike. Gift baskets are delivered to senior citizens during the holidays, and an annual tea is held to raise money for college scholarships, during which Ouida and a group of church sisters prepare an expansive Southern breakfast.

Ouida sends this recipe for a robust Southern-style chili that she makes with dried red beans—a Gulf Coast favorite.

1½ cups dried red chili or other tiny red beans, soaked (see "Getting Soaked" on page 98)

1 red or green pepper

2 onions

3 cloves garlic

1 to 2 hot chili peppers, jalapeño or serrano

½ pound smoked sausage

3 tablespoons corn oil

2 tablespoons chili powder

1 cup coarsely chopped fresh or canned tomatoes

2 tablespoons tomato paste

1 cup light beer or water

1 to 1½ cups chicken broth or Homemade Chicken Stock (see recipe on page 234)

1 bay leaf

1 teaspoon salt

¼ teaspoon freshly ground black pepper

1 cup corn kernels

3 to 4 tablespoons chopped long-leaf parsley or cilantro

Rinse the soaked beans well with cold water and set aside. Core and dice the red or green pepper. Slice the onions and mince the garlic and chili peppers. Cut the sausage into ½-inch chunks.

Heat the oil in a large pot. Stir in the red or green pepper, onions, garlic, chili peppers, and sausage. Sauté 3 or 4 minutes over low heat, stirring. Add the chili powder and sauté 1 or 2 minutes more.

Stir in the tomatoes, tomato paste, beer or water, 1 cup of the chicken broth, bay leaf, salt, black pepper, and the beans. Bring to a boil, reduce the heat to simmer, cover, and cook for 1 hour or until the beans are just tender, adding the remaining chicken broth if necessary.

Add the corn and parsley or cilantro and cook 20 minutes longer or until the corn is tender.

Let the chili set for 15 minutes in a warm place. Reheat if necessary and serve with hot brown rice.

CARIBBEAN PEAS AND BEANS

Serves 4

S ince this dish is such a staple in the Caribbean, you would think that the local inhabitants would know their peas from their beans, but when either one of these legumes is mixed with rice, there is considerable disagreement on exactly what the dish should be called. Regardless of whether you are in Jamaica, Trinidad, Barbados, Antigua, or Puerto Rico, rice is the stable ingredient, but the legume can be tiny red chili beans, large kidney beans, lentils, and even a variety of peas—such as pigeon, congo, and cowpea—as well as black beans, especially in the Latin Caribbean.

In Jamaica, for example, the combination is referred to as Rice and Peas, although it is made with red beans. In other countries the name ranges from Beans and Rice, to Rice and Beans, to Peas and Rice. And rest assured, if you make the mistake and say it "wrong," you will be promptly corrected. Never mind.

This is a delightful combination, and it's a favorite of Ann Birchett and her husband, Butch, who have been visiting the Caribbean annually for the past thirty years and own a time share there.

Ann lives right down the street from the Convent Avenue Baptist Church in Harlem, located on 145th Street, and she has been a member of the church for almost a half century. She is at the church all of the time: for Sunday services, concerts, recitals, political rallies, senior programs. And she is also totally enmeshed in community and civic concerns, from street cleanup campaigns to youth programs to the administration of their tenant-owned apartment building, so much so that, well, some folks say she is a taskmaster.

"I know they say I am always on their case," Ann says philosophically, "but things have to be done right."

Ann is one of those no-nonsense, attentive-to-details persons, and this applies to her cooking as well. She is a creative cook, although she demurs and says she doesn't cook like she once did, conjuring memories of the fabulous spreads she is known for.

Since she is so involved in her church and community, you often see her in winter wearing her mink coat, leaving her lovely apartment with a dish of food sitting in the curve of her arm.

1 cup dried small red chili beans or small dried pigeon, cow-, or congo peas, soaked (see "Getting Soaked" on page 98)

½ pounds chicken parts, such as necks, gizzards, backs

4 cups water

1 onion

2 to 3 cloves garlic

3 or 4 sprigs fresh thyme, or ½ teaspoon dried thyme

2 tablespoons vegetable oil, or 2 or 3 bacon strips

½ teaspoon hot pepper flakes

1 teaspoon salt

½ teaspoon freshly ground black pepper

½ cup coconut milk (see "Coconut Milking" on page 115)

1 cup long-grain brown rice

Rinse the soaked beans or peas and the chicken parts with cold water and place in a large heavy pot. Cover with the water and bring to a boil. Reduce the heat to low, cover, and cook for 45 minutes or until the beans or peas are almost tender, but still crunchy.

When done, set aside 2½ cups of the cooking water and drain the beans or peas and set aside. Remove the chicken parts and discard.

Slice the onion and mince the garlic. Chop the fresh thyme or crush the dried herb. Heat the oil in the pot used to cook the beans or peas. (If using bacon, omit the oil and sauté the bacon until brown and crisp and then remove from the pot, reserving the bacon drippings in the pot.)

Add the onion, garlic, thyme, hot pepper flakes, salt, and black pepper and sauté over low heat for 5 or 6 minutes.

Stir in the coconut milk and 2 cups of the reserved cooking water from the beans or peas. Bring to a boil. Add the rice and reduce the heat to medium-low. Stir in the beans or peas. Cover and cook for 25 to 30 minutes or until the rice and legumes are tender, adding a little of the remaining cooking water if the pan sticks. (If using bacon, crumble and sprinkle over the dish before serving, if desired.)

COCONUT MILKING

I was an adult visiting the Caribbean before I learned that the sweet, clear, slightly sticky liquid that we clamored to drink when my father cracked open a fresh coconut wasn't actually milk but rather coconut water. We usually had fresh coconut during the Christmas holidays, and my mother would grate the meat and use it in her Coconut-Jelly Cake (see recipe on page 307) or coconut custard pie, which were just two of the numerous cakes and pies that she baked during this time of the year.

Years later I learned that the coconut grows virtually everywhere in the West Indies, and that the meat is grated, turned into milk, and used in many dishes, including desserts, soups, stews, and of course in the rice-and-bean dishes (or rice-and-peas!) that grace every meal.

The milk is easy to make: Place the whole coconut into a large bowl and pour over a kettle of boiling water. This softens the shell so it cracks easily. Let the coconut set for 10 minutes.

Drain the bowl, dry the coconut, and wrap in a large kitchen towel. Crack with a hammer and quickly remove the coconut from the cloth and pour the coconut water into a cup. I drink this on the spot as a refreshing tonic as I go about, often saying that I will save it to stir into a soup or sauce, but I never do. (Note: Coconut is high in saturated fat, which increases cholesterol, so reserve this dish for special occasions.)

With a sharp knife, carefully remove both the woody coconut shell and the leathery brown layer covering the coconut meat. Finely grate the coconut with a hand grater or use a food processor. Using 1 cup of grated meat per 1 cup of boiling water for each cup of coconut milk, place the coconut and water into a blender (or food processor) and whirl for about 1 minute or process until the coconut is pulverized.

Allow the mixture to set for about an hour and then strain through a large layer of cheesecloth, squeezing the pulp to extract all of the milk. The milk will keep for a few days in the refrigerator in a tightly covered jar, or you can freeze it in a plastic container to use later.

LENTIL AND TOMATO SOUP

Serves 6

ileen Melia handles the correspondence and takes care of other administrative duties at the Our Lady Queen of Peace Catholic Church in Arlington, Virginia, and she laughs and says that she really has her hand, figuratively speaking, in many pots.

Eileen does cook. And she is also involved in the church's many activities. She is a member of the bereavement committee, participates in the church's social justice program, and teaches Sunday school.

About her church, which is located on South 19th Street, Eileen says: "Our Lady Queen of Peace is a historically black Catholic church that is more than fifty years old. Our parish is a dream come true: the courageous dream of a small band of black Catholics, who in 1945 took Jesus at His word and laid the foundation for a worshipping community that would welcome all as sisters and brothers, as members of the one great family of God. From that humble beginning a parish has evolved in which diversity is counted a blessing and no effort is counted too small to make a difference."

Eileen sends a recipe that is perfect on a cold, wintry day:

1 onion

4 carrots

2 stalks celery

2 cloves garlic

5 cups water

1 cup chopped tomatoes, fresh
   or canned

3 tablespoons tomato paste

½ teaspoon dried thyme

1 tablespoon chopped fresh dill, or
   ¾ teaspoon dried dill weed

1½ teaspoons salt

¼ teaspoon freshly ground black
   pepper, more if desired

1 smoked turkey wing, or ½ pound
   piece of smoked turkey meat

1 cup dried lentils

Chop the onion; scrape and dice the carrots; dice the celery; and mince the garlic. Place the vegetables in a large pot.

Add the water, chopped tomatoes, and tomato paste. Crush the thyme

and add to the pot, along with the dill, salt, black pepper, and smoked turkey.

Bring to a boil. Reduce heat to simmer, cover, and simmer for 30 minutes.

Meanwhile, pick over the lentils, removing any debris or stones. (Lentils do not require soaking.) Rinse well. Stir the lentils into the pot and simmer for 2½ to 3 hours, or until the legumes are tender and the soup is creamy.

Herbed Lentils and Mushrooms

Serves 4

udith Price is the cog that turns many of the wheels at the Canaan Baptist Church in Harlem, and she does her job with a magnetic, overwhelming presence that inspires most people to do their best. She is the church's controller as well as the president of its community enrichment center, which offers a variety of job-training skills and after-school programs for neighborhood youths. The center also runs a catering facility, and operates a banquet hall that features a gospel brunch on Sundays.

On a recent Saturday afternoon Judith and I sat down to exchange church news, and I felt as elated and nervous as I did years ago when the Home Mission Club was held at our house.

I served this lentil dish with grilled fish, rice, and a salad, and I think Judith was pleased.

¾ cup brown lentils
¾ cup green lentils
1 onion
1 red or yellow pepper
2 cloves garlic
1 small cayenne pepper, or less if desired
¼ teaspoon dried thyme
½ teaspoon dried basil
3 tablespoons olive or corn oil

1 bay leaf
3 cups water
½ pound chicken parts, such as necks, gizzards, backs
1 teaspoon salt
½ teaspoon freshly ground black pepper
½ pound fresh mushrooms
3 cups cooked brown rice

Pick over the lentils, checking for stones or debris. Rinse and set aside. (Lentils do not require soaking.)

Slice the onion, core and cut the red or yellow pepper into thin strips. Finely mince the garlic and cayenne pepper. Crush the dried thyme and basil.

Heat 1 tablespoon of the oil in a large pot. Stir in the onion, red or yellow pepper, garlic, chili, thyme, basil, and bay leaf. Sauté for 5 minutes or until the onions and peppers are soft.

Add the water, chicken parts, salt, and black pepper. Bring to a boil, reduce heat to simmer, cover, and cook for 25 to 30 minutes.

Meanwhile, rinse the mushrooms, dry with paper towels, and slice thick.

Heat the remaining 2 tablespoons of oil in a medium skillet. Stir in the mushrooms and sauté for 4 or 5 minutes, or until opaque.

Remove the chicken parts from the pot and discard. Add the lentils to the pot, bring to a boil, then reduce the heat to simmer. Stir in the mushrooms.

Cover and cook for 30 minutes or until the lentils are tender. Watch carefully near the end of the cooking period because the lentils can quickly overcook and become mushy.

Serve the lentils over hot rice.

A Bounty of Peas and Beans

SPLIT PEA AND HAM SOUP

Serves 8 to 10

*P*at Mack is a poet, Sunday school teacher, legal secretary, and meeting planner—and a talented cook. She uses many of her skills at the Glendale Baptist Church in Landover, Maryland. Several of her poems have been put into production by the church's dance ministry, and last year she was asked to write the theme poem for the church's Black History Month celebration, which was titled "A Blessed People of Talent."

She assists often with the kitchen ministry, which serves breakfast on Sundays from 7 A.M. to 10 A.M., and provides dinner on Wednesdays from 5 P.M. to 7 P.M. before prayer meeting and Bible study.

Pat is in her late forties and is the mother of one daughter, JaJuan. Recently she and her husband, Clinton, celebrated their twenty-fifth wedding anniversary. She says that many members of her large extended family attend the church, which was established in 1927 in Washington, D.C. Her maternal grandparents were among the original founders.

On March 18, 1995, Glendale moved into a new building on Central Avenue in Landover. The church pastor, the Reverend Anthony G. Maclin, cut the ribbon on the new church, and the one-thousand-strong congregation marched into its new home.

Pat sends this story: "Glendale Baptist participates in the Self Help and Resource Exchange (SHARE) program, and ironically enough, a few years ago there was a pound of dried split peas in the SHARE package that came in that month. I decided that I would take on the task of transforming those little green and yellow buttons, which are full of nutrients but are so often overlooked and underrated, into a memorable meal. I remembered that I had a big ham bone with lots of meat on it in the freezer.

"So feeling my way through, I created this dish. After encouraging a few church members to sample the finished dish, which I served with my buttermilk cornbread, I now have folks who once swore that they would never eat split pea soup bringing me their ham bones, along with the other necessary ingredients, so I can make them a pot o' soup. In fact, 'Cuz' (my cousin Ronald) keeps me supplied with five bags of split peas just to make sure that my inventory at the church pantry doesn't run out."

For a change of flavors, Pat sometimes substitutes dried black beans for the split beans, and uses smoked turkey instead of ham.

This is her recipe:

1 pound dried green or yellow
   split peas
1 large onion
2 cloves garlic
2 tablespoons olive or vegetable oil
5 cups water
5 cups chicken broth or Homemade
   Chicken Stock (see recipe on
   page 234)

1 meaty ham bone, about ½ pound
1 pound fresh carrots
1 pound all-purpose white potatoes
1 piece of ham, about ½ pound
½ teaspoon salt, if needed
½ teaspoon freshly ground
   black pepper
½ cup chopped flat-leaf parsley

Carefully pick over the peas and remove any stones or debris. Rinse the peas well with cold water and set aside. (Split peas don't require soaking before cooking.)

Slice the onion and mince the garlic. Heat the oil in a large heavy pot, at least 8-quart size. Add the onion and garlic and sauté 4 or 5 minutes.

Add the water, chicken broth, peas, and ham bone and bring to a boil. Reduce heat to very low, cover, and simmer for at least 1½ hours or until the peas are tender and the mixture is creamy. (Pat says that during the winter months she often simmers the pot for 3 or 4 hours.)

Scrape the carrots and cut into 1-inch chunks. Peel the potatoes and cut into 1-inch chunks. Coarsely shred the ham. Stir into the pot the carrots, potatoes, ham, salt (if desired), black pepper, and ¼ cup of the chopped parsley.

Cover and simmer 45 minutes or until the vegetables are tender. Remove the ham bone from the pot. Shred any meat left on the bone and return the meat to the pan.

Discard the bone. Adjust the seasoning, adding additional salt and black pepper if necessary.

Sprinkle the soup with the remaining parsley and serve immediately in warm soup bowls.

A Bounty of Peas and Beans

Variation: This soup is as equally delicious made with a half-pound piece of smoked turkey. For an interesting flavor change, substitute fresh basil for the parsley.

SHARE

SHARE is a nationwide program established in 1990 to help people save money on their grocery bills while strengthening their communities through volunteer services.

SHARE is open to anyone who wishes to participate: "If you eat, you qualify" is the organization's motto.

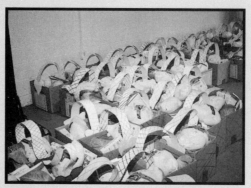

At Glendale Baptist Church in Landover, Maryland, church members prepare SHARE baskets for the needy at Thanksgiving.

Here's how the organization works: Register at your neighborhood site and pay fourteen dollars. Give two hours of volunteer service to the community. Pick up your **SHARE** package on the distribution date and receive approximately thirty dollars' worth of high-quality frozen meat, fresh fruits, vegetables, and staples, saving at least 50 percent off retail cost. Then reregister for the next month.

For information on your nearest **SHARE** sites, call: 1–888-SHARE-SAVE.

Muhammad Supreme Bean Soup

*b*ack in the late 1960s, during the inception of the Muslim influence in African-American communities, I often visited a little restaurant in Harlem on Lenox Avenue near 116th Street that sold both a delicious bean cake and a hearty navy bean soup. The Muslims have long touted the nutritional benefits of navy beans and have created many ingenious recipes using this legume, which they say, along with whole wheat bread and whole milk, provide all the nutrients needed daily.

Those long-ago days came to mind recently when I received Sister Wanda Muhammad's recipe. She is a member of the administrative staff at the University of Islam in Chicago, and several years ago while she was teaching a cooking class at the mosque and school, she collected a cache of recipes from sisters across country.

Sister Wanda sends this recipe for navy bean soup:

1 pound dried navy beans, soaked for at least 8 hours or overnight (see "Getting Soaked" on page 98)	¼ cup corn oil
	¼ cup chopped parsley
	1 tablespoon paprika
	3 tablespoons tomato paste
2 onions	8 cups water
1 green or red pepper	¾ teaspoon freshly ground
3 cloves garlic	black pepper
2 celery stalks	½ teaspoon crushed red pepper
1½ teaspoons dried sage or rosemary	½ pound chicken backs or necks, or smoked turkey wing (optional)
3 carrots	2 to 3 teaspoons salt

Rinse the soaked beans well with cold water, drain, and set aside.

Chop the onions; core and dice the green or red pepper; and mince the garlic. Dice the celery. Finely crush the sage or rosemary. Scrap the carrots and cut crosswise into 1-inch chunks.

Heat the oil in a large heavy pot. Stir in the onions, green or red pepper, garlic, celery, sage or rosemary, and parsley. Sauté for 5 minutes, stirring, or until the onions are soft and translucent.

Stir into the pot the carrots and paprika, and heat 1 minute longer. Add the tomato paste, water, black pepper, crushed red pepper, chicken parts or turkey wing, if desired, and soaked beans. Bring to a boil, cover, reduce heat to simmer, and cook for 3 to 3½ hours or until the beans are tender and creamy.

Stir in the salt and heat 10 minutes longer.

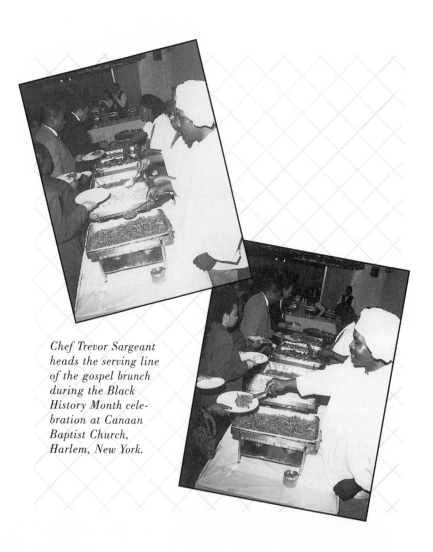

Chef Trevor Sargeant heads the serving line of the gospel brunch during the Black History Month celebration at Canaan Baptist Church, Harlem, New York.

LILLIAN'S THREE-BEAN SALAD

i was sitting with Lillian and Bill Hayes in their backyard, enjoying a late-summer cookout when the church brother brought the news: Lillian had entered her pound cake in a cook-off at the Saint Mark African Methodist Episcopal Church in Corona, Queens, and was named first-prize winner.

We weren't surprised. Lillian is a superb cook, and during the summer months her home garden looks very much like the one she tended years ago in Waycross, Georgia. There are rows of fresh green or snap beans, green peppers, tomatoes, squash, scallions, herbs, and lettuce—all the makings for a beautiful bowl of salad.

Lillian recently made a savory, pretty-as-a-picture bean salad and carried it out to a function at her church, which is located on Northern Boulevard. And although no contest was underway, this dish was a winner, too.

¾ cup dried white kidney or
   cannellini beans, soaked (see
   "Getting Soaked" on page 98)
¾ cup dried red kidney beans,
   soaked
4 cups cold water
1 bay leaf
2 tablespoons lemon juice
2 tablespoons cider or wine vinegar
2 cloves minced garlic

¼ cup chopped parsley or cilantro
2 tablespoons mustard
1 teaspoon salt
½ teaspoon freshly ground
   black pepper
½ cup olive oil
1 onion, thinly sliced
½ pound fresh green beans, cooked
Lettuce leaves

Rinse the soaked beans in cold water and place in a large heavy pot. Cover with the water. Add the bay leaf. Place on the stove and bring to a boil. Reduce heat to low and cook, covered, for 1½ hours or until the beans are tender but not mushy.

While the beans are cooking, prepare the salad dressing: In a large serving bowl, combine the lemon juice, vinegar, garlic, parsley or cilantro, mustard, salt, black pepper, oil, and onion. Beat the vinaigrette with a fork or wire whisk until well blended.

Drain the hot cooked beans and place in the bowl. (Don't cool the beans; they absorb more flavor if tossed with the salad dressing while still hot.)

Cut the green beans in half and stir into the bowl. Toss the beans well with a large spoon, coating with the salad dressing.

Cover the bowl with plastic wrap and chill for at least 2 to 3 hours or overnight.

When ready to serve, rinse, drain, and dry the lettuce leaves and place on a large platter. Spoon the beans onto the lettuce and serve.

OUR ROOTS: GREENS AND OTHER VEGETABLES

*i*f I were Aretha Franklin I would write a love song about greens, composing refrains replete with the many inflections, commands, exclamations, and lyricism I have heard expressed over the years: "A mess of greens. A pot of

greens. Any more greens left? Who ate all the greens? Pass the greens. Wash the greens again. Don't leave no grit on those greens. Cook the greens tender. Those turnips are too bitter—add a white potato, a drop of sugar, some vinegar. You cooking greens today? Save the pot likker. Eat those greens, girl, they're good for you!"

Greens are the centerpiece of the African-American menu, and like much of our eating pattern, they go straight back to West Africa, where many varieties of greens are used in soups and stews. Our ancestors were brought from Africa to the Americas to work the land, whether the Caribbean or Latin America, and alongside the cotton and sugar cane and rice, they planted their soul food: greens.

Hallelujah! When I was a child my mother would simmer a pot of greens long and lovingly, often with a ham bone, and then pass a hot pepper sauce or relish when we sat down to dinner. Sometimes, if she were cooking collards, she would add
a few pods of okra,

"Pastor Appreciation Day" at the Holy Temple Church of God in Christ, Harlem, April 1955. Church pastor, The Reverend Clarence Roberson (extreme right), embraces two young celebrants.

and although I didn't know it then, this was a nutritionally rich dish. Few people know more about the goodness of greens than Delores L. Brandon, a nutritionist and the kitchen manager–administrator at the Hartford Memorial Baptist Church in Detroit, who can talk for days, as the expression goes, about food and its Biblical references, citing "Manna from Heaven," the "Garden of Eden," and "The Last Supper" as examples.

Mrs. Brandon says frankly that she turns to the Scriptures when executing her role at Hartford Memorial, which is to keep the congregation healthy and well fed.

She has a challenging task. The church, which is located on James Couzens Freeway, has some twelve thousand members and at least 250 different clubs and organizations.

"Our bodies are God's gift to us," Mrs. Brandon says firmly, "and when He gives us a gift you have to treat it right. You can sin by eating the wrong foods. If you have high blood pressure then it doesn't make sense to eat a lot of salty ham hocks and fried chicken. You can season those greens with herbs and onions and peppers and bake that chicken. We have to be careful about what we eat. Leviticus is a beautiful book to study to learn a lot about nutrition and food."

Mrs. Brandon sends this tasty and healthy recipe for the greens she often serves at the church:

Mixed Greens

Serves 6

3 pounds collard, turnip, and/or
  mustard greens
2 or 3 cloves garlic
1 red pepper
1 or 2 jalapeño peppers
⅓ cup vegetable oil
3 cups chicken broth or Homemade
  Chicken Stock (see recipe on
  page 234)

1 teaspoon salt
½ teaspoon black pepper
1 teaspoon sugar
2 tablespoons cider or red
  wine vinegar

Buy young, tender greens with small leaves. Avoid those with withered or yellowing leaves. Cut away thick stems and discard.

Stack a dozen or so collard leaves at a time, roll tightly, and then cut the roll crosswise into ½-inch strips. Keep the collards separate from the turnip and mustard greens, because they go into the cooking pot first. (The mustard and turnip greens don't have to be cut into strips.)

Rinse the greens 4 or 5 times, making sure that all the sand or grit is removed. Drain and set aside.

Mince the garlic; core and dice the red pepper; and finely mince the jalapeño. Heat the oil in a large stockpot or saucepan. Add the garlic, red pepper, and jalapeño. Sauté 2 or 3 minutes.

Stir in the chicken broth, salt, black pepper, sugar, and vinegar. Bring the liquid to a boil, reduce the heat, and cook over low heat for 15 minutes.

Raise the heat to high and stir in the collard greens, using a long-handled spoon to turn over the leaves in the boiling broth. When the greens are thoroughly immersed in the liquid, reduce the heat to medium-low, cover the pot, and cook for 15 minutes.

Stir in the turnip and mustard greens, using a long-handled spoon to cover the greens with the pot liquor. Cover and cook 40 minutes longer or until the greens are tender.

SAUTÉED GARLIC GREENS

Serves 6

*t*he Mount Zion United Methodist Church in New Orleans holds
its annual festival on the last Sunday in May, and the event has the air
of an old-fashioned revival, with church members selling and sharing
a staggering array of food: homemade ice cream, all kinds of cakes and pies,
barbecue, fried fish, rice and beans, potato salad, jambalaya, gumbo, and
greens.

Gloria Landry is one of the stalwart members of Mount Zion, and
whenever Albert Stevenson or Emily Moran take to the kitchen, it isn't
long before they have to make room for Gloria. Mrs. Landry sends
this recipe for greens, which is one of her favorite renditions during the
annual festival.

Her recipe is very similar to the garlic-laden greens served in Brazil
with the popular dish called feijoada, which is a pot meal of pork, rice, and
beans. There are more people of African origin in Brazil than in the United
States, and this dish shows that all of Mother Africa's children share a
common soul food.

3 pounds collard greens	*½ to 1 cup chicken broth*
1 large onion	*3/4 teaspoon salt*
2 or 3 cloves garlic	*½ teaspoon freshly ground*
¼ to ⅓ cup vegetable oil	* black pepper*

Pick over the greens and discard any with yellowing or wilted leaves.
Remove thick stems. Stack a dozen or so leaves at a time and then
roll tightly, jelly-roll fashion. Place on a cutting board and cut each roll
crosswise into ½-inch strips. Continue rolling and cutting this way
until all the greens are cut.

Rinse the greens at least 4 or 5 times in a large basin of cold water,
swishing to remove any sand or dirt. Drain well.

Chop the onion and mince the garlic.

Heat a scant 2 tablespoons or so of the oil in a large heavy pot. Place
about a third of the greens at a time in the pot and sauté, stirring, for

5 or 6 minutes, or until the greens are wilted. Remove from the pot.

Add the remaining greens and 1 tablespoon of oil and sauté in the same way. When all the greens are sautéed, add the remaining oil to the pot, stir in the onions and garlic, and sauté 4 or 5 minutes or until the onions are tender. Return the greens to the pot.

Add the chicken broth, salt, and black pepper. Cover and cook over low heat for 30 minutes or until the greens are tender.

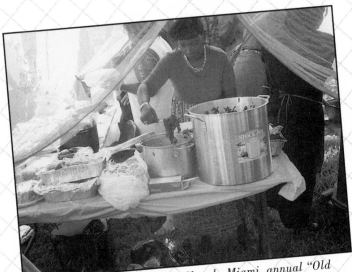

New Shiloh Missionary Baptist Church, Miami, annual "Old Fashion Day." Church member Mary Stewart dips into the pot of greens.

MEAN GREENS

Serves 6

ethesda Full Gospel Church is a nondenominational congregation located on Main Street in downtown Buffalo, New York, at the site of a former movie theater now under renovation. Construction plans call for a bookstore, a library, a special sanctuary for children, a soup kitchen for the homeless, and a full-service restaurant.

The congregation is predominantly African- and Caribbean-American, and one member is Rhea Pierce, who says that she loves the church because it feels as though a revival is always underway. The church members frequently visit one anothers' homes and also gather often at the church for various functions, sharing food and fellowship.

Sister Pierce recently learned a new way to cook greens from her beloved daughter-in-law, Shelda, and she promptly invited over Sister Rita and several other church members for a Sunday-afternoon gathering.

She sends the recipe, which she so aptly named, considering that in black jargon "mean" describes something extraordinarily good.

Here's Sister Rhea's story: "I came home from a vacation in Birmingham, Alabama, to find this delicious improvisation waiting for me in the refrigerator. My son, Darryl Vinson, and his wife, Shelda, whom I consider a daughter, live in Fontana, California, but had been visiting Buffalo while I was down South.

"At first glance I thought the dish was from the Caribbean, but after further investigation, I found it was the result of a 'cook off.' Apparently, my son had received adoration from friends and family on his greens. My daughter-in-law got jealous and decided to 'out cook' him.

"In fact, the other day, I served Shelda's greens to Sister Rita, and she liked them so much that she broke her vegetarian diet. We like to chow down on this dish with a pan of hot, from-scratch cornbread and some buttermilk."

Rhea sends this "mean" recipe:

1 carrots	3 cups water
1 onion	1 teaspoon salt (if desired)
1 green or red pepper	¾ teaspoon black pepper
1 or 2 jalapeño peppers	¼ cup vegetable oil
1 meaty ham bone, or ½ pound smoked ham	3 pounds collard greens
	2 links turkey sausage

Scrape and dice the carrot. Chop the onion; core and mince the green or red pepper; mince the jalapeño. Place the vegetables into a large heavy pot, along with the ham bone or ham, and the water. Add the salt (if desired), black pepper, and the oil. Bring to a boil, reduce heat to low, cover, and cook for 40 minutes.

Meanwhile, pick over the greens and discard any with yellowing or wilted leaves. Remove thick stems. Stack a dozen or so collard leaves at a time and then roll tightly, jelly-roll fashion. Place on a cutting board and cut each roll crosswise into ½-inch strips. Continue rolling and cutting this way until all the greens are cut.

Rinse the greens at least 4 or 5 times in a large basin of cold water, swishing to remove any grit.

Stir the greens into the pot and bring to a boil again. Using a long-handled spoon, turn the greens over and over in the pot liquor until they are completely immersed. Cut the turkey sausage into 1-inch pieces and add to the pot.

Cover and cook over low heat for 50 minutes or until the greens and sausage are tender.

Variation: Turnip and mustard greens can be mixed with the collards. To do so, cook the collards for 20 minutes and then add the turnip or mustard greens, since they require less cooking than collards, which are more fibrous. Also, a half-pound piece of smoked turkey can be substituted for the ham.

COLLARDS AND CABBAGE

Serves 8

artha Hemmans wishes that the kitchen was a little bigger at the Ebenezer Baptist Church in Atlanta, for the simple reason that whenever she and the other church sisters gather there to cook for the homeless, there is a lot of bumping into one another. Oh, they argue about who used this pan and left it dirty, or whether a dish should be cooked this or that way. But mostly they just cut eyes at each other

This is not surprising, considering that the congregation has at least four members who are professional caterers and dozens of others who are excellent cooks. And since the church holds numerous baptisms, homecomings, revivals, receptions, and prayer breakfasts, they often put their skills to good use.

Ebenezer was the family church of the late Reverend Dr. Martin Luther King Jr., and on Sundays people from across the country and around the world come by the busload to attend service. At least seven hundred worshippers crowd into the majestic church, which has mahogany pews and piped organ music. When seats run out, folding chairs are set up in the basement to accommodate the overflow crowd, allowing another three hundred visitors to enjoy the service on closed-circuit TV. And almost every Sunday some group or another is treated to a church dinner planned and executed by Ebenezer's fancy cooks.

Mrs. Hemmans cooks often at the church, which is located on Auburn Avenue, although she demurs and says she is a so-so cook.

In fact, Mrs. Hemmans is just downright self-effacing about most aspects of her life. Besides cooking for the homeless at Ebenezer, she cooks for a program run by the YMCA on Gordon Street and for another ecumenical outreach effort coordinated by the Grace United Methodist Church. But she cooks with heart and soul, love and concern, and has no lofty explanations for her endeavors.

"It's something I particularly enjoy doing," says Mrs. Hemmans in her modest way. "When I joined this church back in 1946 I remember the

senior Reverend King telling us that those of us more fortunate had to give something back to the community."

She pauses for a moment, deep in reflection, and then relates that on any given Sunday during the early 1960s so many people flocked to Ebenezer that you had to arrive early in the morning and stand in line if you wanted to get into the church for the 11 A.M. service. The church pastor at that time was the Reverend Martin Luther King Sr., a staunch civil rights activist whose son had been one of the leading architects of a successful bus boycott by African-Americans a few years before in Montgomery, Alabama.

"I remember after World War Two the senior Reverend King urging us to become involved with civil rights," says Mrs. Hemmans, a retired schoolteacher. "He always worked closely with the community. Urged us to buy land and property and own something. In those days we used to spend all day at the church. We would have Sunday school at 9 A.M., an 11 A.M. service, a 3 P.M. service, BYPU—Baptist Young People Union–sometimes between 3 and 6 P.M., and then the evening service at 7 P.M. Since we were here all day we had to eat, and a lot of people brought food to the church. Today we do most of our cooking at the church."

Mrs. Hemmans's sautéed squash is full of flavor, redolent with onions and herbs. In the middle of the summer she makes an excellent cobbler using the locally grown Elberta peach, and her pie is always succulent and crusty. And Mattie Hodges, a caterer and one of the culinary doyennes at Ebenezer, who is touted as "knowing how to burn," says Mrs. Hemmans's greens are as good as anybody's.

Mrs. Hemmans's recipe:

3 pounds fresh collard greens
1 small head of green cabbage,
    about 1½ pounds
1 onion, or 1 cup chopped
    green onions
1 hot chili pepper, such as cayenne
¼ cup vegetable oil
2 cups chicken broth or Homemade
    Chicken Stock (see recipe on
    page 234)

1 cup water
2 tablespoons vinegar
1 teaspoon salt, or less
½ teaspoon freshly ground
    black pepper
1 small smoked turkey wing

Cut the coarse stems from the collards and discard. Stack a dozen or so collard leaves at a time and roll them tightly, jelly-roll fashion. Place on a cutting board, and using a sharp knife cut each roll crosswise into ½-inch strips. Continue rolling and cutting this way until all the greens are cut. Wash the greens at least 4 or 5 times in a large pan of cold water, swishing to remove any sand or grit. Drain and set aside.

Cut the cabbage into quarters, core, and then shred coarsely. Rinse well, drain, and set aside. (Don't mix the two greens because they require different cooking times.)

Chop the onion and finely mince the chili pepper. Heat the oil in a large stockpot or Dutch oven. Add the onions and chili pepper.

Sauté over low heat for 5 minutes, stirring. Stir in the chicken broth or stock, water, vinegar, salt, and black pepper. Add the turkey wing. Bring to a boil, reduce heat to low, and cook for 20 minutes.

Add the collard greens. Using a large spoon, cover the leaves with the liquid. Bring to a boil again, cover, reduce heat to low, and cook 35 to 40 minutes or until the greens are just tender.

Stir in the cabbage, covering with the cooking liquid. Cover the pot and cook 20 minutes longer, or until the cabbage and collard greens are tender.

Discard the turkey bone and skin before serving, if desired.

STEAMED CABBAGE

Serves 4 to 6

imone Monique Barnes is president of the Young Adult Ministry at the Grace Baptist Church in Mount Vernon, New York, and at age twenty-three she nicely bridges the gap between neighborhood youths and church elders. The church is located on South Sixth Avenue.

A while back she sponsored a "Charge Against Hunger" fashion show at the church, and asked a donation of ten cans of food for the price of admission, so as to raise consciousness about the homeless and the hungry. Last year during the holidays she sponsored a Christmas Outreach Party for local youths living in shelters, group homes, and crowded housing. Part of this expedition involved a trip to the Metropolitan Museum of Art in New York City to view its extensive Egyptian collection.

"The kids went to the museum kicking and screaming," recalls Simone. "But when we got there and I told them to look on the walls and at the images, and they saw that the people looked just like them, I had to drag everybody out of there. They didn't know that Egypt is in Africa. I made them realize that they, too, have a history."

Simone sends this recipe for steamed cabbage:

1 large head of cabbage, red or green, about 2 pounds
1 small red pepper
2 cups chicken broth or Homemade Chicken Stock (see recipe on page 234)

½ teaspoon salt
½ teaspoon freshly ground black pepper
¼ cup olive oil

Discard any tough or withered outer cabbage leaves. Cut the cabbage in half and then cut out the core and discard. Shred the cabbage coarsely. Rinse the cabbage several times with cold water, making sure that it is free of grit. Core the red pepper and cut into strips.

Place the cabbage in a large pot. Add red pepper, chicken broth, salt, black pepper, and olive oil. Bring to a boil. Reduce heat to simmer, cover, and cook about 20 minutes, or until the cabbage is tender.

GOURMET COLLARD GREENS

Serves 8

*b*lack church people who know the Reverend Dr. Arlene Churn usually say two things about her right off: She has this inimitable sense of style, and if you don't watch out she'll give you those stylish clothes she wears right off her back.

Reverend Churn is pastor of the Cathedral of Faith Baptist Church in Camden, New Jersey, and when her vast network of friends aren't talking about her generosity, leadership, abiding faith, and feisty optimism, they talk about how Martha Stewart can't really hold a candle to her.

"I am on the road a lot," says Dr. Churn, "but when I am at home I like to unwind with a few friends. I pull out my best dishes, silverware, and cloth napkins. And I cook because I enjoy my cooking more than I do the food at most restaurants.

"Just think, Kentucky Fried Chicken telling us how to fry chicken. Can you imagine anybody eating that?"

But oh her greens! Dr. Churn sends this recipe:

4 pounds fresh collard greens	2 tablespoons soy sauce
2 cloves garlic	1/2 pound smoked turkey wing
1/2 teaspoon dried marjoram or	or thigh
oregano	1 teaspoon salt (if desired)
3 bacon strips, or 1/4 cup vegetable	1/2 teaspoon freshly ground
oil	black pepper
4 cups chicken broth or Homemade	1 cup dry white wine
Chicken Stock (see recipe on	2 hot chili peppers (optional)
page 234)	

Cut the coarse stems from the greens and discard. Stack a dozen or so leaves at a time and then roll tightly, jelly-roll fashion. Place on a cutting board, and using a sharp knife cut each roll crosswise into 1/2-inch strips. Continue rolling and cutting this way until all the greens are cut.

Wash the greens at least 4 or 5 times in a large basin of cold water, swishing to remove any sand or grit. Drain and set aside.

Mince the garlic and crush the marjoram or oregano.

Place the bacon strips in a large pot and fry over medium heat until crisp. Remove the bacon from the pot and discard, reserving the bacon drippings in the pot. (If using vegetable oil, heat in the pot.) Stir in the garlic, dried herb, chicken broth, soy sauce, turkey wing or thigh, salt (if desired), and black pepper.

Bring to a boil. Reduce the heat and cook, covered, over medium-low heat for 15 to 20 minutes.

Stir in the collard greens. Bring the pot to a boil again, using a long-handled spoon to immerse the greens in the liquid.

Stir in the wine, cover, reduce the heat to low, and cook 45 to 50 minutes or until the greens are tender.

At serving, if desired, dice the hot peppers and pass along with the greens.

OUR GREENS: A PRIMER

We used to pick greens fresh from the garden, dripping with the morning dew, but migration and urbanization over the past fifty years have moved most African-Americans a long ways from those backyard garden plots of yesteryear. But greens remain firmly planted in our heritage and sealed on our palates. And thanks to jet cargo, today a wide variety of greens are available year-round at supermarkets, vegetable stands and trucks, and at farmers' markets.

Volunteer Carolyn Drake carries a tray of food out of the freezer at the Hartford Memorial Baptist Church in Detroit.

Start by buying at least a half pound of greens (or more) per person. All greens have to be trimmed, plus they shrink during cooking, so allowing eight ounces per serving isn't very much. When you buy greens, select bunches with small tender leaves so that you can cut cooking time to the minimum as well as save nutrients. Also, make sure to avoid greens with coarse stems and wilted, yellowing leaves; these have lost flavor and nutrients.

Fresh, washed-and-drained greens will keep in the refrigerator, in plastic containers or bags, for two or three days. After that they begin to loose flavor and turn yellow. However, greens freeze well and will keep for two or three months in the freezer. To do so, wash well, drain, and then pack in plastic bags or containers and freeze.

Here's a primer on greens:

Collards: A fibrous vegetable that can require long cooking when mature. So look for tender, small, sparkling green leaves. If you can only find mature leaves, strip and discard the coarse, tough stems and ribs.

Collards are delicious with green onions and hot chili pepper relish made with vinegar (see recipe for Hot Pepper Relish on page 153).

Dandelion: Dandelion greens, when very young and tender at the first breath of spring, are delicious raw, mixed with lettuce in a salad. As these greens get older they get bitter. Blanch the mature greens for 2 minutes in boiling water to lessen the bitterness, and then simmer in broth.

Kale: This green has crisp, curly, dark green leaves, and the smaller the leaves the better. Kale is similar in texture to collards but has a more intense flavor. Avoid bunches with limp or yellowing leaves.

Mustard Greens: These have pale green, delicate leaves with frilly edges, and if I were pushed to name my favorite greens, I would choose this variety, but don't tell anybody I said that. They have a slightly bitter taste but are not quite as intense in flavor as dandelion.

Turnip Greens: When garden fresh and young, turnip greens are fork tender after a brief cooking. They are tangy and bitter, have flat leaves, and also boast a root that is packed with nutrients. They are delicious combined with other greens, such as collards, or cooked with white potatoes, which cut their sharp flavor.

Broccoli Rabe: Despite its name, this leafy vegetable, which has flowering stalks that resemble tiny heads of broccoli, is a member of the turnip family. It is also sometimes called Chinese flowering cabbage. The flowering stalks should be green, not yellow.

Unless garden fresh, broccoli rabe can be bitter. To tame flavor, blanch this way: Put on a pot of water and bring to a rolling boil. Add the greens, blanch for 3 minutes, drain, and then simmer with chicken stock and herbs and a sliver of smoked turkey or ham.

Spinach: This nutritious green cooks in a few minutes flat. It is also great raw in salads. Look for firm, dark leaves, and avoid those that are waterlogged and slimy.

PLOTTING OUR GARDEN

Since my family lived close to the land, the demands of our garden stretched from season to season. In February we planted green onions or scallions, white potatoes, and sometimes green peas or English peas, as Mama called these pods. By the first week of May, but certainly no later than mid-May, our onions, new potatoes, and peas were ready to pick, and when company came for Sunday dinner, we would combine the three vegetables for a delectable dish.

During the first week of March we planted turnips, cabbage, and collards, and eight or so weeks later, after the last frost of the year, they were simmering in a pot on the back of the stove. Mama always said that a dusting of frost made greens sweet and tender.

Our biggest planting occurred during the first week of April, usually before Good Friday, and we always prayed that the last frost of the year was behind us, since digging up wilted plants and starting all over again would have added countless hours to our stretched workday. At this time we would set out tomatoes, crowder peas, squash, butter beans, snap or green beans, sometimes black-eyed peas, occasionally beets, never carrots or lettuce, always okra, hot peppers, corn, and of course, our beloved sweet potatoes, both the light yellow and orange-red flesh variety.

After that planting we would cultivate and tend our patch and count our blessings. By mid-June we were slicing green tomatoes, tossing with cornmeal and frying until crispy and brown, long before this delicious fare became the name of a popular movie. By the first of July the rest of the tomatoes on the vine were juicy red and full of flavor.

The crowder peas and butter beans were ready by the last of June, and a couple weeks later, we could pull a few pods of okra off the vines and mix the two together for a pot of good eating. By midsummer we had squash and beets. Late summer brought sweet, sweet corn, and everything that hadn't been picked from the garden and eaten would be packed into jars and canned for the winter.

No two families ever planted or picked on the same exact schedule, for although we were communal, each household was a separate entity and had its own way of doing things. Sometimes around Labor Day we would dig up the sweet potatoes, while some families would let the potatoes remain in the ground until late fall. We didn't do this; Daddy said if the tubers remained in the ground much past mid-September, they would sprout and become chalky and woody. The late-digging families said the longer the sweet potatoes stayed in the ground, the sweeter the root.

And once the last sweet potatoes were out of the bountiful earth, we would plant our fall crop of collards, turnips, or mustard greens or cabbage, so that we could enjoy garden-fresh greens again in the dead of winter. A month or two later this cycle of work and reward would begin again, as unwavering as the seasons.

I was reflecting on these memories recently during a conversation with Irene Thomas, who cooks as much as anybody at the Tenth Street Baptist Church in Washington, D.C., and knows four times as much about home gardening.

Mrs. Thomas has been cooking for more than twenty years at the Tenth Street Baptist, which is located on R Street in northwest Washington, and there are few people there, or anywhere else for that matter, who care more about food than she does. That's saying a lot, considering that Tenth Street Baptist pulsates with activities and food is a centerpiece of that action.

Mrs. Thomas and her husband, Clifford, both retired, cultivate four vegetable gardens: three at their home in northwest Washington, D.C., and the fourth on the Rappahannock River in Fredericksburg, Virginia, where they have a vacation trailer home. They grow everything in their garden quartet that my family grew, plus three or four different types of lettuce, eggplants, cucumbers, and green peppers. And all the vegetables she doesn't eat or give away, she freezes or cans.

The other day she was making chow-chow. I became so besieged with memories of home that I ran out to the farmers' market and bought up a sackful of vegetables and did the same. When I was a child I loved this

pickled relish; the briny vegetables were pungent and crisp, and turned everyday fried chicken and chops into Sunday fare. Sometimes Mama would stir in a little chopped hot pepper to the chow-chow, and serve it with the cooked collards, for hot pepper greens. At other times she would add it to potato salad.

Mrs. Thomas sends this recipe, which she says she also learned how to make from her mother years ago when she was a child growing up in Shelby, North Carolina. Regardless of how many jars of chow-chow she cans during the summer, someone is sure to ask for the last jar.

"The other night I had an appreciation dinner here at my home for two church members," she says crisply. "One of the guests had tasted my chow-chow before and wanted me to go downstairs to check to see if I had a jar left."

Not surprisingly, she *didn't* have a jar left.

The preacher is coming! A feast is laid at the home of Gregory and Sheila Coleman, members of the Big Bethel African Methodist Episcopal Church in Atlanta, Georgia.

CHOW=CHOW

Makes about 8 pints

1 medium green cabbage, about
   2 pounds
2 red peppers
4 green peppers
4 onions
6 green tomatoes
1/3 cup non-iodized salt
Cold water, about 8 cups

8 hot sterilized pint-size jars
   (see page 148)
1 tablespoon pickling spice
1 tablespoon mustard seeds
6 cups cider vinegar
2½ cups sugar
2 tablespoons turmeric
1 teaspoon powdered ginger

Choose vegetables that are garden fresh and free of blemishes. Select a
tight head of cabbage with green, tender leaves. Rinse the vegetables
several times, making sure all are completely free of debris or grit.

Lay the cabbage on a cutting board and cut into quarters. Cut out the
core and discard. Lay the cabbage flat on the cutting board and shred finely.
Rinse 2 or 3 times with cold water and drain.

Core and dice the red and green peppers; thinly slice the onions; and
chop the green tomatoes.

Place the vegetables in a large glass or earthenware bowl. (You will
probably have to use two bowls.) Sprinkle with the salt, and add
just enough water to cover the vegetables. Using a large spoon, toss
the vegetables well.

Cover the bowl with a cloth or plastic wrap and allow the vegetables to
remain in the salt brine overnight, preferably in the refrigerator or in a
cool place.

The next morning, drain the vegetables well and set aside. Prepare the
sterilized jars.

Meanwhile, tie the pickling spice and mustard seeds in a small piece
of cheesecloth or any other white cotton fabric. (Canning purists do this to
keep from biting down on seeds and berries when eating the chow-chow.
The bag is removed from the relish before canning. It is perfectly

acceptable to can the vegetables with the spices and I usually do; Mrs. Thomas doesn't.)

Combine in a large, heavy, stainless steel or enamel pot the vinegar, sugar, turmeric, ginger, and the bag containing the pickling spice and mustard seeds. (Don't use an aluminum, copper, or iron pot because the interaction of the vinegar and salt with these metals will discolor the vegetables.)

Place the pot on high heat and bring the mixture to a boil, stirring to dissolve the turmeric. Reduce the heat to low, and cook, stirring, for 10 minutes, or until the sugar and turmeric are completely dissolved.

Add the drained salted vegetables—the cabbage, red and green peppers, onions, and green tomatoes—and mix well. Cook the vegetables over medium-low heat for just 10 minutes, stirring constantly. Watch carefully because the mixture can stick and burn easily.

Remove the pot immediately from the heat. Remove the cloth bag of spices and discard. Pack the vegetables into the hot sterilized jars, leaving ½-inch space at the top of each jar. Seal at once.

GETTING CANNED

There are several varieties of canning jars on the market, but whatever type you choose, they should be checked for cracks, nicks, and chips before using. In addition, if the jars have lids, make sure that the rubber seal hasn't worn away and that the screw bands are not warped or bent.

Many of the popular clamp-type canning jars have rubber rings, which help seal out air. Check to make sure that the rings aren't stretched out of shape. In other words, if your canning equipment is not in pristine condition, don't use it; go shopping first. All canning equipment should be airtight to prevent air and bacteria from seeping in and spoiling the produce later.

After inspecting, wash the jars, lids, and screw bands in hot soapy water, and then rinse well. Insert a rack into a large, deep, heavy pan or canning pot. Place the jars upright on the rack, along with the lids and screw bands.

Add enough water to cover the jars, and then cover the pot. Set the pot on high heat, bring to a boil, and boil rapidly for 15 minutes. Turn off the heat but leave the jars and other equipment in the hot water until you are ready to fill them with the vegetables.

Avoid touching the mouth of the jars when removing from the hot water. Use clean tongs to transport the lids and screw bands.

BATTER=FRIED VEGETABLES

Serves 6 to 8

ecently, one of the church deacons at the Canaan Baptist Church in Harlem asked Deaconess Ernestine Bradley, the church's executive chef, to cater his daughter's wedding reception. Since this was a youngish crowd, Deaconess Ernestine said that she decided to serve what she calls "pickup food"—an array of tasty tidbits such as shrimp cocktail, Buffalo chicken wings, beef kabobs, deviled eggs, cheese straws, marinated tomatoes, and batter-fried vegetables, which the guests quickly devoured.

Deaconess Ernestine has a wide-ranging menu. If the gathering is small and personal, she may just cook chicken 'n' dumplings. Sometimes she jumps into the church's van and searches through the streets of Harlem for a truck loaded with fresh produce, and if successful, will buy up several bunches of turnips with roots, or a bag or two of crowder or black-eyed peas, and set the pots to boiling, just like she did years ago when she was growing up in Orangeburg, South Carolina. Another sister will bake an upside-down pineapple cake or a sinfully delicious German chocolate cake, and they will chuckle and promise only to eat one slice themselves, but they know better. Canaan Baptist is located on 116th Street.

Deaconess Ernestine says that these dishes remind her of the past, and as she tries to remember just how some of the traditional dishes were made, she adds a little of this seasoning, a smidgen of another. "I don't want to forget my roots," she says smiling.

She sends this recipe for vegetable fritters:

2 pounds carrots, zucchini,
   cauliflower, or broccoli, or a
   mixture of the vegetables
2 cups all-purpose flour
½ teaspoon salt
¼ teaspoon black pepper

2 tablespoons melted butter
   or margarine
2 eggs
1 to 1¼ cups milk
Oil for deep frying, about 3 cups

Chefs Ernestine Bradley and Trevor Sargeant preside over the table for the Black History Month celebration during the gospel brunch at Canaan Baptist Church in Harlem, New York.

Wash the vegetables several times and then drain and pat dry with paper towels. Scrape the carrots and cut into 2-inch sticks. Cut the zucchini into 2-inch sticks. Separate the cauliflower or broccoli into small florets, no more than about 1½-inch size. Set aside.

Combine in a medium bowl the flour, salt, black pepper, butter or margarine, and eggs. Mix well.

Gradually stir in 1 cup of the milk until just blended. The batter should be thick enough to coat and cling to the vegetables. You may not need to add the remaining ¼ cup of milk. Don't overmix.

Cover the bowl and chill the batter for at least 1 hour. (The batter can be refrigerated for several hours or overnight.)

To fry, heat the oil in a deep heavy pot or skillet until a deep-frying thermometer reads 375 degrees.

Remove the batter from the refrigerator and beat until smooth. Using long-handled tongs, dip several pieces of the vegetables into the batter, covering all over, and then place on a plate.

Now still using the tongs, gently immerse the vegetables into the hot oil.

Fry for 2 or 3 minutes, turning the pieces over in the fat. When golden brown, remove from the oil and drain on paper towels. Keep warm in an oven set at 250 degrees.

Fry the remaining vegetables in the same way.

FRIED GREEN OKRA

Serves 4

y brother Levord and his wife, Laura, and their teenage son, Lee, live in Choctaw County, Alabama, closely attached to the land. Laura always has some handicraft project underway, and Levord grows grapes and makes wine, for which he has won several prizes in local and regional contests.

Levord, who is a deacon at Shiloh Baptist, also teaches Sunday school and is enmeshed with numerous church activities, from community outreach programs to fund-raising events.

Laura sings in the choir, and whenever there is a funeral dinner, homecoming, church picnic, or any other social event, she is there with a basket of food, and her vegetables are usually fresh from the garden.

Laura sends this recipe for fried okra, which is just as popular in the South, and as delicious, as fried green tomatoes:

2 pounds fresh okra	*⅛ teaspoon cayenne*
¾ teaspoon salt	*½ cup cornmeal*
½ teaspoon finely ground	*½ cup corn oil or vegetable*
black pepper	*shortening*

Buy small, tender pods of okra that are green and glistening, avoiding woody pods with coarse seeds. Rinse the okra, drain well, and then dry with paper towels. Cut off the tips of the okra and discard, and then cut the okra pods crosswise into ½-inch pieces.

Sprinkle the okra with the salt, black pepper. and cayenne. Pour the cornmeal into a plastic or brown-paper bag. Add the okra and shake the bag well, covering the okra with the cornmeal.

Remove the okra from the bag and put into a large strainer or colander, then shake gently to remove all excess cornmeal. This is important: If there is too much cornmeal in the frying pan the okra will not fry quickly and will become heavy and soggy.

Pour about half of the oil into a large heavy skillet and heat until quite hot. Add about one third of the okra and fry quickly until golden brown, turning over with a slotted spoon. This should take no more than 5 minutes. Remove the okra from the pan, drain on paper towels, place on an ovenproof platter and keep warm in an oven set at 250 degrees.

Continue frying the remaining okra in the same way, adding more oil as needed. But make sure that the oil is hot again before adding another batch of okra to the pan.

Serve hot, with garden-fresh sliced tomatoes.

Hot Pepper Relish

Makes about 1½ cups

*a*nn and Lutillie Stepney are retired schoolteachers and between them they have thirty-eight godchildren, enough to fill two classrooms. Well, almost.

The Stepneys are members of the Mount Bethel Baptist Church in Gulfport, Mississippi, and for the past thirty years they have devoted much time, effort, and energy to their community and their church.

Until recently Ann was a church usher and also served as a counselor for the church's youth department. Lutillie is a retired high school football coach, and he has kept many young men on a straight-and-narrow path with his inspiring messages, exemplary behavior, and fatherly concern.

"I think it's now time to let some of the younger women take over my role," says Mrs. Stepney, who is in her early fifties. "All those years when I was an usher I was so busy I didn't get a chance to really enjoy the service. The other Sunday I got a chance to sit and meditate during service for the first time in years."

Ann makes this pronouncement and then laughs and adds that after she has rested for a while, she is sure to be pressed into duty for some other committee at Mount Bethel, which is located on 30th Avenue. And, sure enough, just last Thanksgiving the couple was at the church helping prepare a brotherhood meal for the infirm and shut-in.

Ann sends this recipe for hot pepper relish, which she has also passed along to the young sisters at the church, where somebody is always cooking:

12 hot chili peppers, such as cayenne or Jamaican peppers	¼ teaspoon salt
2 cloves garlic	¼ teaspoon freshly ground black pepper
½ onion	¾ cup cider vinegar

Chop the peppers finely and mince the garlic. (Wear rubber gloves if you think your eyes will tear, for you don't want to wipe your eyes with fingers covered with hot pepper juice!)

Finely dice or grate the onion. Place the peppers, garlic, and onions into a small stainless steel or enamel saucepan. Stir in the salt and pepper. Add the vinegar.

Cook over low heat for 10 minutes.

Remove from the heat and pour the relish into a sterilized pint jar. Seal, let cool, and store in a cool place until ready to use.

Keep the relish refrigerated after opening. Use sparingly. Remember: This stuff is hot!

HOT STUFF

I know many African-Americans who rarely sit down to a meal without having a bottle of hot sauce on the table, or a few pods of hot pepper chopped into a fiery relish, and the same goes for our sisters and brothers in the Caribbean and Africa. We sprinkle hot sauce on fish, ribs, chops, and chicken; stir hot pepper relish into our greens; and also add a little heat to a pot of peas and beans with a pod or two of hot minced peppers.

Admittedly, hot peppers and sauce do boost flavor, but they are also rich in vitamins A and C and packed with healing powers.

The membranes of hot chili peppers contain a chemical called capsaicin, which researchers say stimulates the flow of mucous and helps relieve colds. It also helps thin the blood and thereby prevents the clotting that can lead to heart attacks and strokes. And more than that, capsaicin encourages the brain to release endorphins, which make us feel good, just like a good Sunday sermon.

Today hot chili peppers are available in an assortment of colors, sizes, and shapes, spilling out of vegetable stands like an artist's palette.

The most commonly available chilies, in ascending order of heat, are: poblano, jalapeño, serrano, cayenne, Scotch bonnet (also called Jamaican peppers), and habañero, which is considered the fiercest and hottest of all chilies.

SUMMER SQUASH CASSEROLE

Serves 4

attie Hodges is one of the leading cooks at the Ebenezer Baptist Church in Atlanta, and she is just as self-assured about her skills as her good friend Mrs. Hemmans is retiring and diffident about hers. Over the years she has worked at a bakery and at several restaurants and cafés, and until her retirement a few years ago, she spent more than twenty years in food service for the Atlanta public school system. And since she is the yang to Martha Hemmans's yin (or vice versa), she says quite frankly that she is a food fanatic.

"I cooked my first meal when I was five years old," she says matter-of-factly. "I grew up out in the country in Hancock County, about 120 miles from Atlanta. My mother and I were at home alone and she was about to give birth to my brother. My mother was sick and hungry. My aunt was due to come over and cook in a few minutes. It got late; she wasn't there by 10 A.M. I told Mama to drink a glass of milk and I would do the cooking. I had been watching her cook before then. She would let me help a little bit, so that I could feel independent.

"So I went into the kitchen and made bread, fried ham, cooked eggs, got the syrup. I got it all done. I was only five. We had an old wood-burning stove in the middle of the room that had a reservoir on the side where you could boil up to three gallons of water. The stove had a pipe that ran across the room and through a hole to the outside.

"By the time my aunt came we were sitting at the table eating. She said, 'Who came over and cooked that meal?' I said, 'I did.' She was shocked, and said, 'Wonder if you didn't get burned.' I didn't.

"I remember that day as clear as yesterday. When I tell people that story they look at me like I am crazy. But it is true. I've been cooking ever since I was five. Today I spend 90 percent of my time in my kitchen. I love my kitchen and I love to cook."

But she doesn't cook for just anybody. Whenever she feels like it, she caters private parties for a very select clientele. She also serves on Ebenezer's Gourmet Committee, which has the daunting task of

overseeing the vast array of food prepared and served at the church.

Besides that, Mrs. Hodges often joins Mrs. Hemmans, Mrs. Davis, Mrs. Dean, and Mrs. Jones in the kitchen at Ebenezer. Sometimes, she says, the women have so much fun she thinks she is five years old again.

Mrs. Hodges sends this delectable recipe for summer squash:

2 pounds straight neck or zucchini
squash
1 large onion
1 small red or green pepper
1 stalk of celery
1 large firm red tomato, or
3 plum tomatoes
2 sprigs fresh oregano, or
½ teaspoon dried oregano
3 tablespoons butter or vegetable oil

¾ teaspoon salt
½ teaspoon freshly ground
black pepper
1 cup soft bread crumbs from
leftover bread
1 tablespoon vegetable oil or
melted butter
½ cup grated natural-aged
Cheddar or Parmesan cheese

Preheat the oven to 375 degrees.

Butter a 1½ quart baking dish and set aside.

Rinse the squash, cut off stems, and discard, and then cut crosswise into ¼-inch thick slices. Place the squash in the top of a steamer over boiling water and steam for about 10 minutes or until tender but still crispy. (You can also cook the squash directly in the water, but steaming keeps it from becoming waterlogged.) Remove the squash from the heat, drain, and set aside.

Meanwhile, thinly slice the onion; core and dice the red or green pepper; chop the celery and the tomatoes. Chop the fresh oregano or crush the dried herb.

Pour the water from the bottom of the steamer. Heat the butter or oil in the pan. Stir in the onion, red or green pepper, celery, and herb. Sauté 5 minutes over medium heat or until the onions are translucent.

Stir in the tomatoes, salt, and black pepper and sauté 2 or 3 minutes longer. Add the drained squash and mix well. Remove from heat.

Spoon the squash mixture into the buttered baking dish.

In a small bowl, mix together the bread crumbs, oil or butter, and cheese. Scatter the mixture over the top of the squash. Place the dish in the hot oven on the middle shelf and bake for 18 to 20 minutes or until the top is crusty and lightly browned. Serve hot.

GARDEN OF SQUASH

Mattie Hodges remembers the squash, so young and tender in the middle of summer during her youth. She would cut the vegetable into chunks and quickly sauté in bacon drippings with green onions for a mouth-watering dish that only took a minute to prepare. Since every family had a garden, some folks grew one variety of squash while another family grew a different type, and although nobody planned this, it seems as though no two families ever planted the same variety during the exact same year.

And the colors were also so different, ranging from deep green to yellow to creamy white. There were, as she now knows, a variety called straight, another known as crookneck, and a pale green hat-shaped variety known as pattypan, as well as zucchini.

Sautéed Summer Squash

Serves 4

*a*nn Birchett cuts a familiar presence along Convent Avenue in Harlem, as she makes her way from her home to the Convent Avenue Baptist Church and to various community centers and programs. Often she has a dish of food tucked in her arm, including this old-fashioned way with summer squash.

2 pounds pattypan or crookneck
  squash or a mixture of two
½ teaspoon salt
½ teaspoon freshly ground
  black pepper
1 onion

1 small red or green pepper
2 or 3 fresh basil leaves, or
  ½ teaspoon dried basil
3 to 4 tablespoons vegetable oil or
  bacon drippings

Rinse the squash, drain well, and pat dry with paper towels. Cut off stems and discard and then cut the squash into ¼-inch slices crosswise. Sprinkle the squash with the salt and black pepper.

Slice the onion; core and dice the red or green pepper; chop the fresh basil or crush the dried herb.

Heat the oil or bacon drippings in a large heavy skillet. Add the squash, onion, red or green pepper, and basil. Cook over medium heat for 10 to 15 minutes or until the squash is tender, turning occasionally so as to brown evenly.

This dish is equally delicious served hot or at room temperature. To reheat, place in a heavy skillet and heat over a medium-low heat for 5 minutes, stirring occasionally.

SQUASH SALAD

Serves 6 or more

*M*arion Wells is a member of the West Hunter Street Baptist Church in Atlanta, where she is involved in many church projects. A retired schoolteacher, she took on the challenging task of collecting favorite recipes from church members a while back.

She sends this recipe for squash, which is a favored dish in the South, almost as popular as greens.

8 crookneck squash
1 large onion
1 green pepper
2 large tomatoes
½ cup Vinaigrette Sauce, or more if
* desired (see recipe on page 174)*

Lettuce leaves, washed and drained
* and chilled*
2 tablespoons chopped long-leaf
* parsley or cilantro*

Rinse the squash and steam over boiling water for 10 minutes or until tender. Or place the squash in a large saucepan or Dutch oven, cover with water, bring to a boil, then reduce the heat, cover, and cook for 10 minutes or until the vegetable is tender but still crisp.

Drain the squash and cool. Cut the cooled squash crosswise into ⅛-inch slices. Thinly slice the onion; core and dice the green pepper; cut the tomatoes into thin wedges.

Place the squash in a large bowl. Add the onion, tomatoes and green pepper. Pour over the Vinaigrette Sauce and mix well.

Chill the salad in the refrigerator at least 2 hours, preferably overnight.

At serving, arrange the lettuce leaves on a serving platter. Top with the marinated vegetables and then sprinkle with chopped parsley or cilantro.

SWEET, SWEET POTATOES

African-Americans enjoy sweet potatoes in so many ways: baked straight from the oven, syrupy, steamy and succulent; peeled and candied with sugar and spices until they shine like satin; sliced and fried and caramelized into charred goodness; mashed for pies and soufflés; deep fried and salted for briny, fleetingly sweet potato chips.

Our love for sweet potatoes goes way, way back. Slaves on plantations roasted sweet potatoes in hot ashes and enjoyed them as a treat whenever they were afforded the opportunity, since rations were meager at best. Before the slave trade there were festivals in Africa marking the planting and harvesting of yams, which have a peel similar to sweet potatoes but usually with white or cream-colored flesh. Yams actually belong to another botanical family, though almost everyone confuses the two. We African-Americans mostly eat sweet potatoes; in the Caribbean the slightly chalky tubers are actually yams.

Regardless, I could eat a plain baked sweet potato, either hot or cold, every day, and sometimes I do. These tubers are full of beta-carotene or the plant variety of vitamin A, and they are so high in fiber.

Irene Thomas, who grows most of her vegetables and cooks more than she intends to at the Tenth Street Baptist Church in Washington, D.C., sends this recipe:

BAKED SWEET POTATOES

Serves 4

4 large sweet potatoes
1 to 2 teaspoons vegetable oil or
  shortening

Butter or margarine (if desired)

Preheat the oven to 400 degrees.

Wash the sweet potatoes, drain, and dry with paper towels. Cut off any blemishes or sprouts. Cut off the end tips, if desired.

Rub the potatoes sparingly all over with the oil or shortening. (If you add too much oil the potatoes become soft and mushy during the baking.)

Place the potatoes in a large ungreased roasting pan. Bake in the hot oven for about 50 minutes or until the potatoes are soft, turning over once or twice to bake evenly.

Remove the potatoes from the oven and let set for about 10 minutes so the steam can evaporate, resulting in a firmer textured hot potato. Serve with butter or margarine, if desired.

Glazed Sweet Potatoes

Serves 6 to 8

rs. Ollie Hutchins swept into my life more than eighteen years ago, and that is the only way I can describe the arrival of this grand woman who was eulogized during services last year at the Mount Calvary United Methodist Church in Harlem, as an "elegant, complex, Christian lady." The church is located on Edgecombe Avenue.

She helped me raise my son, Roy, and she did so with her uptown style and boundless love, enveloping him with music, the arts, sports, and an uncompromising code of ethics. Oh, she could be a taskmaster, and she was picky and particular about most things, including food.

A few days before her funeral repast, her daughter, Delores Lee, a schoolteacher and my dear friend, reminded me that her mother loved sweet potatoes and gave me her favorite recipe. While I was preparing this dish, Roy reminded me that Mrs. Hutchins had simply gone to sleep and for once, forgot to wake up. We loved her.

I carried this recipe to her funeral repast:

8 to 10 small sweet potatoes, about 3 pounds
½ cup dark brown sugar
½ cup white sugar
1 cup water
½ teaspoon ground cinnamon, or more if desired
½ teaspoon ground nutmeg or allspice
2 whole cloves
4 tablespoons butter or margarine

Preheat the oven to 325 degrees.

Scrub the sweet potatoes and rinse well. Peel the potatoes and then cut crosswise into ⅜-inch-thick slices.

Butter a 2-quart casserole or shallow baking dish. Arrange the potatoes in overlapping layers in the pan. Set aside.

In a medium saucepan, combine the brown sugar, white sugar, water, cinnamon, nutmeg or allspice, cloves, and butter or margarine. Heat over low heat for five minutes, stirring.

Pour the glaze over the potatoes, covering all the potatoes with the sugar mixture. Cover the dish with a lid or aluminum foil.

Place the dish on the middle shelf of the hot oven. Bake for 1 hour or until the potatoes are tender, gently ladling the glaze over the potatoes once or twice during the baking.

Remove from the oven. Let stand for a few minutes in a warm place for the glaze to set. If serving later, reheat at 300 degrees for 20 minutes or in a microwave.

SWEET POTATO FRIES

Serves 4

Mama often put out a platter of these crunchy fries whenever the Home Mission Club members gathered at our house. I remember eating far too many of these delightful "chips," which were sometimes sprinkled with salt and at other times with sugar. Both versions are delicious.

4 sweet potatoes
3 cups cooking oil

Salt or brown or white sugar
(if desired)

Scrub and rinse the potatoes. Drain and pat dry with paper towels. Cut away any blemishes or sprouts.

Preheat the oil in a deep heavy pot or skillet until it reaches 375 on a deep-fry thermometer.

Meanwhile, cut the unpeeled potatoes into ½-inch-thick slices lengthwise, and cut again lengthwise into strips as for French fries.

Dry the potatoes again with paper towels, since they will leak moisture once cut.

Add a handful of the potato strips at a time to the hot oil and cook for 4 or 5 minutes or until golden brown and tender, turning with long-handled tongs as they fry.

Remove the potatoes from the oil, drain on paper towels, and keep warm in a 250-degree oven while frying the remaining potato strips.

At serving, sprinkle with either salt or white or brown sugar, if desired.

ONE POTATO, TWO POTATOES

Although sweet potato dishes bear our culinary signature, we also set our tables and pack our church food baskets and boxes with very fine white potato dishes, too. Years ago in my family, new potatoes and green or string beans was a favorite combination during the summer when our garden was in full harvest. On special occasions my sister, Helen, who was a cook at a local café, made the best mashed potatoes ever—creamy but fluffy, and too rich with butter and cream. Sometimes on Saturday afternoons Mama would cut up a batch of white potatoes into finger-size strips and fry until crispy and golden and delicious.

Our favorite dish, though, was potato salad—an improvisational mixing of a root vegetable with mayonnaise, onions, pickles, hard-cooked eggs, peppers, olives, capers—or whatever strikes the cook's fancy.

Like macaroni and cheese, we African-Americans have made this dish our own, and today, I can't imagine a backyard barbecue, church picnic, family reunion or Saturday afternoon fish fry without several bowls of creamy potato salad.

POTATO SALAD FOR A CROWD

Serves 25 or more

thought of the many church gatherings I have attended when Dava Albert's recipe for potato salad arrived. Dava is a young, dedicated churchwoman, age twenty-four, who works with youths at the Mount Olive Baptist Church in McLoud, Oklahoma, which is near Oklahoma City.

Mount Olive is a small country church with some 150 members, including Dava's parents, Robert and Emily Morris, and her sister, Gina, and brother, Arthur. Her mother is the church's clerk.

Whenever there is a homecoming or anniversary celebration, one of the church brothers brings out a smoker from home and the men, including Dava's father, smoke the ribs, chicken, beef briskets, and hot dogs, while the church sisters bring out the vegetables and side dishes.

"We fill those pews with our neighbors and friends," says Emily. "Recently we had our homecoming and invited five churches. We fed everybody. We never sell food unless it is a fund-raiser."

Dava sends a recipe for potato salad and these words. She writes:

"Church picnics are the most remembered group activity within a church family, more so than almost any other activity the congregation as a whole can participate in. Many people have attended church picnics and gotten married later or found jobs from just conversation and the power of networking. Positive, supportive information is shared more at church picnics than at other activities.

"I always look forward to our

Guests sample a tempting array of dishes at the Black History Month celebration held by Canaan Baptist Church in Harlem.

yearly picnic. The weather usually cooperates and everyone in the church brings members of other churches and their families to come eat, sing, and fellowship. The food is always great and I can't remember one dish at any picnic that I didn't truly love."

Dava's recipe for this potato salad serves twenty-five or so. The recipe can be doubled or tripled for an even larger crowd.

10 pounds all-purpose white
  potatoes
1 teaspoon salt
1 dozen eggs (or more, if desired)
2 green peppers
2 or 3 stalks celery
2 onions
4 to 5 cups commercial mayonnaise
  or Homemade Mayonnaise
  (see recipe on page 224)

¼ to ½ cup prepared mustard
2 teaspoons salt
1½ to 2 teaspoons freshly
  ground black pepper
4 cups pickle relish
1 cup chopped drained pimentos
Paprika
Chopped parsley
Celery leaves (optional)
Olives (optional)

Rinse and scrub the potatoes, and trim off any blemishes. Cut the potatoes in half but don't peel. Place in a large pot, cover with water, and add the salt. Bring to a boil, reduce heat to medium-high, cover, and cook 25 to 30 minutes or until the potatoes are tender but not mushy. (Unless you have a very large commercial-size pot you will have to cook the potatoes in batches.)

While the potatoes cook, place the eggs in another pot, cover with cold water, bring to a boil; reduce the heat and simmer, uncovered, for 12 to 15 minutes.

After 12 minutes of cooking, crack one egg to see if it is fully cooked. If so, remove the remaining eggs from the heat, drain, and crack and peel under cold running water. Dry with paper towels and dice.

Core and mince the green pepper; finely chop the celery; chop the onions. Combine the green pepper, celery, and onion in a large mixing bowl. Stir in the mayonnaise, mustard, salt, black pepper, relish, and the pimentos.

When the potatoes are done, remove from the heat, drain, and let cool a few minutes. When the potatoes are cool enough to handle, peel and then dice into ½-inch pieces.

Add the potatoes while they are still warm to the mayonnaise mixture. Add the diced eggs. Using a large wooden spoon, mix well, but stir lightly so as not to mash the potatoes.

Cover the bowl and chill the potato salad for at least 3 or 4 hours, but preferably overnight.

At serving, turn the potato salad onto several platters. Sprinkle with a little paprika and chopped parsley. Garnish with celery leaves and whole olives, if desired.

Lemony New Potatoes

Serves 4

*d*eborah Sherow spends many hours at the Greater Saint Mary Baptist Church in Tyler, Texas, and since she is a consummate cook, many of those are spent in the kitchen, which the church recently expanded and renovated.

She sends this recipe for new potatoes, which, when I was a child, was a harbinger of the sparkling jewels that the earth would bring forth during the summer and fall:

2 pounds new potatoes
4 tablespoons butter or margarine
2 tablespoons lemon juice
2 tablespoons chopped parsley
 or basil

1 teaspoon grated lemon rind
½ teaspoon salt
¼ teaspoon freshly ground
 black pepper

Wash and scrub the potatoes. Don't peel the potatoes, but cut a thin strip around the center, making a band—a fancy touch.

Place the potatoes in a medium saucepan and cover with water. Bring to a boil, reduce the heat to medium, cover, and cook 10 to 12 minutes, or until the potatoes are tender. Watch carefully, and don't overcook. Drain the potatoes and set aside.

Dry the saucepan and combine in the pan the butter or margarine, lemon juice, parsley or basil, lemon rind, salt, and black pepper. Heat over low heat for 2 or 3 minutes, stirring.

Return the potatoes to the pan. Spoon the butter-lemon mixture over the potatoes, coating well. Cover the pan and heat over medium-low heat for 5 minutes, or until the potatoes are hot.

POTATO BREAKFAST SLICE

Serves 4 to 6

auline Grier is the president of the Deaconess Club at the Holy Trinity Baptist Church in Philadelphia, Pennsylvania, and often she and the other women gather at breakfast or at brunch to talk church and community concerns. The church is located on Bainbridge Street.

Mrs. Grier likes to keep the menu simple, and she does so by serving a slice of this savory pie, which combines the familiar breakfast foods of eggs, ham, cheese, and potatoes. Fruit juice and coffee are offered, and after a brief session, the women move on to the rest of their busy day.

Note: Mrs. Grier says that she usually prepares the pie crust and cooks the potato the night before the meeting, so that she only has to assemble the pie and pop it into the oven the next morning.

4 all-purpose white potatoes	3 eggs
1 (9-inch) pie crust (see recipe on page 320)	2 tablespoons milk
	½ teaspoon salt
2 tablespoons vegetable oil	¼ teaspoon black pepper
1 sliced onion	3 or 4 slices cheese such as
1 tablespoon chopped parsley	provolone, mozzarella, or
½ pound thinly sliced baked ham or smoked turkey	cheddar

Scrub the potatoes, cut away blemishes, and then place in the top of a steamer and boil for 30 minutes or until tender. Drain, cool, peel, and cut into thin slices.

Preheat the oven to 425 degrees.

Prepare the pie crust. Prick the pie crust all over and then brush with egg white. Place the pie crust in the hot oven on the lower shelf and bake for 10 minutes or until the crust is lightly browned. Remove the pie shell from the oven and set aside.

Reduce the oven heat to 375 degrees.

Heat the oil in a medium skillet. Add the onion and parsley and sauté 5 or 6 minutes or until the onions are soft and translucent. Remove from the heat.

Arrange the potato slices in the baked pie crust, overlapping in a neat pattern. Spoon over the sautéed onions and parsley, and then top with the sliced ham or turkey.

In a small bowl, lightly beat together the eggs, milk, salt, and black pepper. Pour the egg mixture over the potatoes, onions, and ham or turkey. Top with the sliced cheese, covering the surface completely.

Place the dish in the hot oven on the middle shelf and bake for 20 minutes, or until the eggs are set and the dish is piping hot.

Remove from the oven, let set for a few minutes in a warm place, and then cut into slices.

COLE SLAW AND OTHER COOL SALADS

Cole slaw is almost as popular at African-American gatherings as potato salad, and there are as many versions as cooks in the kitchen. The main ingredient is a tender head of cabbage that is shredded or grated and combined with a creamy dressing. Purists use homemade mayonnaise while the health-conscious use a vinaigrette sauce made with olive or vegetable oil, which is low in saturated fat. (A vinaigrette sauce is also fine for lettuce and other vegetable salads.)

After that the imagination soars. Over the years at church and family gatherings I have enjoyed cole slaw tossed with a variety of ingredients—including walnuts, pecans, raisins, grated carrots, caraway and sesame seeds, and slivers of smoked ham or turkey. And once on New Year's Day in Atlanta, the cole slaw was combined with black-eyed peas for good luck and prosperity.

Whatever the ingredients, this is another example of turning one of our beloved greens—cabbage—into a pungent, jazzy creation.

CREAMY COLE SLAW

Serves 6

Susie B. Waxwood, who at age ninety-five is as sprightly as many women half her age, sends a delightful recipe for cole slaw that was developed by the late Daisy Reeves, one of the founders of the Ladies Aid Society, a missionary group, at the Witherspoon Street Presbyterian Church in Princeton, New Jersey. The club today is known as the Women's Association.

Mrs. Waxwood, who has been a member of the church since 1935 and is the former executive director of the Princeton YWCA, remembers that during the 1940s and '50s, one of the highlights at the church was the club's annual Harvest Home Dinner. The event, held in October, was attended by scores of people and the money raised was used for the upkeep

Hartford Memorial Baptist Church in Detroit holds Baccalaureate Day. Kitchen staff prepares for visitors. Left to right: Elma Williams, Delores Brandon, the church's kitchen manager–administrator, and Carolyn Drake.

of the church, which today has some two hundred members.

"The food was always delicious," recalls Mrs. Waxwood. "We would start off with platters of celery sticks, carrot curls, and olives, and then move on to roast turkey, mashed potatoes and gravy, succotash, candied sweet potatoes, Harvard beets, cakes and pies, buttered rolls, and of course, Daisy's cole slaw, which was creamy and crunchy. They have a lot of social events at the church today, but not like those Harvest Home Dinners of years ago."

1 large head of green cabbage, about 2 pounds
1 green pepper
1 onion
3 tablespoons cider vinegar
Pinch of salt
Pinch of black pepper

2 teaspoons sugar
1 teaspoon dry mustard
½ cup commercial mayonnaise or Homemade Mayonnaise (see recipe on page 224)
¼ cup sour cream

Choose a heavy head of cabbage with tight, crisp green leaves. Place the cabbage on a cutting board and cut into quarters. Rinse the cabbage well with cold water and drain until dry or spin to dry in a lettuce spinner.

Wrap the cabbage in toweling and allow to crisp overnight in the refrigerator. When the cabbage is dry and crisp, cut away the core and then shred finely.

Core and finely dice the green pepper and chop the onion. Combine the vegetables in a large bowl.

Make the dressing: Combine in a small bowl the cider vinegar, salt, black pepper, sugar, dry mustard, mayonnaise, and sour cream. Beat together with a fork or wire whisk until well-blended.

Pour the dressing over the vegetables and toss to mix well. Cover the bowl with plastic wrap and chill again for 2 or 3 hours or overnight.

Broccoli Cashew Salad

Serves 4

during the week the Reverend Vincent Adams shakes the pots and pans at a supermarket restaurant on the Gulf Coast in Biloxi, Mississippi, where he works as a chef. On Sundays he goes to church. Reverend Adams is an associate minister at the Saint James Baptist Church in Gulfport, Mississippi, which is located on 25th Street, and the chaplain of a local Army Reserve Unit.

He sends this recipe for a broccoli salad with a vinaigrette dressing that he developed for the church's Kitchen Committee:

1 head broccoli	¼ cup salad dressing or Vinaigrette
1 red pepper	Sauce (recipe follows)
1 green pepper	1 cup cashew nuts
2 carrots	

Trim off any tough broccoli stems and discard. Cut the remaining broccoli stalks into 2- to 3-inch florets. Core the red and green peppers and cut into ¼-inch wide strips. Scrape the carrots and shred coarsely.

Steam the broccoli over boiling water for about 5 minutes or until just tender. Drain and cool.

Combine in a large bowl the broccoli, peppers, and carrots.

Pour the salad dressing or Vinaigrette Sauce over the broccoli and vegetables, and then chill for at least 1 hour. At serving time, toss the salad with the cashew nuts.

Vinaigrette Sauce

Makes about 1¼ cups

This basic salad dressing adds zing and zest to tossed salads as well as to cole slaw, chicken or shrimp salad. Store in a jar with a lid and it will keep for at least a week in the refrigerator.

2 cloves garlic

1 tablespoon soy sauce

¼ cup cider or red wine vinegar

1 cup olive oil

¼ teaspoon salt

¼ teaspoon freshly ground black
  pepper

2 teaspoons prepared mustard

Mince the garlic and combine in a small bowl with the soy sauce, vinegar, olive oil, salt, black pepper, and mustard. Beat with a whisk or fork until well blended.

Use immediately or place in a jar with a tight lid and refrigerate. Shake when ready to use.

GOING FISHING

One quick look at the map of the United States shows why African-Americans over the years often literally snatched the day's dinner from the sea, and in doing so held numerous celebrations and gatherings around our catch, including the traditional fish fry, which still reigns supreme at black churches from coast to coast. This country is divinely blessed with an abundance of inland rivers, lakes, streams, and bayous, plus shorelines that extend from New England to the Florida Keys, along the Gulf Coast, and the breadth of the West Coast, from Baja to Alaska.

These inland and ocean waters brim with cod and haddock, monkfish, swordfish, flounder, sole, clams and crabs, mussels and oysters, crappies, walleyed pike, perch, striped bass, butterfish, porgy, whiting, red snapper, pompano, grouper, mullet, catfish, trout, redfish, crayfish, shrimp, mako shark, yellowfin, salmon, sturgeon—and the list goes on and on.

We African-Americans went fishing in these waters and netted a kettle of good cooking. If we lived on the coast of South Carolina or on the Gulf Coast of the South, we combined our catch with herbs and onions and garlic and whatever else was available, and created fish stews and gumbo. Sisters at black churches in the Chesapeake Bay region boiled crabs in a potful of spicy seasoning. On the coast of Louisiana and Texas the crabs were replaced by crayfish and shrimp, but the savory seasonings remained the same. Inlanders, in the Midwest and especially in the South, fried fish in a cast-iron skillet or pot, and if it were a Saturday afternoon fish fry on the churchyard, in a great big black iron pot that would hold somebody's laundry on Monday morning.

No matter, fish is good for you, whether fried, baked, or broiled, and we have known that for years. All fish contain polyunsaturated fats called omega-3 fatty acids, and studies show that these oils lower blood cholesterol levels and help prevent clotting of the arteries, which can lead to heart attacks and strokes. The important consideration to remember when frying fish is to use vegetable oil and not lard, which is rendered pork fat. All animal fat is loaded with cholesterol, which is linked with heart diseases.

COOKIN' FISH GOOD

Like meat and chicken, fish can be fried, grilled, broiled, sautéed, boiled, steamed or braised, baked or smoked, or stir-fried, but no cooking method is actually better than the other, since each method results in a different flavor and texture. However, some cooking methods are easier than others, and the method that we African-Americans are masters of, frying, is the most difficult.

Personally, I find that broiling or baking fish in an oven is quick and simple and involves little fuss or bother. All you have to do is heat the oven or broiler, season the fish, oil the broiler or baking pan, and brush the fish with a little oil and soy sauce to prevent drying during cooking. (Don't use butter for broiling because it burns easily under intense heat.)

If you are broiling you can easily adjust the distance of the heat source from the food, which is a key element to success. Thin fillets weighing six to seven ounces each can be placed three or four inches from the broiler heat and broiled in about five minutes. If I am doing fish steaks, I cut them about ¾-inch thick, and broil six inches from the heat for about five minutes per side.

Small whole fish weighing about 1½ pounds are ideal for broiling, although I think larger fish are better baked, since the cooking is easier to control. Remember that a whole fish has to be moved farther from the broiler heat—six to eight inches—than thin fillets so that the inside cooks before the skin chars and burns.

A fish weighing less than two pounds should broil for about eight minutes per side, but the only way to make sure it has cooked long enough is to check for doneness. To do so, using a knife or fork, flake the fish at its thickest part. If the flesh is white and opaque and moist, the fish is done.

Baking is ideal for large whole fish, and to produce a crisp skin the heat should be quite high, at least 425 degrees. Since this is dry heat, baste the fish several times during the baking with a little oil mixed with a liquid, either beer, wine, or vegetable or fish stock (see recipe on page 67).

The general rule for baking a whole fish is to bake ten to twelve minutes per pound. Or, measure the fish at its thickest part and cook ten minutes per inch of thickness.

Ideally, a three-pound fish should bake for thirty minutes or so, but the only true way to gauge for doneness is to test the fish by piercing with a fork or knife, and if the flesh is opaque but still moist, the fish is done. (Recently the trend at chi-chi restaurants across country calls for removing the fish from the oven once it is opaque, save for a translucent line running along its thickest part. The notion is that the fish will finish cooking on its way to your plate. I don't particularly care for half-done fish, but I do concede that doneness is a matter of personal preference.)

Pan sautéing is as easy as broiling or baking, and particularly suitable for firm-textured fish, such as swordfish, red snapper, salmon, tuna, monkfish, sea and striped bass, and shellfish, such as shrimp and scallops.

The key to success is to use a heavy large skillet, at least twelve or thirteen inches in diameter, or better yet, use a cast-iron griddle that sits over the burner.

Oil the pan or griddle rather generously with oil, or with a mixture of oil and butter, and then heat until very hot. Add the fish, making sure not to crowd the pan, and sear quickly on both sides. Once lightly browned, reduce the heat, and add other seasonings, such as capers or onions or peppers, and finish sautéing until the fish test done when flaked with a knife or fork.

Next to frying, grilling over hot charcoal is the most challenging fish-cooking method to master, but like with most pursuits, experience helps. Again, don't attempt to grill fish weighing more than two pounds; it's easier to bake or steam large whole fish. And if possible, adjust the distance of the fish from the heat, depending on the thickness of the fish. Thick fish steaks should be placed six inches or more from the heat, while thin fillets can be placed four inches from the heat. Test for doneness by piercing the fish with a knife or fork. (See "Grilling Is Hot" on page 192.)

A few other caveats to remember when grilling fish:

- Allow the charcoal to turn completely ashy before placing the fish on the grill.
- Use a spotlessly clean, oiled grill.
- Oil the fish lightly to keep it from sticking to the grill.
- Dab the fish frequently with marinade to keep it from drying out during the grilling, and move it about often by inserting a thin, wide, metal spatula under the fish.
- Consider grilling the fish in an oiled shallow pan set on the grill, rather than placing the fish directly on the rack over the charcoal.

Or fry the fish. The fish fry is such a hallowed black church tradition that I used to hear my father recount many incidents and episodes of the past: . . . and then use such and such fish fry at such and such church as the connecting point of reference. No wonder, fried fish is so delicious. And despite the bad rap about fried foods being high in fat, recent studies show that when fish or chicken is fried quickly at a high temperature and drained, it actually absorbs very little fat.

The first thing you need to fry fish right is a good heavy pot or skillet and the bigger the surface area, the better. Down South, when I was growing up the church sisters used to say that the fish should "float" in the hot oil. And don't listen to anybody who tells you that you can fry a small batch of fish in a small saucepan and it tastes just as good—it doesn't.

After the pot issue is settled, the other elements, such as the type of frying oil and the proper coating, can get sticky. Some fryers prefer old-fashioned lard—high cholesterol and all—since they say it produces a very crisp crust. Others prefer vegetable shortening, and there are also the safflower, peanut, and corn oil partisans, primarily because all of these have a high smoking point.

I found that canola oil renders a very crispy, light-tasting fried fish, while olive oil, which is great for salad dressings, doesn't work well for deep frying. Olive oil has a low smoking point and more than that, the fish ends up oily and heavy in texture. And any oil you use should reach at least three inches up the side of the pan, and the cooking surface should be as wide as possible so that the fish can "float."

Mama used to coat fish with a mixture of cornmeal and flour, but Aunt Mary used nothing but finely ground cornmeal. Other women back home used finely crushed saltine crackers or commercially prepared bread crumbs. People who like crusty fried fish dip the fish in a batter made of flour, egg, and milk, and then fry. Battered fish requires a slightly lower frying temperature, for it is important that the fish gets done before the batter overbrowns and burns.

Whatever breading you use, the oil should be piping hot before you add the fish, and unless you are an experienced cook, the best way to gauge the temperature is with a deep-frying thermometer. For best frying, let the oil reach at least 375 degrees, and if it drops after frying a few pieces of fish, let the temperature rise again before frying another batch. (If the fish has been dipped in a heavy batter, fry at 365 degrees.)

Harriet Rakiatu-Campbell, a member of the Women's Ministry Choir at the Mount Moriah African Methodist Episcopal Church in Annapolis, Maryland, at a pot-luck fund-raising event.

Even after the thermometer reads 365 or 375 degrees, once you put in the fish, the temperature falls immediately. So unless you are frying in one of those big black laundry pots, you can't put in many pieces of fish at once. If you are using a twelve- or thirteen-inch skillet or pot, fry no more than a half-pound of fish, or two or three fillets, at once, and don't crowd the pan.

Drain the fish on paper towels as soon as you lift it from the hot oil. Keep the fish warm, and let the temperature rise back to 375 degrees before adding more fish.

When all is done and the splattered oil is cleaned up, get out the hot sauce, ketchup, and lemon wedges, and enjoy this old-time treasure. Velma Mosley, who is just as zealous about food as she is about the community and church, sends a delectable fried-fish recipe.

Mrs. Mosley is a member of the Greater Hopewell Baptist Church in Swan, Texas, and whenever there is a social function at the church, she arrives with a covered dish.

She is an expansive and friendly woman who reflects the essence of the expression "If you want something done right give the job to a busy person." A nurse by training, she works with civil rights organizations, knocks on voters' doors for African-American candidates, serves as an advocate for the mentally and physically disabled, and spearheads fund-raising events for local community projects.

Mrs. Mosley is also a consummate cook. She sends a recipe for spicy fried fish:

TEXAS FRIED FISH

Serves 4

3 pounds small whole catfish
1 cup milk
¾ teaspoon salt
1½ teaspoons Cajun seasoning or paprika (more if desired)
½ teaspoon freshly ground black pepper
½ cup very fine ground cornmeal
Vegetable or corn oil for frying, at least 3 cups
Lemon wedges

Scale and gut the fish. Cut off the heads and discard. Rinse the fish well with cold water and drain. Split the fish down the middle lengthwise for fillets, but don't skin. Place the fish in a large bowl and pour over the milk and let soak for at least 30 minutes.

Drain the soaked fish well and then pat as dry as possible with paper towels. If the fish is wet the oil will sputter and the fish will fall apart.

Going Fishing

Sprinkle the fish with the salt, Cajun seasoning or paprika, and black pepper. Pour the cornmeal into a brown paper or plastic bag. Add the fish and shake to coat evenly with the cornmeal. Remove from the bag, shaking to remove any excess coating. Set the fish aside.

Pour the oil to a depth of at least 3 inches into a large heavy cast-iron skillet or Dutch oven. Heat the oil over high heat to 375 degrees.

Carefully lower two or three fish fillets into the oil and cook for 2 or 3 minutes on each side, turning often. Using long-handled tongs, remove the fish from the hot oil, drain on paper towels, place on a platter, and keep warm in an oven set at 250 degrees.

Allow the temperature of the oil to rise back to 375 degrees before adding more fish. Continue frying this way until all the fish is fried. Serve with lemon wedges and Hush Puppies, if desired (recipe follows).

Variation: Fish for frying should be small in size and firm in texture. Other good choices for frying are mullet, whiting, porgies, flounder, croaker, grouper, and butterfish.

HUSH PUPPIES

*t*he story goes that this recipe got its name years ago during a fishing trip that turned into a fish fry, which is not unusual in the South. To quiet a barking dog, the owner threw a spoonful of cornmeal batter into the oil, let it turn brown, and then threw it at the pet with the admonition: Hush, puppy!

So much for food lore. For authentic flavor, fry the fish first, keep warm, and then fry the hush puppies in the same oil.

Jacqueline Evans, who directs the Women Ministry's Choir and is the minister of music at the Mount Moriah African Methodist Episcopal Church in Annapolis, Maryland, sends a wonderful recipe for these down-home favorites:

1½ cups yellow or white cornmeal

½ cup all-purpose flour

½ teaspoon salt

2 teaspoons baking powder

*¼ cup melted butter or vegetable
  shortening*

⅓ cup finely minced green onions

2 tablespoons chopped parsley

*1 minced small hot chili pepper,
  or less*

1 beaten egg

¾ to 1 cup milk

Vegetable oil, at least 3 cups

Sift the cornmeal, flour, salt, and baking powder into a medium bowl. Set aside. Heat the butter or shortening in a small saucepan. Add the green onions, parsley, and chili pepper. Sauté for 5 minutes or until the onions are soft.

Add the onion mixture to the cornmeal and flour. Stir in the egg and milk and mix well. The batter should be a little stiffer than regular cornmeal batter. Set the batter aside while heating the oil.

Heat the vegetable oil to 375 degrees. Drop the batter by tablespoonful into the hot oil. Don't overcrowd the pan. Fry the hush puppies until golden brown, for about 3 minutes, turning frequently with a long-handled tong.

Remove the hush puppies and drain on paper towels. Keep warm in a 250 degree oven. Repeat the process until all the batter is fried.

Going Fishing

Oven-Fried Fish

Serves 4

deaconess Ernestine Bradley is the executive chef at the Canaan Baptist Church in Harlem, which boasts a catering service and a formal dining room that seats three hundred. She cooks for many social events at the church—weddings, receptions, recitals, baptisms—as well as prepares private dinners for the church's dynamic minister, the Reverend Wyatt Tee Walker. But no gathering is more popular than the church's Gospel Express Banquet, which is held periodically on Sundays at the church, which is located on 116th Street.

Deaconess Ernestine and her staff cook a potpourri of dishes for the various events held at the church, including this crisp but moist oven-fried fish:

2 pounds fish fillets, such as
*   whiting, porgies, mullet, flounder,*
*   or red snapper*
Juice from 1 lemon
2 or 3 teaspoons paprika
½ teaspoon salt
½ teaspoon freshly ground
*   black pepper*

1 egg white, beaten
¼ cup milk
¾ to 1 cup plain bread crumbs
¼ to ½ cup canola oil
Lemon wedges

Rinse the fillets well under cold water. Squeeze the lemon juice over the fish and then sprinkle with paprika, salt, and black pepper. Set aside.

In a medium bowl, combine the egg white and milk and beat until well blended.

Spread the bread crumbs on a plate or tray. Dip the fish first in the egg-milk mixture, and then roll into the bread crumbs, coating evenly. Shake off excess crumbs. Set the fish aside for 30 minutes to allow the coating to dry.

Preheat the oven to 425 degrees.

Pour the oil into a large roasting pan. Place the pan into the hot oven and heat for 5 minutes. Carefully remove the pan from the oven and immediately place in the fish fillets in a single layer.

Return the pan to the oven and place on the lower shelf. Oven-fry the fish for 8 minutes. Using a large metal spatula, carefully turn over each fillet, and oven-fry for 7 to 8 minutes or until the fish is golden brown and flakes easily when pierced with a fork.

Remove from the oven, drain on paper towels, and serve piping hot with lemon wedges.

CARIBBEAN-STYLE BAKED RED SNAPPER

Serves 4 to 5

oycelyn Clarke is a nutritionist and registered dietitian and it is not surprising that she is always touting the health value of fish. But besides that, Joycelyn hails from the Caribbean island of Antigua, and when she was growing up the bounty of the sea was daily fare.

Joycelyn lives in New York City now and occasionally she is called upon to spread the good news about health and food at the Allen African Methodist Episcopal Church in Jamaica, Queens, where she has been a member for more than a dozen years.

The church, which is located on Merrick Boulevard, is involved in many activities and programs. A while back Joycelyn distributed nutrition information at a Woman's Day program held at the church, and recently she was a panelist during a health forum. And since she is also a fine cook and caterer, over the years she has rolled up her sleeves and made an array of healthy dishes for after-service snacks at the church's Shekinah Youth Chapel.

Joycelyn sends a tropical recipe for fish that literally jumps off the plate with flavor and goodness.

1 whole red snapper, 3½ to 4 pounds

1½ teaspoon salt

½ teaspoon freshly ground black pepper

1 clove finely minced garlic

5 tablespoons vegetable oil or melted margarine

1 red pepper

1 small chili pepper

3 or 4 scallions

2 or 3 sprigs thyme, or ¼ teaspoon dried thyme

1 small chayote squash, also known as christophine and cho-cho

¾ cup soft bread crumb

¼ cup lime or lemon juice

1 tablespoon Worcestershire sauce

Preheat the oven to 425 degrees.

Scale and gut the fish, leaving the head on. Cut a slit down the length of the belly of the fish, opening up the fish like a book. Rinse the fish well with cold running water, drain, and pat dry with paper towels.

Sprinkle the fish with the salt and black pepper, and then rub all over with the garlic and 1 tablespoon of the oil or margarine. Set aside.

Core and dice the red pepper and chili pepper. Chop the scallions and the thyme, or crush the dried herb. Peel the chayote, split lengthwise, and using a sharp knife, cut out the vegetable's opaque core and discard. Cut the chayote into tiny cubes.

Heat 2 tablespoons of the oil in a medium skillet. Add the red pepper, chili pepper, scallions, thyme and chayote. Sauté over medium-low heat for 4 or 5 minutes or until the vegetables are tender.

Remove from the heat, add the bread crumbs to the mixture, and toss lightly with a fork until well blended.

Loosely place the stuffing on the larger side of the fish, filling in the cavity of the head as well. Fold over the other side of the fish. (It doesn't matter if the stuffing spills over the sides of the fish.)

Combine in a small bowl the remaining 2 tablespoons of oil, lemon juice, and Worcestershire sauce.

Generously rub a shallow roasting pan or baking dish with oil. Place the fish in the pan and set in the middle shelf of the hot oven. Pour about half of the sauce over the fish.

Baste occasionally with the remaining sauce while baking for 35 to 40 minutes or until the fish is lightly brown and the flesh is opaque when flaked at its thickest part with a fork.

Variation: Chayote squash or christophine is commonly available at Hispanic markets and Caribbean-specialty shops and at most large supermarkets. A fine substitute for this vegetable is zucchini or yellow squash.

Going Fishing

GRILLED FISH

Serves 4

n the early 1980s, while living in the Bay Area of California, a friend once invited me to a church picnic held by members of the Downs Memorial United Methodist Church in Oakland. Along with the barbecued ribs, these health-conscious Californians had also placed two or three types of small whole fish on the grill. A few mesquite wood chips were thrown over the charcoal, and the result was a lightly charred, succulent fish that was robust with flavor.

I cadged this recipe from one of the church brothers, and have been enjoying fish grilled over wood ever since:

4 small whole fish, 10 to 12
   ounces each, such as porgy, trout,
   mullet, striped bass, red snapper,
   or monkfish
⅓ cup vegetable oil
1 teaspoon salt
½ teaspoon freshly ground
   black pepper

2 cloves crushed garlic
½ teaspoon dried thyme
Juice of 2 limes or lemons
2 tablespoons soy sauce
2 tablespoons spicy mustard

Build a fire using hardwood charcoal briquettes and water-soaked wood chips. (See "Grilling Is Hot" on page 192.)

Meanwhile, scale and gut the fish. Cut off the heads, if desired. Rinse the fish well with cold running water, drain, and pat dry with paper towels.

Rub the fish all over, including the cavity, with 2 tablespoons of the oil, and then sprinkle with salt and black pepper and rub with the garlic. Crush the dried thyme and rub all over the fish.

Combine in a bowl the lime or lemon juice, soy sauce, mustard, and the remaining oil.

Generously oil a shallow baking pan.

Close the fish and place in the pan. Drizzle half of the sauce over the fish.

Place the pan on the grill at about six inches from the heat. Grill the

SOUL FOOD

190

fish for 7 minutes or until the underside becomes deep brown and lightly charred, inserting a large metal spatula from time to time under the fish to keep it from sticking to the pan.

Using the spatula, carefully turn over the fish. Drizzle over the remaining sauce.

Grill the fish for 5 minutes longer, and then test for doneness by piercing the fish at its thickest part with a knife or fork.

If the flesh is opaque, the fish golden brown all over, and the juices run clear, the fish is done. Watch carefully at this point and don't overcook the fish. Serve immediately.

The Reverend Lucille Medley eyes the crowd at the holiday dinner following a performance of "The Messiah" at the Metropolitan Missionary Baptist Church in Chicago.

Going Fishing

GRILLING IS HOT

These are several types of wood sold today for grilling, including cherry, apple, peach, walnut, pecan, alder, sassafras, and the highly popular mesquite, which swept this country's culinary landscape more than a decade ago. The mesquite trend also spawned a slew of smoking equipment, such as kettles, smokers, grills, and hibachis, and turned open-fire cooking, which half of the world has been doing for eons, into a new backyard pastime.

Today smoking aficionados blow smoke about wood chips, sounding like wine connoisseurs: Mesquite is assertive; hickory is strong; walnut wood is medium-bodied; apple and cherry are mild in flavor.

Wood smoke does impart a delicious flavor to fish, poultry, and meat. For best results, drop a few handfuls of wood chips—about 2 cups—or a few wood chunks in a pot of water and soak for 30 or so minutes. If a heavier smoke flavor is desired, soak for an hour or longer. The water prevents the chips from burning so fast and renders more smoke.

When lighting the fire, pile the charcoal in the center of the grill, using about 30 briquettes for 3 to 4 pounds of fish or chicken. Hardwood charcoal that requires a starter cooks slower and gives off less fumes than the self-igniting variety, which is pre-soaked with fluid starter.

Hardwood charcoal can be ignited with fluid starter, with nontoxic lighter cubes, or in a can-shaped gadget called a chimney starter, which uses crumpled newspaper to ignite the briquettes. Once burning, the charcoal is transferred to the grill.

You can also pile the charcoal into the grill and ignite with an electric starter, but if you are building a fire at the state park or a picnic or camping site, this gadget won't do you any good. In that case, start the grill fire without a starter, the old-time way: Tear off a dozen pieces of paper—about the size of a half sheet of letter-size paper—using newspaper, a brown bag, or even the charcoal bag. Twist the paper tightly into strips.

Pile the twisted paper strips into the center of the grill and top with a couple handfuls of twigs or sticks, or dried wood chips—not water soaked—such as oak or hardwood, or dried leaves and vines from fruit or nut trees. (Avoid resinous wood twigs from pine or fir or evergreen trees; they impart an acrid flavor to food.)

Arrange 15 or 20 briquettes over the twigs and paper, stacking like a pyramid. Ignite the pile with a match. Once the coals are burning, add the remaining briquettes specified in the recipe. If the fire fails to start on the first try, start again. Patience counts here.

Allow the briquettes to burn until they are glowing and ashy. This usually takes 25 to 30 minutes. Spread out the ashy charcoal into a single layer and throw on a handful of well-drained wood chips or chunks. The fire is now ready for grilling.

Pan-Sautéed Curried Salmon

Serves 6 as an appetizer; 4 as a main dish

In black Baptist parlance, the Reverend Sharon Keeling is a "convention baby," which means that she began attending the annual gathering of the National Baptist Convention, USA, when she was in her mother's arms. Over the years she has prayed with, preached to, and broken bread with scores of church members across the country.

And she says laughing that she has also been both hugged and scolded during countless cookouts, missionary breakfasts, receptions, suppers, and family dinners at the homes of churchfolks who still have trouble remembering that she is no longer "just Sharon."

But she accepts this, and respectfully listens (or at least pretends to) whenever they lovingly chastise her about everything from the length of her dress—"That skirt is too short to wear up in that pulpit," to the goings and comings of her teenage daughter, Kimberly.

The Reverend Keeling is an associate minister at the Convent Avenue Baptist Church, which is located on 145th Street in Harlem, New York, and she is also the president of Keeling Enterprises, a Manhattan-based public relations firm that specializes in services to ecumenical organizations.

Recently I hosted a gathering with the Reverend Sharon Keeling to discuss the concerns of Keeling Enterprises, which, among its many services, arranges workshops, seminars, retreats, and events for ecumenical organizations and institutions as well as drafts proposals for grants and assistance. AIDS awareness is also a concern, and Reverend Keeling provides family counseling and assistance with funeral arrangements.

Breaking bread with Reverend Keeling is always inspirational. I served a salmon dish and she promised to pass on the recipe to her "convention baby," Kim.

This is the recipe:

1½ pounds salmon fillet, cut into
2-inch pieces
½ teaspoon salt
½ teaspoon freshly ground
black pepper
2 teaspoons soy sauce

1 clove garlic
2 teaspoons curry powder
1 tablespoon fresh chopped dill, or
1 teaspoon dried dill
2 tablespoons olive oil
Lemon wedges

Sprinkle the salmon with the salt, black pepper, and soy sauce. Mince the garlic and rub into the salmon, along with the curry powder and dill, coating evenly.

Heat the oil in a large heavy skillet. Add about half of the salmon pieces and sauté over medium heat for 2 to 3 minutes on both sides or until the fish is flaky and tender. Remove the fish from the pan and place in a warm serving platter.

Sauté the remaining salmon the same way. Serve with lemon wedges.

FRESHLY FISHED

Ideally, any fish you buy should have been snatched out of the water within the past forty-eight hours. So buy from a reputable market that has a heavy turnover. Fresh fish deteriorates quite rapidly, and if it isn't kept chilled and then sold quickly, it becomes smelly and slimy and milky, and if fillets, the edges crack and curl and turn light brown.

So use your eyes and nose when buying fish. If you feel that the fish isn't fresh, trust your instincts and lean over and sniff. Fresh fish smells of the ocean—salty and briny. Stale fish smells like ammonia—don't buy it.

Check out the fish gills and scales. The gills should be red and glistening, and if the gills are dull pink or brownish, pass up the fish. The scales should be shiny and bright, clinging tightly to the fish skin. And the fish should be cold, preferably sitting on ice rather than swimming in it, which can cause flavor loss.

Going Fishing

SALMON CAKES (CROQUETTES)

Serves 4

azel Knox remembers that years ago services at the all-black Bethpage Presbyterian Church in Concord, North Carolina, were considerably sedate, but the food served was just as finger-lickin' good as that at the other black churches in the community.

Hazel's family lived a little ways from the church, up in the mountains in a village named Asheville. She says that some of her fondest memories include coming down to the city to attend service at Bethpage, which her family has belonged to for several generations. She sends these words:

"When I was growing up in the mountains of North Carolina, I used to listen to stories told by my grandmother, Bertie Thompson, about her mother and all the wonderful cakes and pies she would bake. Whenever there were special occasions at the church, or just friends stopping by, there would be lots of pastries and other goodies.

"But Grandma Bertie's specialty was her salmon cakes, or croquettes, which were easy to carry out to church. This dish has stayed to this day with the Knox family, who lived for decades in the mountains of North Carolina."

When I was growing up, from time to time Mama would treat us to croquettes for breakfast, and my memories of this dish are just as keen as Hazel's. Mama served the salmon cakes with grits, scrambled eggs, hot pancakes, and fruit syrup, and we thought we were at a hotel banquet.

Hazel sends this recipe:

1 pound cooked salmon, canned
 or fresh
1 small onion
1 beaten egg
½ cup soft bread crumbs
1 tablespoon Worcestershire sauce
¼ to ½ teaspoon hot sauce

¼ teaspoon black pepper
1 cup shredded sharp Cheddar
 cheese
1 tablespoon finely chopped parsley
¼ cup flour
4 tablespoons butter or margarine
Lemon wedges

If using canned salmon, drain and pick over carefully to remove dark cartilage and bones. Finely chop the onion.

Using a fork, flake the salmon and then combine in a medium bowl with the onion, egg, bread crumbs, Worcestershire sauce, hot sauce, black pepper, cheese, and parsley.

Using about one-third cup salmon mixture for each cake, shape the mixture into rounds, about ½-inch thick.

Sprinkle the flour on a plate or board. Dredge the patties in the flour, coating well, but dusting off excess flour.

Place the patties in the refrigerator and let set for 30 minutes or longer.

Heat the butter or margarine in a large skillet until foamy and hot. Add the patties and brown on both side, cooking about 5 minutes.

Remove the salmon cakes from the pan and drain on paper towels. Serve warm immediately, with lemon wedges.

NOT IN VEIN

Actually, there is nothing wrong with eating the thin, dark vein that runs along a shrimp's back, considering that many people do when shrimp is boiled in the shell.

However, a deveined shrimp looks so much nicer on a plate, especially if you are preparing a fancy dish. And it is easy to do. Here's how:

Using your fingers, strip off the shrimp shell, leaving the tail intact, which makes the shrimp look more impressive. Now either lay the shrimp on a cutting board or hold it in your hand.

Using a sharp knife, cut a small slit along the vein and then lift it out with the tip of the knife. Scrape away any residue and rinse the shrimp well. Save the shells to make fish stock (see recipe on page 67).

NETTING SHELLFISH

The first time I ate shrimp I was visiting my brother John and Aunt Mary on the Gulf Coast and was presented with a spiny crustacean that was plunged in a pot of boiling water that had been seasoned with plenty of onions, garlic, herbs, and a heavy dose of cayenne.

John had already cooked corn and potatoes in the broth, and as soon as the shrimp turned deep pink, he lifted them out with a strainer and dumped into a bowl. We went out into the backyard, spread newspapers, and John showed me how to extract the sweet white meat, which was fiery from the cayenne. We feasted and talked for hours.

I have eaten a lot of shellfish, and particularly shrimp, since that time, and so have other Americans. Shrimp is the most popular shellfish in the United States, so much so that a famous food editor, Craig Claiborne, once extolled, "If there is anything out of the ocean with more virtues than shrimp, I'd be hard put to name it."

That statement may be a little hyperbolic, but shellfish in general makes a dramatic presentation. It is also low in calories, a good source of protein, not as high in cholesterol as once thought, and can be cooked in a flash. In other words, jewels from the sea.

As far as marine biology is concerned, shrimp, crabs, and lobsters are classified as crustaceans because they have a crust-like covering, while oysters, clams, scallops, and mussels, which are protected by a shell, are mollusks.

Wendell Holmes developed a recipe for shrimp that he serves at a wide range of social events. He is a caterer and also heads the Kitchen Ministry at the Glendale Baptist Church in Landover, Maryland.

Every Wednesday evening Wendell prepares the food for a dinner that is served prior to the church's prayer service and Bible study. As he moves about the kitchen, he often thinks of his father, the late Benjamin Holmes.

His father worked as a chef at a local hospital and had a catering business on the side. Back in the late 1960s, when Wendell was a young man, he used to go with his father when he catered parties, receptions, and other social events at various churches in Washington, D.C., and at country clubs in the suburbs. At first his job was washing dishes, but after a while his father began to teach him the fine points of cooking, and soon Wendell was his right-hand man.

"When I was teenager I didn't like cooking at all," recalls Wendell, who is now forty-nine. "But after my father passed I found myself enrolling in food courses at a local community college. Now I can't think of anything else I would much rather do."

Wendell sends this spicy and herbaceous recipe that can either be cooked on an outdoor grill or under an oven broiler:

BARBECUED SHRIMP

Serves 4

2 pounds jumbo shrimp
½ teaspoon salt
¼ teaspoon freshly ground
  black pepper
1 cup ketchup
½ cup red wine
¼ cup hoisin or soy sauce
2 tablespoons Worcestershire sauce
2 tablespoons dark molasses

2 tablespoons sunflower oil
1 clove garlic
1½ teaspoons dried marjoram
  leaves
1½ teaspoons dried oregano leaves
Lemon wedges
Parsley sprigs

Peel and devein the shrimp (see "Not in Vein" on page 198). Rinse the shrimp with cold water. Dry with paper towels. Sprinkle with salt and black pepper and set aside.

Combine in a medium saucepan the ketchup, wine, hoisin or soy sauce, Worcestershire sauce, molasses, and the oil. Mince the garlic. Crush the dried marjoram and oregano. Add the garlic and the herbs to the pan.

Place the pan on medium-high heat and bring to a gentle boil. Reduce the heat to very low, cover, and simmer, stirring occasionally, for about 30 minutes. If the sauce thickens, stir in a little more wine or water.

Preheat the broiler.

Lightly oil a large broiler pan. Place the shrimp on the pan in a single layer. Brush generously with the barbecue sauce. Set about 6 inches from the heat. Broil for 2 minutes. Remove the pan from under the broiler. Using tongs or a fork, turn over each shrimp. Brush generously again with the barbecue sauce.

Set the pan back under the heat and broil for 2 minutes longer or until the shrimp are tender and pink. Serve immediately with lemon wedges. Decorate the platter with parsley sprigs.

Note: Hoisin is a thick, reddish brown, sweet, spicy sauce made from soybeans. Sometimes called Peking sauce, it is delightful for grilling shellfish. If not available, substitute soy sauce, which is also made from soybeans.

The shrimp can also be broiled in the shell. Using kitchen scissors, cut the shrimp shell down the back, along the vein. Then using a knife, cut along the vein and lift it out, leaving the shell intact. Rinse the shrimp well. Coat with the barbecue sauce and broil for about 3 minutes per side or until golden and pink.

PICKLED SHRIMP

Serves 6 as an appetizer

LaVinia Hairston sends this delightful, pungent shrimp recipe from her church, Grace Presbyterian, in Martinsville, Virginia, via Buffalo, New York. LaVinia, a lawyer, lives in Buffalo, but her family roots and church affiliation go back more than one hundred years to Grace Presbyterian, of which she is still a member.

LaVinia spends a month in Martinsville during the summer, and the highlight of her visit is reuniting with family and friends at Grace Presbyterian, located on Fayette Street, which her great-grandfather joined in the early 1880s.

2 pounds large or jumbo shrimp	½ cup cider vinegar
1½ quarts water	¼ cup olive oil
2 tablespoons pickling spices	¼ to ½ teaspoon hot pepper flakes
1 onion	½ teaspoon salt
1 red or green or yellow pepper	½ teaspoon freshly ground
1 or 2 cloves garlic	black pepper
2 tablespoons fresh dill, or	
1 teaspoon dried	

Peel and devein the shrimp (see "Not in Vein" on page 198). Rinse with cold water.

Pour the water into a large pot. Add the pickling spices. Bring to a rolling boil. Add the shrimp and cook for 2 to 3 minutes or until they are pink and tender. Watch carefully and don't overcook. Drain the shrimp and set aside.

Prepare the pickling marinade: Thinly slice the onion; core and cut the fresh pepper into thin strips; mince the garlic; and chop or crush the dill.

Place the vegetables in a large glass bowl. Add the vinegar, olive oil, hot pepper flakes, salt, and black pepper and mix well. Stir in the drained shrimp. Let cool completely, cover with plastic wrap, and chill overnight.

At serving, drain the shrimp, mound on a platter, and provide round toothpicks so that guests can help themselves.

THE DANCE OF FREEDOM

God put rhythm in our feet, and when they touch the ground,
We glide, we slide, and we shuffle around
Our dance is our heritage, straight from motherland
It starts in our feet and works up to our hands

Then our heads get ta movin', and our arms go ta swingin'
Yes, we're in our own world, when we're dancin' and singin'

Our steps are passed down by each generation
The high kicks, the swift turns
In smooth syncopation

As light as a feather, a breath of fresh air
Chassé, plié, spin around like a flare!

Oh, the beauty, the wonder, our dance tells a story
Of a people who toiled hard, but who now dance in Glory!

They danced in the fields, they shouted 'round the fire
Each movement gave way to their longing desire
That somehow, some day, sweet freedom would bring
A new dance, a new life, and a new song to sing!

So, dance on, proud, black folks, and then dance some more
Let your black, rhythmic feet take you up to that door
Where we'll all dance together, 'round the Great Master's
    throne
Then we'll have a new dance, as He welcomes us home!

—*Patricia Mack* (1996)

Going Fishing

SHRIMP-FRIED RICE

Serves 2 to 3

g wendolyn W. Terrell recently collected into a booklet two hundred recipes from the fine cooks at the Saint Paul United Methodist Church in Oxon Hill, Maryland, and sold the booklets during a fundraising drive for a brand-new church.

This is not surprising. She says very little happens at the church, located on Saint Barnabas Road, unless food is involved, and the church sisters had a ready cache of recipes. She sends two recipes, one that she often carries out to church functions, and another from Pauline Purnell, who is never shy about bringing out covered dishes, either.

Mrs. Terrell also sends this report:

"Saint Paul is thought to be the oldest black congregation in the Baltimore Conference of United Methodist Churches. Records show that in 1791, Saint Paul was known as the 'original organization of this society of Negro adherents and dedicated worshippers.'

Members of the Saint Paul United Methodist Church in Oxon Hill, Maryland, celebrate the completion of their new church.

"We started out as a small congregation and, through the years, have maintained a small-church, close-knit, family atmosphere. From the beginning, the rolls of Saint Paul have always been filled with dedicated, faithful, hardworking members. Many socials, weddings, and programs have taken place within these walls, not to mentions the dinners.

"Saint Paul is known for being the church home of some of the best cooks on the East Coast. This is a reputation well deserved and cherished."

Now, now, sisters and brothers, these dishes really are delicious:

1 pound large shrimp
3 cups water
1 bay leaf
2 tablespoons vegetable oil
1 cup sliced fresh mushrooms
½ cup diced celery
½ cup chopped green onions

1 teaspoon finely minced ginger
2 eggs, beaten
3 cups cooked rice
3 tablespoons soy sauce
¼ teaspoon freshly ground
    black pepper

Peel and devein the shrimp (see "Not in Vein" on page 198), then rinse and set aside.

Pour the water into a large saucepan and add the bay leaf. Place on high heat and bring to a rolling boil. Add the shrimp and cook for 2 to 3 minutes or until the shrimp turn pink and are tender.

Remove the shrimp from the heat and drain. Cut the shrimp into ½-inch pieces and set aside.

Heat the oil in a large skillet over medium heat. Add the mushrooms, celery, green onions, and ginger. Sauté, stirring, for 4 to 5 minutes.

Push the vegetables to one side of the pan. Pour the beaten eggs into the skillet and scramble, stirring from the bottom of the pan.

Add the cooked rice, shrimp, soy sauce, and black pepper, mixing all the ingredients together.

Heat, stirring over medium-low heat for 5 minutes or until the mixture is heated through. Serve with a green salad and hot bread.

Best Crab Cakes Ever

henever Pauline Purnell serves these crab cakes at the Saint Paul United Methodist Church, there is cause for shouting.

1 pound fresh lumpfish crab meat
⅔ cup soft bread crumbs
2 eggs, lightly beaten
2 teaspoons Worcestershire sauce
1 teaspoon Old Bay seasoning
¼ teaspoon freshly ground
   black pepper

½ cup flour
2 tablespoons vegetable oil
2 tablespoons butter or margarine
Lemon wedges

Carefully pick over the crab meat and remove all cartilage and discard.

In a medium bowl combine the crab meat, bread crumbs, eggs, Worcestershire sauce, Old Bay seasoning, and black pepper. Form the mixture into 8 cakes, using about ⅓ cup mixture per cake.

Spread the flour on a large plate or board. Roll the crab cakes lightly into the flour, coating well, but dust off excess flour. Set the cakes in the refrigerator to chill for 30 minutes.

When ready to sauté, heat the oil and butter or margarine in a large heavy skillet. Add the crab cakes and sauté over medium heat 2 to 3 minutes on both sides or until they are golden brown. Serve with lemon wedges.

SUNDAY CRAB MEAT SALAD

Serves 4 to 6

Pat Mack wears many hats at the Glendale Baptist Church in Landover, Maryland, and I am not talking about those fine chapeaus the church sisters are known for. Several of Pat's poems have been put into production by Glendale's Dance Ministry, and recently her poem "The Dance of Freedom" was selected for publication in Iliad Press's twenty-fifth anthology.

Pat also teaches Sunday school and often assists with the Kitchen Ministry, which cooks for both the homeless and for church functions. Her brother, Wendell Holmes, a caterer, heads the ministry.

Pat sends this special recipe for crab salad:

1 pound fresh lump crab meat
¾ cup chopped celery
2 to 3 tablespoons chopped onions
¼ cup pickle relish or chopped
    olives
¾ cup commercial mayonnaise or
    Homemade Mayonnaise
    (see recipe on page 224)

2 tablespoons lemon juice
1 tablespoon Worcestershire sauce
½ teaspoon Old Bay seasoning
¼ to ½ teaspoon freshly
    ground black pepper
Lettuce leaves
Lemon wedges
Tomato wedges

Pick over the crab meat, making sure to remove and discard any cartilage or bones. In a large bowl combine the crab meat, celery, onions, and relish or olives. Set aside.

Combine in a small bowl the mayonnaise, lemon juice, Worcestershire sauce, Old Bay seasoning, and black pepper. Mix well.

Pour the mayonnaise mixture over the crab meat and mix well. Cover the bowl with plastic wrap and chill at least 2 hours.

At serving, arrange a bed of lettuce leaves on a platter. Top with the crab meat salad. Garnish with the lemon and tomatoes wedges.

Going Fishing

FISHING FOR GUMBO

Few members of the Mercy Seat Baptist Church remember my Aunt Mary, but the ones who do say she was a woman of so many interests that it was hard to define exactly what she did and didn't do. Actually, Aunt Mary liked to fish, cook, work the crossword puzzles in the *New Orleans Picayune-Times* and host the Missionary Club meeting, and since she wasn't the least bit modest, she considered herself an expert at all of these pastimes.

Truth is, our family considered Aunt Mary a "worldly woman." She was my father's sister, who in the early 1920s moved from Clarke County in Alabama to the Gulf Coast near Biloxi, Mississippi, then moved to Los Angeles, and then returned to the Gulf Coast sometime in the early 1940s. Nearing middle age, she married a jazz trumpet player from New Orleans and opened up a hair-dressing shop at her house, which had six heavy-bearing pecan trees in the backyard.

In 1949, when my oldest brother, John, was a very young man, he went to visit Aunt Mary and never returned home, and as soon as I reached my teens, I, too, fell under her charm and always spent summers with her.

I thought her life was touched by magic. Throughout her house there were framed copies of her cosmetology diploma, and scores of photographs of her only child, her daughter Victoria, and of Victoria's only child, Mary Ethel, who lived in faraway Los Angeles. Her husband, a thin, fair-skinned, brooding man with a strange, hoarse voice, had a fine reputation in New Orleans jazz circles, and he was always picking up his horn and blowing a few bars, though he was much too contentious to give us the pleasure of hearing a full number. One of his sons was also a professional musician, and Aunt Mary talked constantly about his music engagements and adventures. Victoria and Mary Ethel would telephone from Los Angeles on Sunday evenings and during such moments Aunt Mary's laughter would spread through the house.

To me her house was as grand as the French château I had read about. This was the late 1950s and through the eyes of a provincial adolescent I saw a lumpy chesterfield sofa in nape-worn velvet, elegantly revealing its age and pedigree. Two overstuffed side chairs covered with floral cretonne flanked the sofa, and there was a glass-topped, rectangular walnut coffee table displaying another compendium of photographs. An old Victrola dominated one corner, and several cluttered end tables held porcelain lamps with tattered fringed shades, and this was the room where we gathered when we worked the crossword puzzles and listened to the phonograph.

The day Aunt Mary made gumbo for the Missionary Club ladies remains in my mind as vivid as yesterday's chain of events. I had never eaten this dish before, and since she loved showing off, she began spouting about the intricacies of gumbo, its origin, and who in the community knew how to make good gumbo and who didn't—which was all of her neighbors, as far she was concerned.

For most of the day before the meeting she scurried about in the kitchen, chopping the celery and onions and pepper, cleaning shellfish, stirring the roux or the gravy base, tasting the broth for flavor. From time to time she would throw back her head, set her arms akimbo, and lecture about the subtleties of this famous dish, with that ever-present Lucky Strike stuck in the corner of her mouth. (She lived to be eighty-eight.)

"Most folks think that you just throw a whole bunch of stuff in a pot and you got a gumbo," she would say. "A gumbo is like a good stage production, you got to make it act by act. In layers. If you don't do that you end up with a real mess."

And with that said, she would throw back her head laughing, extinguish her cigarette, wash her hands, and continue putting on her show.

Shortly before 2 P.M. on the appointed day, her "buddies," as she called the middle-aged women who formed her circle, filed up the cement walkway onto the front porch, which was painted forest green. Aunt Mary whispered, as if she were afraid they would hear, "Here

Going Fishing

they come," and in a matter of seconds I heard the screen door rattling, followed by a crisp rap.

Aunt Mary motioned me toward the front door and then turned and whirled toward the kitchen. I went and opened the door into the faces of Mrs. Maybell, Mrs. Esther, Mrs. Cora, and two other club members, both of whom were named Mrs. Ruth.

"Hi child." "Hi girl." "Hi Hon." They greeted me offhandedly, almost in unison, and while I was struggling to say something polite and respectful, as I had been taught, they brushed past me and into the center of the room.

One of the women finally yelled in the direction of the kitchen, breaking the silence, which for a few seconds had hung as solemnly as a sphinx: "How you doin', Mary? What you cook today?"

"Gumbo!" Aunt Mary said triumphantly, bounding out of the kitchen. She leaned over and set a big steaming bowl of the dish on a mat in the center of the old mahogany dining room table.

Gulf Coast Gumbo

Serves 10 to 12

2 pounds medium shrimp
6 ears fresh corn
1½ pounds smoked beef sausage
2 pounds okra
2 stalks celery
2 large onions
3 to 4 cloves garlic
1 can (28 ounces) undrained
   tomatoes
½ cup vegetable oil
¼ cup chopped parsley
1 teaspoon hot pepper flakes (more
   if desired)

1 teaspoon dried thyme
½ cup unbleached flour
4 bay leaves
1 tablespoon salt
1½ teaspoons freshly ground
   black pepper
5 cups boiling water or hot Fish
   Stock (see recipe on page 67)
3 cups shucked oysters
1 pound crab meat
2 tablespoons gumbo file

Peel and devein the shrimp (see "Not in Vein" on page 198). Remove the husk and silk from the corn. Cut the corn crosswise into 1-inch chunks. Cut the beef sausage and okra crosswise into ½-inch slices. Chop the celery and the onions. Mince the garlic. Coarsely chop the tomatoes, saving the canned juice. Set aside the shrimp, okra, corn and tomatoes.

Using a large heavy pot or kettle (at least 10 quarts), heat the oil. Add the sausage, celery, onions, garlic, parsley, and hot pepper flakes. Crush the dried thyme and add to the pot. Sauté over low heat 7 to 8 minutes or until the onions are soft and translucent.

Push the vegetables and sausage to the side of the pot. Stir in the flour and cook, stirring, over low heat, 5 to 6 minutes longer, or until the flour turns beige in color but not brown. This is the roux. Watch carefully and don't allow the flour to burn or brown.

Add the tomatoes with the tomato juice, the okra, bay leaves, salt, and black pepper. Bring to a boil, reduce the heat to low, and cook, covered, 30 minutes, stirring occasionally.

Without increasing the heat, add the boiling water or fish stock and the corn. If the gumbo is bubbling, reduce the heat a bit, and then cook, covered, for 30 minutes.

Add the shrimp, oysters, and crabmeat and cook for 30 minutes, stirring occasionally, or until the shrimp are pink and tender and the gumbo is flavorful.

Stir in the gumbo file and cook for only 2 minutes, stirring. Remove the gumbo from the heat immediately and let set in a warm place 10 to 15 minutes. Don't reheat the gumbo after adding the file; it will become gummy. Serve with Perfectly Steamed Rice (recipe follows).

Note: If fresh crabs are available, select 1½ dozen medium crabs that are alive and wiggly. Fill a large 8-or 10-quart heavy pot half full with water and bring to a rolling boil. Plunge the crab into the water and cook for about 2 minutes, or just until they turn bright red. Remove the crabs immediately from the hot water and rinse under cold running water.

To clean the crabs, lay each one on a chopping board, grab the top shell, pull it away from the body, and discard. Turn the crab on its back, lift up the apron, pull off, and discard. Lift up the flaps at each end and pull out the spongy underbelly and discard. Using a sharp knife, split each crab in half crosswise. Rinse again with cold running water. Add the crabs to the gumbo along with the shrimp and oysters.

PERFECTLY STEAMED RICE

Serves 10 to 12

2 quarts water
2 teaspoons salt
½ teaspoon black pepper

¼ cup olive oil
2 tablespoons lemon juice
4 cups long-grain white rice

Combine in a large saucepan the water, salt, black pepper, oil, and lemon juice. Cover and bring to a rolling boil. Stir in the rice.

Reduce the heat to medium-low. Cook for 15 minutes. Turn off the heat and leave the rice on the same burner for 10 minutes or until the water is absorbed and the rice is tender.

Flake the rice with a fork before serving.

The dining room rapidly fills at the church anniversary celebration held at Christian Hope Baptist Church in Philadelphia.

Going Fishing

GOOD GRAVY: THE ROUX

The first time I heard Aunt Mary use the word "roux" I was sure she was just putting on airs, using some fancy French word for gravy. She was forever saying that Uncle John was a Creole, so she had a tendency to affect New Orleans manners. Anyway, as my interest in food increased, I soon learned that this shortening-and-flour paste is the basis of much of the cooking on the Gulf Coast, New Orleans, and South Carolina, and yes *roux* is the official name.

The roux is used to thicken gumbo, stews, sauces, and gravies, and it can be either white or brown, depending on the cooking technique and flavor desired. However, both versions are made with the same ingredients—flour and oil or butter—but the product changes character as heat is applied.

Basically, the mixture of flour and oil should be blended and cooked gently over low heat in a heavy skillet, from 5 minutes or so, or until much longer. White roux, which is often used in dishes such as fish and veal stews, should not color, while a brown roux should reach the color of hazelnuts, or deep tan. However, a brown roux has to be watched carefully, for if you let it burn it loses its thickening power and also imparts an acrid, bitter taste to the liquid.

A white roux should always be cooked long enough to get rid of the raw taste of flour, and this requires a very low heat. The roux should also be stirred frequently while cooking, to distribute the heat and to allow the flour to swell evenly, so that it can later absorb the liquid that will be added to thicken the gravy.

If you keep cooking a white roux it eventually turns brown, and in the process loses about half of its thickening power. For example, 2 tablespoons of white flour cooked with 2 tablespoon of oil or butter will thicken 2 cups of liquid, but if you brown the flour, you will need to reduce the liquid to 1 cup.

Basic White Roux: Heat 2 tablespoons butter or vegetable oil in a small skillet. Stir in 2 tablespoons of all-purpose flour. Cook, stirring over low heat for 5 to 7 minutes. Don't allow the mixture to brown.

Use the roux to thicken 2 cups of sauce or gravy. Stir into the liquid and mix well.

Basic Brown Roux: Heat 3 tablespoons butter or vegetable oil in a small skillet. Stir in 3 tablespoons of all-purpose flour. Reduce the heat to very low and cook, stirring frequently, for 10 to 12 minutes, or until the roux reaches a rich, golden brown. Watch carefully and don't allow the roux to burn.

Use the roux to thicken 2 cups of gravy or sauce. Stir into the liquid and mix well.

Browned Flour: Many gumbo experts, like my brother John, who learned how to make this dish from Aunt Mary, prefer to use a brown roux made with browned flour, which John says imparts an ethereal, nutty flavor to the broth.

The flour is placed in a heavy skillet and browned without oil. The key is very low heat and frequent stirring with a wooden spoon. The flour should brown in 25 to 30 minutes.

When the flour is the color of hazelnuts, remove from heat. If not using immediately, cool and store in a tightly covered jar in a cool place. Use to thicken sauces and gravies and gumbo.

Going Fishing

CHICKEN AND OTHER FINE BIRDS

*L*ong before fast-food chains and the gourmets got into the chicken business, this fowl was a special treat in African-American communities. We could eat it practically every day and for Sunday dinner, too. And we kept on licking our fingers and enjoying this bird, even when the larger

community made us the subjects of caricatures and insults. Oh, we all remember the images made of us. Chicken-eating, watermelon-loving Negroes have fueled many jokes. Never mind.

We have always known when a good thing is good. Chicken is delectable, relatively low in calories and cholesterol, and can be enjoyed in so many ways: baked, fried, poached, barbecued, smoked and grilled, or smothered

Church member Letha Tubbs enjoys the holiday dinner at Metropolitan Missionary Baptist Church in Chicago.

with gravy or simmered with dumplings.

When I was growing up in the South the women in most families each had their way with chicken, and of course, their way was the right way. Baked chicken was rubbed, either with sage, paprika, or cider vinegar, or slathered with butter and baked plain with a dusting of salt and black pepper. Chicken for frying was soaked in either buttermilk or sweet milk or evaporated milk, and then dipped in a batter, or coated with flour or a mixture of cornmeal and flour. Oven-fried chicken was often dipped in milk and then rolled in crushed cornflakes or saltine crackers, and almost every family had a "secret" recipe for barbecued chicken.

I grew up on the kind of chickens that gourmets today refer to as "free-range." Our chickens were raised in the backyard where they pecked on grass and grains, strutted about, and then were restricted in a coop for a few days before they were put to rest for the frying pot or oven. And thanks to this range of movement, the chickens were much more fibrous, "meaty," and flavorful than the mass-produced chickens of today, which are penned and seldom, if ever see, the ground.

However, chicken has soared in popularity over the past two decades, and the number of free-range breeders is increasing. Like gospel, this is good news, for it also means that the price of free-range chicken, which in the past has been considerably more expensive than mass-produced chicken, is not as steep as it used to be. My advice is to shop around and buy the best chicken you can afford. The flavor of a good, rich-tasting chicken is worth the few extra dollars.

But always pay attention to your selection. Avoid chicken that is bruised, slimy, or with an offensive odor. If the chicken is packaged, check and make sure that the "sell by" expiration date hasn't passed. Also check and make sure that the counter where the chicken is stored is cold; chicken sitting in a warm place can quickly "go off."

Once you take the chicken home, refrigerate immediately. If you are not going to cook the chicken the same day, remove the innards from the cavity, discard any packing, rinse the chicken with cold water, and using either freezing containers or freezer paper or aluminum foil, freeze the bird. When you are ready to cook the chicken, defrost the chicken in the refrigerator, not on the kitchen counter; this usually takes overnight or at least 8 hours or so. After thawing, rinse the chicken again and proceed with the recipe for country-style chicken smothered with onions and gravy that was sent by Florene Thomas, who is an usher at the Starrville Church of the Living God in Winona, Texas.

Mrs. Thomas is also a caterer, and she is expected to bring out a dish to every potluck dinner or social gathering held at the church, which is located on Highway 271.

Starrville has a long history of rallying its members for a cause. According to church records, Starrville was organized in 1909 under a brush arbor. A few years later a structure was built, but unfortunately, in 1916 the building was destroyed by a storm.

Chicken and Other Fine Birds

However, the congregation prevailed and a new wood-frame house of worship soon stood on the same ground.

Today, Starrville Church of the Living God is solid as a rock. A brick building was constructed in 1968 and the congregation is as committed as ever.

Mrs. Thomas sends this recipe for a classic black-church chicken dish, which remains a favorite at her church.

Flo's Smothered Chicken

Serves 4

1 chicken, 3-3½ pounds
1 teaspoon salt
½ teaspoon freshly ground
*   black pepper*
½ cup flour
1 celery stalk
2 onions

2 cloves garlic
½ teaspoon dried thyme
2 tablespoons oil
2 cups chicken broth or Homemade
*   Chicken Stock (see recipe on*
*   page 234)*

Cut the chicken into serving pieces: the breast into halves, the legs and thighs separated, plus the wings, for a total of 8 pieces. Trim away any visible fat and discard. Rinse the chicken well under cold running water. Pat dry with paper towels.

Sprinkle the chicken with the salt and black pepper. Place the chicken into a plastic or brown bag. Pour the flour into the bag and shake well to cover the chicken all over. Remove the chicken from the bag and dust off excess flour. Save 1 tablespoon of the flour to use to thicken the gravy.

Dice the celery; slice the onions; and mince the garlic. Crush the thyme. Set aside.

Heat the oil in a large skillet that has a cover. Add the chicken and sauté over medium-low heat for about 20 minutes, turning occasionally to brown evenly. When golden brown, push the chicken to the side of the pan. Add the reserved tablespoon of flour and sauté, stirring, until deep browned.

Add the celery, onion, garlic, and thyme to the skillet and sauté for 5 minutes, stirring occasionally, or until the vegetables are tender. Sir together the chicken and vegetables.

Add the chicken broth. Bring to a gentle boil. Reduce the heat to very low, cover, and simmer the chicken for 20 to 25 minutes, or until the chicken is fork-tender and the juices run clear when pierced.

Chicken and Other Fine Birds

THE LADIES' CHICKEN SALAD

Serves 6

Mabel Kinzer remembers that when members of the Philathea Club met at her family's home, her mother, the late Mabel James, cooked as though she was preparing for a hotel banquet. Mrs. James was a member of several social and civic clubs, but none was more important to her than the women's group known as the Philathea Club at the Providence Baptist Church in Greensboro, North Carolina. The church is located on Tuscaloosa Street.

"The women were all very good friends, but they were very competitive and in some ways very comical," recalls Mabel, who lives today in Manassas, Virginia, and is a member of the Little Union Baptist Church in Dumfries, Virginia. "There were about thirty church members in the club. A member's standing in the group was determined to some degree by how many of the women came out to her house for the meeting.

"My mother would work for two or three days getting the house ready. Everything would be sparkling and polished. She would make something she called 'Russian tea,' which was an infusion of fruit juices, tea, and cloves and cinnamon. She would steep this all day and the air would be scented with this wonderful aroma. I used to stand and watch them in amazement."

Mabel says her mother's menu usually included sliced turkey, baked ham, often Waldorf salad, sometimes shrimp salad, greens, hot rolls, a pineapple upside-

Church nurses Mary M. Combs (left) and Ledora Moore at the holiday dinner at Metropolitan Missionary Baptist Church in Chicago.

down cake (see recipe on page 333), plus chicken salad served with homemade mayonnaise.

She sends this recipe:

1 chicken, 3 to 3¼ pounds
1 onion
2 cloves garlic
4 cups water
½ teaspoon salt
½ teaspoon freshly ground
  black pepper
2 stalks celery

2 hard-cooked eggs
½ cup pickle relish
½ to 1 cup Homemade
  Mayonnaise (recipe follows)
1 tablespoon spicy brown mustard
Lettuce leaves, washed, dried,
  and chilled

Cut the chicken into serving pieces: the breast into halves, the legs and thighs separated, plus the wings, for a total of 8 pieces. Trim off and discard any visible fat. Slice the onion and mince the garlic.

Place the chicken in a large pot. Add the water, the onion, garlic, salt, and black pepper. Place over medium-high heat, bring to a boil, cover, reduce heat to simmer, and cook the chicken, turning occasionally, for 30 to 40 minutes or until fork-tender and the juices run clear.

Remove the chicken from the heat, drain, and cool. Save the broth to use later in soups and stews or to cook greens and other vegetables.

Place the chicken on a cutting board and remove the skin and bones and discard. Discard the onions. Cut the chicken into 2-inch strips.

Finely mince the celery. Dice the hard-cooked eggs. In a large bowl combine the chicken, celery, eggs, and the pickle relish.

In a small bowl mix together the mayonnaise and mustard. Beat with a whisk or fork until creamy and well blended.

Pour the sauce over the chicken and vegetables and mix well. Cover the bowl with plastic wrap and chill the chicken salad for at least 1 hour.

At serving time, line a large platter with lettuce leaves. Top with the chicken salad. Serve with hot biscuits or yeast rolls.

Variation: Years ago, chicken salad was elevated to a high-art creation at black church meetings, sorority and social club luncheons, and fashion shows. Various ingredients were mixed with the chicken, including pickles, capers, olives, walnuts, pecans, or slivers of baked smoked ham. A particular exquisite version of this classic dish is made with baked instead of poached chicken. (See recipe for Roast Chicken on page 250.)

HOMEMADE MAYONNAISE

Makes a scant 1¼ cups

This recipe takes a little time but the reward is worth it: creamy, pungent, richly flavored mayonnaise, free of stabilizers and fillers.

1 egg yolk
½ teaspoon dry mustard, or 1 tablespoon prepared mustard
¼ teaspoon salt
¼ teaspoon freshly ground black pepper

1 tablespoon cider or wine vinegar
1 cup olive oil or other vegetable oil, or ½ cup each
1 tablespoon lemon juice

Place the egg yolk, mustard, salt, pepper, and vinegar in a small bowl. Using an electric mixer, beat the mixture on high speed for about 5 minutes or until slightly thickened.

Add the oil, 1 teaspoon at a time, beating 10 to 15 seconds after each addition. Continue beating this way until at least ¼ cup of the oil has been added and the mixture has thickened and formed an emulsion.

Once thick, begin adding the oil in a slow, steady stream, beating continuously.

Caution: Don't add the oil too quickly or the mayonnaise may curdle. If this happens, set the mayonnaise in a bowl of warm water and beat briskly until it emulsifies again.

Once all the oil is beaten in and the mayonnaise is thick and creamy stir in the lemon juice.

The mayonnaise will keep for a few days in the refrigerator in a tightly covered jar, but not much longer.

SOUTHERN FRIED CHICKEN

Serves 4

ven before Deaconess Eva Mae Grace knew exactly what she was going to cook and take out to the church for "Old Fashion Day" at the New Shiloh Missionary Baptist Church in Miami, she had already laid out her clothes. She had decided to wear a white bonnet in remembrance of her mother who died five years ago, cotton stockings like the ones women used to twist into a tight knot just below the knees, and a long blue-jean skirt that almost swept the floor. Her husband, David, had decided on a pair of overalls, but even the night before the celebration he hadn't found the brogan shoes he had been looking for, primarily because he was too busy at the church helping build a tent on the grounds.

And besides that, the Grace family still had more cooking to do. Mrs. Grace had bought six bunches of turnip greens from a trucker who hauls in vegetables from Georgia, and they had to be picked over and washed, and then cooked and seasoned the old-fashioned way with a ham bone.

Church members David and Eva Grace in costume for the annual "Old Fashion Day" celebration at the New Shiloh Missionary Baptist Church in Miami, Florida.

Chicken and Other Fine Birds

This was the second Saturday in December and at Thanksgiving when the family had visited her hometown of Whiteville, North Carolina, which is near Wilmington, she had bought a sack of sweet potatoes and some crowder peas. She had already made sweet potato pies and was getting ready to cook the peas. Late that Saturday afternoon she stuck the last of the peach cobblers in the oven, and while they were baking, she steamed the potatoes for the potato salad that the family was also carrying to the church, which is located on Northwest 95th Street.

Mr. Grace is a deacon at Shiloh and has worked at many restaurants and hotels in Florida as a cook, and now works in maintenance at a famed local hotel. He is no stranger to the kitchen. Shortly before 9 P.M. he seasoned two big slabs of roast beef, and since the pies were done, the kitchen now pretty much belonged to him.

Once the beef was roasting in the oven he checked to see if he had enough film for his 35mm camera, and also flicked on his video camera to make sure it was working so that he could capture all of the splendor of this annual event. Then Deacon Grace lamented that he wished that their son, Larry, the oldest of their nine children and a professional photographer who lives and works in Minneapolis, had come home for the day so that he could have taken the pictures.

"This is a wonderful day of fellowship and family," says Mrs. Grace, full of enthusiasm, "and every year it gets bigger and bigger. People come out by the hundreds. It's like the old-fashioned camp meeting we used to have years ago out in the country."

Mrs. Grace still had to fry chicken, but since she is pretty fussy about this Southern specialty, she had decided to wait until Sunday morning to do so. That way, she said, the chicken would be crisp and succulent when she laid it out on the table under the tent along with the staggering array of other foods.

"People check out what you bring," she says chuckling. "There will be every food you can imagine: barbecue, roast pig, collard greens, all kinds of cakes and pies. Everybody tries to outdo each other."

Mrs. Grace is so accustomed to doing too many things at once that

even when weariness began edging her voice, she dismissed the notion that she was tired, saying softly, "I love to cook and so does my husband."

She laughed in her quiet way and added, "I consider people who eat my food my patients, and I taste and doctor it up if it isn't right."

Mrs. Grace has spent much of her life as a caregiver, first as a nursing assistant at a local hospital, and for the past thirty-nine years as a teacher's assistant with the Dade County school system, where she helps students with employment and college opportunities.

She was ordained a deaconess eighteen years ago, after a counseling session with the church pastor, the Reverend Arthur Jackson Jr., and felt this was her calling, too. For two years she served as president of the Deaconess Ministry.

"I love to talk to people, to listen to their needs and concerns," she says soberly. "I love Sunday school, love the church, communion, helping the handicapped, visiting the sick. I love children—children are my heart. I always say that the Lord smiled on me with my nine children."

Mr. and Mrs. Grace are both sixty and have been married for two thirds of their lives: forty years. They talk deferentially about each other and of their seven sons, two of whom are chefs at local restaurants, and of their two daughters, whom Mrs. Grace says, laughing again, "can't boil water."

Although there are certainly many talented cooks in this family, it's conceded that Mrs. Grace is the expert at frying chicken. She sends this recipe for Southern-style chicken that is crispy and spicy and absolutely delectable:

1 chicken, 3¼-3½ pounds
1 cup buttermilk
1 teaspoon salt
1 teaspoon paprika
2 to 3 teaspoons finely ground
*   black pepper (less if desired)*

¾ cup flour
3 cups sunflower or other vegetable
*   oil or shortening*

Cut the chicken into serving pieces: the breast into halves, the legs and thighs separated, plus the wings, for a total of 8 pieces. Save the neck, gizzard, liver, and back to use in soup or chicken stock, or do like my mother used to do, and fry them right along with the rest of the chicken.

Trim away any visible fat and discard. Rinse the chicken well under cold running water. Place the chicken in a large bowl, cover with buttermilk, and marinate for 1 hour. Drain and dry with paper towels.

Sprinkle the chicken with the salt, paprika, and black pepper.

When ready to fry the chicken, pour enough oil into a deep, heavy cast-iron skillet or pot to a depth of at least 3 inches. Place the pan on high heat, and using a deep-frying thermometer, heat the oil to 360 degrees.

Meanwhile, pour the flour into a plastic or brown paper bag. Place the chicken in the bag and shake the bag to completely coat the chicken with the flour. Remove the chicken and dust off any excess flour.

When the surface of the oil is rippling and the thermometer registers 360 degrees, add several pieces of the chicken at a time, beginning first with the legs and thighs, then the wings, and finally the breast. Don't overcrowd the pan.

Fry the chicken until it is golden brown and the juices run clear when pierced with a fork. The thighs and legs should cook in 20 to 25 minutes, the wings in 18 to 20 minutes, and the breast in 15 minutes or so.

If the temperature drops below 360 degrees, let the oil heat back up before adding more chicken. Remove the chicken from the hot oil and drain on paper towels. Keep warm in an oven set at 200 degrees.

Variation: Many Southern cooks say that the special trick to crispy fried chicken is that the pan has to be covered during half of the cooking period. Mrs. Grace favors this method, which can get tricky, but does produce a crackling-like skin.

For best results, heat the oil to about 350 degrees, add a few pieces of chicken, cover the pan, lower the temperature a bit, and cook the chicken, covered, for 5 minutes. Remove the cover, turn the chicken, and cook, covered, for 5 more minutes.

Uncover the chicken for the remaining cooking period and continue cooking until the chicken is golden brown and the juices run clear when pierced with a fork.

A CHICKEN IN EVERY POT

When Mama made Chicken 'n' Dumplings on Sundays before church service, she would rise early, put the hen in a large pot, cover with water, add seasoning, and let the bird simmer for a couple of hours. We raised chickens, and our hens were grain-fed and fibrous, and with the impatience of youth, I thought she was going to cook the bird forever.

My mother's hands were seldom idle, and while the chicken was simmering and emitting wonderful aromas, she would make the dumplings. I would watch her stir the batter together, roll out the pastry, and cut it into little strips.

Nothing went to waste in my family, and when the hen was just tender, Mama would pour some of the broth into mason jars and store in the icebox to use for gravies and soups.

She would then drop the dumplings into the pot and simmer until the dough turned translucent and pearly and tender. I would watch her, wondering how in the world I was going to wait until after church service to eat my favorite meal.

I thought of these memories when a recipe for this dish arrived from the Reverend Jim Holley, who is the pastor of the Historic Little Rock Missionary Baptist Church in Detroit, Michigan.

The Reverend Holley is also a talk radio show host, an entrepreneur, and the recipient of a doctorate. His populist doctrines and sermons resound with the rallying cry of economic empowerment for the African-American community. He is heard from 12 to 3 P.M. on Saturdays and from 12 to 1 P.M on Sundays on WCHB (1200 AM) in metropolitan Detroit, dispensing information about everything from investment tips to community service to health advice.

"I try to keep my congregation and the community informed," says the Reverend Holley, "so that they can make politicians accountable, so that they can talk to each other about particular issues, so that they can get together and do business. I am a strong advocate of black enterprise. I am a strong advocate of education. That's why I try to pass on any information and inspiration that concerns the African-American community."

The Reverend Holley preaches his message to some 2,800 members from the pulpit at the Little Rock Baptist Church, which is located on Woodward. When he assumed leadership of the church twenty-five years ago, it had forty-three members.

Today the church operates a nearby homeless shelter that can accommodate four hundred people; runs a chartered school for grades kindergarten through five; operates an on-site job-training program; and produces a "Country Preacher" line of cookies and potato chips, which are sold both retail and wholesale, including to a major airline. It also recently broke ground for a shopping center that will be located across the street from the church.

Reverend Holley says that the money from the sale of the cookies and potato chips is used to finance the education of eighty young church members at colleges and universities across the country.

"We try to be involved in the lives of people," he says. "My church is the church of the masses. We try to elevate our people. We practice what we preach."

Virtually every Sunday Reverend Holly leaves the pulpit and heads for the church's fellowship hall. And he is especially pleased when some sister prepares Chicken 'n' Dumplings.

He sends this recipe, which is just like Mama's:

Serves 4 to 5

1 chicken, 3¼-3½ pounds
1 onion
2 ribs celery
1 bay leaf
2 or 3 sprigs parsley

1½ teaspoon salt
¼ teaspoon freshly ground
*   black pepper*
¼ to ½ teaspoon dried thyme
5 cups water

Remove the innards from the chicken. Discard the liver but save the gizzard and neck. Trim off any visible fat from the chicken and discard. Cut the chicken into serving pieces: the breast into halves, the legs and thighs separated, plus the wings, for a total of 8 pieces.

Rinse the chicken parts under cold running water. Rinse the gizzard and neck. Slice the onion and cut the celery stalks into several pieces.

Place the chicken, gizzard and neck included, into a large pot, at least 6-quart size. Add the onion, celery, bay leaf, parsley, salt, and black pepper. Crush the thyme and add to the pot.

Cover with the water and bring to a boil. Lower the heat and simmer, turning occasionally, for 40 minutes or until the chicken is tender and the broth is well flavored. Discard the bay leaf.

While the chicken cooks, make the dumplings (see recipe below). When the chicken is tender, drop the dumplings into the broth and cook over low heat for 20 minutes or until the dumplings are done and the chicken is fork-tender.

Variation: Traditionally, Chicken 'n' Dumplings is made with a hen, which ranges from 4 to 8 pounds in size and is not as readily available today as a broiler-fryer. They are also fibrous and require long cooking. To prepare the above recipe the traditional way, choose a 4- to 4 ½-pound hen, cover with 8 cups of water, and simmer for about 2 hours or until fork-tender. When the hen is done, remove 2 cups of the broth from the pan before adding the dumplings, to prevent the dish from being too "soupy."

Never-Fail Dumplings

Makes 3 to 4 dozen dumplings

2 cups flour
½ teaspoon salt
1 egg, beaten

6 to 8 tablespoons chicken broth
(from the cooking pot)

Sift the flour and salt into a medium bowl. Add the egg and chicken broth. Using a fork, stir lightly, only until batter is combined. Form dough into a smooth ball, adding a little more flour if it is still sticky.

Divide the dough into 3 portions. Lightly flour a pastry board or cloth. Roll out each portion of dough into a very thin sheet. Let the sheets of dough set for 20 minutes to dry and then cut into 1 × 3-inch strips.

Drop the dumplings into the pot with the chicken.

CHICKEN CREOLE

Serves 4

Patricia Butler is an associate minister at the First Missionary Baptist Church in Handsboro, Mississippi, on the Gulf Coast. She is also a licensed chaplain and she is just as likely to conduct a Bible study at the local jail as she is at a drug addict's home.

Pat is also a fine cook, and whenever the church holds a barbecue or picnic, she arrives with a covered dish. The food of the Gulf Coast is a mélange of many ethnic influences: Cajun, Creole, African, and European, and it is savory and delicious.

Reverend Butler sends this recipe for a chicken dish made with okra—an indigenous vegetable of Africa.

1 chicken, 3¼-pounds	*2 tablespoons vegetable oil*
½ pound smoked sausage	*¼ teaspoon cayenne*
1 onion	*2 cups chicken broth or Homemade*
3 to 4 tomatoes	*Chicken Stock (see recipe*
2 to 3 cloves garlic	*on page 234)*
3 or 4 sprigs fresh thyme, or	*½ pound fresh or frozen whole*
½ teaspoon dried thyme	*okra pods*

Cut the chicken into serving pieces: the breast into halves, the legs and thighs separated, plus the wings, for a total of 8 pieces. Rinse the chicken well under cold running water and pat dry with paper towels. Trim away any visible fat from the chicken and discard.

Cut the sausage into bite-size pieces. Slice the onion; coarsely chop the tomatoes; and mince the garlic. Chop the fresh thyme or crush the dried herb.

Heat the oil in a large heavy pot. Add the chicken, a few pieces at a time, and brown over medium-high heat. Remove from the pot and brown the remaining chicken the same way, removing when brown.

When all the chicken is browned, add the sausage and sauté 4 or 5 minutes, turning to brown evenly. Stir in the onion, tomatoes, garlic, thyme, and cayenne. Sauté 2 or 3 minutes, stirring.

Return the chicken pieces to the pan. Add the chicken broth or stock and bring to a boil. Reduce the heat to low, cover, and cook for 30 minutes or until the chicken is almost done.

Cut off and discard the woody end tips of the fresh okra. Stir the pods into the pot and cook 20 minutes longer or until the okra is tender and the chicken is done. Serve with rice.

Homemade Chicken Stock

Makes about 2 quarts

Since Mattie Hodges spends so much time in her kitchen cooking, she doesn't like to rush around at the last minute preparing chicken stock, especially if she is fixing a dish to carry out to the Ebenezer Baptist Church in Atlanta, where she seems to spend equally as much time.

Besides that, she and her husband, Edward Hodges, a deacon at Ebenezer whom she met at the church in 1945 and went on to marry, are always having some backyard cookout at their home for some church group.

Nothing goes to waste in her house, and she makes her chicken stock from chicken and turkey innards that she saves and freezes until she has enough on hand to make a rich and flavorful stock. When her freezer supply runs out, she occasionally goes searching for a hen so that she can make a pot of stock just as her mother did years ago back home in Waycross, Georgia.

She says she uses the stock for gravy, soups, stews, to make cornbread dressing, and for simmering rice, potatoes, and vegetables. She uses the chicken for sandwiches, in chicken or macaroni salad, or she tosses chunks of the chicken with stir-fried vegetables or adds to a rice pilaf.

Sometimes she takes out half of the broth from the pot and drops in some dumplings with the chicken, for another old-time treat.

Regardless, her recipe is rich and flavorful, and far better than anything you get from a can. This recipe uses a broiler-fryer chicken.

1 broiler-fryer chicken, 3 pounds
1 onion
4 ribs celery
2 or 3 carrots
2 cloves garlic
1 bay leaf

2 or 3 sprigs parsley
½ teaspoon salt
¼ teaspoon freshly ground
   black pepper
10 cups water

Cut the chicken into serving pieces: the breast into halves, the legs and thighs separated, plus the wings, for a total of 8 pieces. Rinse the chicken well under cold running water.

Discard the liver but save the gizzard and neck. Trim off visible fat from the chicken and discard.

Slice the onion, cut the celery and carrots into 2-inch chunks. Mince the garlic. Place all of the chicken—including the gizzard and neck—in a large stock pot, about 8-quart size. Add the onion, celery, carrots, garlic, bay leaf, parsley, salt, and black pepper.

Add the water and bring to a boil. Lower the heat, cover, and simmer about 1½ hours or until the chicken is tender and the broth is well flavored, turning the chicken in the broth several times during the cooking.

Using tongs or a slotted spoon, remove the chicken from the stock and drain. Strain the chicken broth and store in refrigerator in covered containers or jars until ready to use, or place in plastic containers and freeze.

Use the chicken for chicken salad (see recipe on page 223).

KEEPING THE OVEN HOT

The kitchen at the Hartford Memorial Baptist Church in Detroit is jokingly referred to as the "hot seat," and this is probably said because the mammoth church has some 250 different clubs and organizations, and on any given day one of those groups holds some type of reception, service, or fellowship that requires food.

Officially, Delores Brandon oversees this culinary beehive. As kitchen manager–administrator she is in charge of all the food served at the church. On some occasions she and her staff prepare the food, at other times it is catered, and sometimes the church members don aprons, roll up their sleeves, and venture into the "hot seat" to prepare a meal themselves.

The most noticeable invasion occurred recently on New Year's Day when Mrs. Brandon had the unenviable task of managing the temperaments and talents of seventy to one hundred volunteers who cooked and served a multicourse feast for up to seven hundred people at the church, which is located on James Couzens Freeway.

Being a food professional, she handles these invasions with aplomb, and if there is any static or hot air, it is about presentation. Eye appeal is important to her. She doesn't like food cooked and served any old way, as my mother often said.

"I love food," Mrs. Brandon says matter-of-factly. "I love what food is built around: happiness, sharing, being together, common ground. So I am particular about eye appeal—how food looks—about the economics of food. I am also concerned about universal taste and nutrition. I think it is careless and lazy to put out an unattractive pot of food. You are what you eat. Food should look good and taste good."

So you can rest assured that whenever Delores Brandon sends out a platter of baked chicken, the pieces have been arranged just so and then sprinkled with paprika and perhaps decorated with a cluster of parsley, or a little pile of carrot strips fashioned into roses. Her greens are no soggy mess floating in water, either. She seasons the greens with chicken

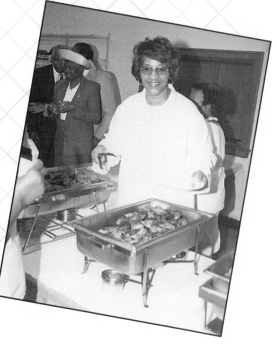

Carolyn Drake (left) and Mary Mathias in the kitchen at Hartford Memorial Baptist Church in Detroit.

Delores Brandon, the kitchen manager–administrator of the Hartford Memorial Baptist Church, Detroit, stands at the ready at the serving table.

broth, onions, and a little vegetable oil and then throws in a handful of chopped red peppers for flavor and added color.

She wouldn't think of serving boiled potatoes without giving the dish a sprinkling of parsley or some other herb, and her tossed salad is a picture-perfect medley of crisp, drained, chilled lettuce, mixed with an array of fresh vegetables and served in a pretty bowl.

Mrs. Brandon has been a member of Hartford Memorial since 1979, and like many other church members, she brought her professional skills to the church and did volunteer work in the arena she knew best: the kitchen. She had been trained since she was knee-high for this position,

Chicken and Other Fine Birds

beginning at home with her mother, Priscilla Williams Maxwell, who for years was a chef for a prominent family in Detroit. At an early age Mrs. Brandon was learning about sauces and silverware and serving dishes, and that probably explains in part why she is so meticulous today about food being "served properly," as she says all the time.

She later bolstered her home training with study in food management and nutrition at the university level, and over the years she has worked as a food manager at a half-dozen local institutions and establishments. In late 1993, the pastor at Hartford Memorial, Dr. Charles G. Adams, decided that Mrs. Brandon's expertise was needed full time, and offered her the position as kitchen manager administrator.

Today she has a full plate, considering that food is such an integral part of church life at Hartford Memorial. The kitchen there rivals many three-star restaurants. It's at least one thousand square feet, and has a convection oven, two commercial stoves, walk-in refrigerators, two large steam tables, and a staggering collection of pots and pans that gets plenty of use.

"When we get together in the kitchen at Hartford we have the best time," Mrs. Brandon says. "We have a beautiful relationship. Cooking is peaceful and spiritual."

Mrs. Brandon sends this recipe:

Baked Chicken and Gravy

Serves 4

1 chicken, 3¼ to 3½ pounds
1 teaspoon salt
½ teaspoon white pepper
2 teaspoons paprika
1 clove garlic
¼ cup vegetable oil or melted
   margarine

2 tablespoons cornstarch
2 tablespoons hot water
2 cups chicken broth or Homemade
   Chicken Stock (see recipe on
   page 234)
2 tablespoons chopped parsley

Preheat the oven to 375 degrees.

Place the chicken on a cutting board and split down the middle lengthwise. Trim away any visible fat and discard. Rinse thoroughly with cold water, drain, and pat dry with paper towels.

Sprinkle the chicken with ¾ teaspoon of salt, the white pepper, and paprika. Mince the garlic and rub all over the chicken.

Oil a 9 × 13-inch shallow roasting pan. Place the chicken, skin side up, in the pan. Pour over the oil or margarine. Place on the lower shelf and bake in the hot oven for 20 minutes, basting occasionally with the pan drippings.

Turn the chicken over and bake 20 to 25 minutes longer, or until the chicken is browned and done and the juices run clear when pierced with a fork. Remove the chicken from the oven and from the roasting pan.

Drain off all but 2 tablespoons of the pan drippings. Mix together in a medium bowl the cornstarch and water. Stir in the chicken broth and the remaining ¼ teaspoon salt.

Place the pan with the pan drippings on medium-low heat. Stir in the chicken broth–cornstarch mixture, scraping up crusty bits in the pan.

Raise the heat a little and cook the sauce for 5 minutes or until the gravy is bubbling hot and thickened. Lower the heat, return the chicken to the pan, and spoon the sauce over the chicken. Heat 4 or 5 minutes longer.

Place the chicken on a warm serving platter. Pour the gravy on and sprinkle the chicken with the chopped parsley.

Chicken and Other Fine Birds

Paprika Baked Chicken

Serves 4

t is often said that no two church sisters cook chicken exactly alike, and the only thing that I can say about the baked chicken prepared by Mrs. Brandon and Esther Mae Archie is that both dishes are delicious.

Mrs. Archie is a member of the Metropolitan Missionary Baptist Church in Chicago, where she is deeply involved with the church's street witness team, an outreach ministry.

She sends a recipe for baked chicken that is a nutritionist's delight: skinless and redolent with peppers and onions.

1 chicken, 3¼ to 3½ pounds	*2 teaspoons paprika*
1 teaspoon salt	*2 large onions*
¼ teaspoon freshly ground	*2 red or green peppers*
black pepper	*¼ cup vegetable oil*

Preheat the oven to 400 degrees.

Oil a 9 × 13-inch roasting or broiler pan and set aside.

Using a sharp knife, trim off any visible fat and skin the chicken. Discard the fat and skin. Cut the chicken into serving pieces: the breast into halves, the legs and thighs separated, plus the wings, for a total of 8 pieces.

Rinse the chicken well with cold water and then pat dry with paper towels. Sprinkle with the salt, black pepper, and paprika.

Slice the onions and core and dice the red or green pepper.

Place the chicken in the roasting or broiler pan. Drizzle over the oil. Scatter the onions and red or green peppers over the chicken. Cover the pan with heavy-duty aluminum foil, sealing the foil along the edges of pan.

Place the pan on the lower shelf of the hot oven and bake for 15 minutes. Remove the pan from the oven. Lift up the foil, and using long tongs, turn the chicken, reseal the foil, and return to the oven. Bake for 10 minutes longer or until the chicken is almost done.

Remove the chicken from the oven and raise the oven temperature to broil. Preheat the broiler for at least 5 minutes.

Remove the foil cover. Using a fork or tongs, lift the chicken from under the onions and peppers and place on top of the vegetables; this keeps the vegetables from charring during the broiling.

Place the chicken under the hot broiler at about 6 inches from heat. Broil 3 to 4 minutes or until lightly golden. Turn the chicken over, and broil 3 minutes more, or until the pieces are golden brown and the juices run clear when pierced with a fork.

Molasses Baked Chicken

Serves 4

*d*addy always helped Mr. Ras make molasses, and was rewarded with several gallons of syrup in return for his work. When we had church company on Sundays, Mama would take a little of the molasses and gingerly brush it on a ham, pork loin, or whole chicken before baking, creating a golden, crusty glaze that turned ordinary fare into a very special dish.

This was her favorite way with chicken, which I liked as much as the Reverend Barlow did.

1 chicken, 3¼ to 3½ pounds
1 teaspoon salt
½ to 1 teaspoon allspice
   or cinnamon.

2 tablespoons cider vinegar
2 tablespoons dark molasses or
   dark syrup
2 tablespoons spicy brown mustard

Preheat the oven to 400 degrees.

Cut the chicken into serving pieces: the breast into halves, the legs and thighs separated, plus the wings, for a total of 8 pieces. Trim off any visible fat from the chicken.

Rinse the chicken under running water, drain, and pat dry with paper towels. Sprinkle the chicken with the salt and black pepper and allspice or cinnamon.

In a small bowl combine the vinegar, molasses or dark syrup, and mustard. Mix well with a fork or wire whisk.

Coat the chicken with the mixture, rubbing well into the skin and flesh.

Lightly oil a large roasting pan. Place the chicken in the pan. Set the pan on the lower shelf of the oven and bake for 20 minutes or until the pieces are golden brown.

Using long-handled tongs, turn the chicken and bake for 20 minutes longer. It is done when the chicken is glazed and golden and the juices run clear when pierced with a knife.

KWANZAA CHICKEN

Serves 4 to 6

Kwanzaa is a Swahili word that means "the first fruits of the harvest," and it incorporates elements of harvest festivals celebrated throughout Mother Africa. The holiday, celebrated by increasingly more African-Americans each year, begins on December 26 and runs through New Year's Day. It is guided by these seven principles: *umoja* (unity), *kujichagulia* (self-determination), *ujima* (collective work and responsibility), *ujamaa* (cooperative economics), *nia* (purpose), *kuumba* (creativity), and *imani* (faith).

The centerpiece of the celebration is the Kwanzaa table, which holds baskets filled with fruits and vegetables—symbols of a collective harvest—

Simone Monique Barnes, president of the Young Adult Ministry, serves a potpourri of food for the Kwanzaa feast at Grace Baptist Church, Mount Vernon, New York.

Renee Barnes (left) with daughter Simone Monique Barnes, president of the Young Adult Ministry, at the Kwanzaa celebration held by Grace Baptist Church in Mount Vernon, New York.

and a seven-branch candleholder. On each of the seven days of Kwanzaa, a family member lights a candle and discusses one of the principles, beginning with *umoja* on the first day, and ending with *imani* on the last day of the celebration, which features a multicourse meal.

Simone Monique Barnes, who is president of the Young Adult Ministry at Grace Baptist Church in Mount Vernon, New York, celebrated her last Kwanzaa with a gathering of friends, family, and church members.

Simone is twenty-three and something of a wunderkind. Besides her church commitment, she attends college and takes cooking classes at a local school.

During her Kwanzaa celebration she served a spicy, glazed chicken, Caribbean rice, smothered red cabbage, mixed green salad, beef in tomato sauce, punch, and a potpourri of desserts: chocolate cake, cheesecake, apple pie, and carrot cake. And the guests shook their heads in wonderment.

Simone sends this recipe:

4 pounds small chicken thighs
¼ cup soy sauce
1 teaspoon cumin
½ teaspoon salt

½ teaspoon black pepper
1 or 2 cloves garlic
2 tablespoons vegetable oil
Parsley sprigs (optional)

Preheat the oven to 400 degrees.

Generously oil a large roasting pan and set aside.

Trim away visible fat from the chicken and discard. Rinse with cold water, drain, and pat dry with paper towels.

Rub the chicken all over with the soy sauce, and then sprinkle with the cumin, salt, and black pepper. Mince the garlic and rub into the chicken.

Place the chicken in the roasting pan in a single layer. Drizzle over the oil.

Bake the chicken in the hot oven for 20 minutes. Turn the chicken and bake 20 minutes longer or until browned golden and glazed and the juices run clear when pierced with a fork.

Place on a platter and decorate with parsley sprigs, if desired.

WEST AFRICAN CHICKEN (POULET AU YASSA)

Serves 4

Several years ago Delores Lee visited Senegal and discovered this delicious, spicy recipe for chicken. Recently she made this dish for a potluck supper held at the Saint John Baptist Church, which is located on 152nd Street in Harlem. She then went about collecting clothes for the homeless.

Delores Lee is the daughter of the late Ollie Hutchins, the woman who guided my son, Roy, to young adulthood, and like her mother, she is a dedicated churchwoman.

She is a member of Saint John's Missionary Society; vice president of the Scholarship Committee, which assists college students with miscellaneous expenses; and is both a schoolteacher and a Sunday school teacher. Every Thanksgiving she bakes turkey and makes cornbread dressing for a dinner that the church prepares for the homeless and the homebound.

"Years ago when we began this program we fed mostly single men," recalls Delores. "Now we are feeding just as many women and children and families. So you see that the need is growing."

There are many versions of this lemony chicken dish in West Africa, where it is often served with rice or couscous. (Couscous, a staple dish in North and West Africa, is made from 100 percent durum wheat semolina. It is delicate, light and quick-cooking: Bring 1 cup water to a boil, season with salt and black pepper and add a little olive oil. Stir in 1 cup couscous, mix and let set, covered, off heat, for 5 minutes before serving.)

Delores sends this recipe:

3½ pounds chicken legs and thighs

3 or 4 sprigs oregano or marjoram,
  or ½ teaspoon dried oregano or
  marjoram

1 teaspoon salt

¾ teaspoon freshly ground
  black pepper

4 to 5 tablespoons corn or peanut oil

¼ cup lemon juice

1 cup fresh shredded coconut

2 large onions

2 cloves garlic

2 hot chili peppers

2 cup coarsely chopped plum
  tomatoes

1 bay leaf

Preheat the broiler.

Trim away any visible fat from the chicken and discard. Wash the chicken under cold water and dry with paper towels. Chop the fresh oregano or marjoram or crush the dried herb. Rub the herb all over the chicken and then sprinkle the chicken with the salt and black pepper.

Generously oil a shallow boiler pan. Place the chicken in the pan in a single layer. Drizzle 2 tablespoons of the oil over the chicken.

Set the pan under the broiler, 6 inches from the heat. Broil the chicken for about 5 minutes or until golden brown. Turn and brown 5 minutes longer on the other side. Remove the pan from the oven. Pour the lemon juice over the chicken. Sprinkle the coconut over the chicken and set aside.

Reset the oven and preheat to 400 degrees.

Slice the onions; mince the garlic; and finely dice the chilies. Heat the remaining oil in a medium skillet. Add the onions, garlic,

Tables are set with an African design motif for the Black History Month gospel brunch at Canaan Baptist Church in Harlem, New York.

and chilies and sauté over medium heat for 5 minutes or until the onions are soft and translucent.

Stir in the tomatoes and bay leaf and cook over low heat, stirring, for 15 minutes longer.

Return the chicken to the oven and bake for 15 minutes. Turn the chicken, pour the tomato sauce on top, and bake until the chicken is tender and brown, about 15 minutes.

Remove the bay leaf before serving. Serve over rice or couscous.

Chicken and Other Fine Birds

ALWAYS ON SUNDAY

There were five boys and five girls in Elnora Dean's family back in Fort Worth, Texas, and even today she believes that having so many people in the family provided her with the basics of how to cook and entertain. She remembers that the boys did the outside work and the girls took care of the house, and by age eight she was standing on a wooden box cooking at the stove.

Today Mrs. Dean is the director of hospitality at the Westminster Presbyterian Church in Los Angeles, and much of her time is spent creating recipes, planning menus, shopping, cooking, and decorating the church's fellowship hall for a wide variety of functions and services. She plans the menus and cooks for funeral repasts, helps pass out bags of groceries to the homeless on Fridays, and coordinates the efforts of a dozen or so church organizations, since some club or other serves food at the church every Sunday.

"Food is part of our fellowship," Mrs. Dean says evenly. "Every Sunday after service we always have food. That way we get to touch and know each other and rub shoulders and socialize; things we don't do during the service."

The Westminster Presbyterian Church, which was founded in 1904 expressly for African-Americans, is located on West Jefferson Boulevard in South Central Los Angeles, in a cream-colored wood-and-cement building with a Spanish motif. The sanctuary has dark brown mahogany pews, gold rugs, off-white walls, and lovely deep-brown ceiling beams. Whenever there is a special event at the church, Mrs. Dean decorates the tables in the fellowship hall with flowers and centerpieces to create a special effect or theme, and since she is so particular about the serving of food, this can take hours.

Mrs. Dean remembers that a decade ago when one of the church members called and asked her to head the Hospitality Committee, she was serving a salad and a platter of spicy chicken wings to a few ladies from her bowling league at her home in La Mirada, California.

"I told him that I was already on several committees but he kept on insisting that I take the position," she recalls.

It wasn't until she was reminded that nobody at Westminster cared as much about food as she did that she relented and accepted the nomination.

Mrs. Dean is a retired registered nurse and her husband, Owen, is a retired engineer, and they seemed to have put down two sets of careers and picked up another, since they cook and entertain all of the time. Their two grown children and their two grandchildren are always at their home, and she chuckles and says that when they visit they act like they haven't eaten in a week.

She collects recipes and pastes them in a photo album between cellophane layers so that they are protected from splatters when she, as she puts it, "tinkers about in the kitchen." And what she enjoys most is making over her compendium of recipes, and then passing on the new versions to whoever is cooking for some function in the church kitchen at Westminster.

"Cooking is a head job," she says with unusual enthusiasm. "I like to get into the kitchen, experiment, and add bits and pieces and see what I come up with."

Mrs. Dean has a wide-ranging repertoire of dishes that she serves at home and at Westminster, but no food holds quite as many childhood memories as chicken.

She remembers that on Wednesdays during the very busy week, the females in her family would fry a couple of chickens and the meal was casual and more hurried. Sunday was another matter.

The family sat down to dinner to baked chicken that was crispy and brown and succulent and looked as regal as holiday turkey. The chicken was served with cornbread dressing and plenty of vegetables. And when candied yams, beets, and a fresh peach, pear, or apple relish were added to the meal, the day would take on a festive note.

"In those days chicken was a delicacy to us," Mrs. Dean recalls.

She sends this recipe:

ROAST CHICKEN

Serves 4

rs. Dean says she has three or four recipes for oven-roasted chicken and usually uses whatever ingredients she has on hand or whatever strikes her fancy. Sometimes she rubs the chicken with dried oregano, Italian seasoning, and lemon pepper; at other times she uses seasoned salt, lemon, and freshly ground black pepper.

Often she rubs the chicken with a tablespoon or so of chopped fresh herbs, and at other times, she simply roasts the old-fashioned way, with just a sprinkling of salt and black pepper.

She sends this recipe for chicken baked with lemon, which she has "tinkered" with for years. And since she particularly enjoys cooking with wine, she adds a judicious amount to the pan gravy served with the chicken.

1 chicken, 3½ pounds	1 teaspoon paprika
1 clove garlic	1 onion
2 tablespoons vegetable or olive oil	1 whole lemon
1 teaspoon salt	½ cup dry white wine
½ teaspoon freshly ground black pepper	½ cup chicken broth or Homemade Chicken Stock (see recipe on page 234)
½ teaspoon dried oregano or thyme	

Preheat the oven to 325 degrees.

Remove the innards from the chicken cavity and freeze for later use in a stock or soup. Wash the chicken in cold water and pat dry with paper towels.

Mince the garlic.

Rub the chicken all over with the oil, then rub with the garlic, salt, black pepper, the oregano or thyme, and paprika, covering the cavity as well.

Cut the onion into quarters. Pierce the lemons all over with a fork. Place the onion and the lemon into the cavity of the chicken and close the opening with round toothpicks. Tie the legs of the chicken upright with twine or wire twist, and tuck the chicken wings toward the back of the chicken.

Generously oil a shallow roasting pan. Place the chicken, breast side down, in the pan. Bake for 20 minutes. Turn the chicken breast side up and bake for 40 to 50 minutes longer, basting every 15 or so minutes with the pan drippings. Bake until it is golden brown and tender.

To check for doneness: Pierce the thigh, and if the juices run clear the bird is done; or insert an instant-read thermometer into the fleshiest part of the thigh, and if the thermometer reads 180 degrees the chicken is done. If not, cook 10 minutes longer and test again.

Remove the chicken from the oven and let it rest in a warm spot for 10 minutes. Remove the toothpicks and twine or wire twist; discard along with the stuffing.

At serving, pour the wine and chicken broth into the roasting pan. Place over medium heat and bring to a boil, scraping up the browned bits. Season with salt and pepper if needed. Strain the gravy into a sauce bowl and serve with the chicken.

Barbecue Chicken

Years ago at family gatherings, invariably somebody would go down into the woods, grab a few hickory, oak, or pecan limbs, and throw the branches on top of the glowing coals that were heating up to cook the ribs and the chicken. Eventually the conversation would turn to the fine points of the task at hand, and usually the men would talk at length about just how the sauce should be made, exactly when the meat and chicken should be placed on the fire, and who really was the best barbecue cook for miles around.

Barbecue is just as much a part of our culinary history as potato salad, and I must confess that I love the aroma and taste of food infused with the smoke of wood, and then swabbed with a rich and spicy tomato-base barbecue sauce.

Barbecue is the high art of soul food, and over the years I have met people who would tell you all manner of their personal affairs but wouldn't think of revealing their secret recipe for barbecue sauce. The sauces come in many guises: almost sweet from a generous amount of brown sugar or molasses; fiery hot from chili peppers; as thick and supple as honey; tart from a generous dash of lemon juice or vinegar.

Elnora Dean sends a delicious recipe for barbecue sauce that is just as studied as the rest of her cooking. It is spicy but not incendiary.

Mrs. Dean is the director of hospitality at the Westminster Presbyterian Church in Los Angeles, and she has developed at least a dozen recipes for chicken to serve at the church's numerous social or fellowship gatherings.

She sends these recipes:

3½ to 4 pounds chicken thighs or legs, or both
1 teaspoon salt
½ teaspoon freshly ground black pepper

2 cups Barbecue Sauce (recipe follows)

Pile about 3 dozen hardwood charcoal briquettes pyramid-fashion in the center of a barbecue grill, preferably one that has a cover. Ignite and allow the charcoal to burn until they are glowing and ashy, and then spread into a single layer.

Meanwhile, soak 2 cups of wood chips or 3 or 4 wood chunks in a pan of water. (See "Grilling Is Hot" on page 192.)

Trim all visible fat from the chicken and discard. Rinse the chicken with cold water. Pat dry with paper towels. Sprinkle with salt and black pepper.

Lightly oil a roasting pan. Place the chicken in the pan. Drain the wood chips or chunks and scatter a handful or one or two chunks over the hot, glowing charcoal.

Set the pan on the grill on a rack about 6 to 8 inches above the coals. Cover and cook for 40 minutes, turning the chicken every 10 minutes.

When the chicken is almost done and lightly browned, coat with 1 cup of the barbecue sauce. If possible, scatter the coals so that the heat is no longer so intense.

Cover the grill and barbecue the chicken 15 to 20 minutes longer, basting occasionally with the remaining cup of sauce, and turning often.

BARBECUE SAUCE

Makes about 4 cups

2 cups ketchup
⅔ cup chili sauce
1 cup beer
¼ cup mustard
¼ cup Worcestershire sauce
¼ cup dark brown sugar
¼ cup cider vinegar

1 tablespoon lemon juice
1 tablespoon vegetable oil
1 tablespoon soy sauce
½ teaspoon hot pepper sauce
½ teaspoon freshly ground
    black pepper

In a medium saucepan combine the ketchup, chili sauce, beer, mustard, Worcestershire sauce, brown sugar, vinegar, lemon juice, vegetable oil, soy sauce, hot pepper sauce, and black pepper.

Bring to a gentle boil, stirring briskly. Reduce heat to simmer, and cook, stirring often, 15 to 20 minutes. If the sauce becomes too thick, stir in a little more beer or water.

Sauce Variation: The herb rosemary makes a delightful sauce for barbecue chicken. Combine in a bowl ¼ cup vegetable oil; ½ cup lemon or grapefruit juice; 2 tablespoons soy sauce; 2 cloves minced garlic; 2 teaspoons paprika; and 1½ tablespoons finely chopped fresh rosemary, or 1 teaspoon crushed dried rosemary.

Brush the chicken generously with the sauce, place on the grill, and cook for 40 to 50 minutes, basting occasionally with the remaining sauce, following directions above.

TALKING TURKEY

Just a couple of decades ago turkey was enjoyed primarily during the holidays, but today it has flown the coop and is available year round, and you no longer have to buy the whole bird either. You can purchase ground turkey for burgers and spaghetti sauce, turkey breasts to bake and slice for sandwiches or to grill for cutlets, turkey legs for roasting or barbecuing, and smoked turkey wings, necks, and thighs for seasoning greens and peas and beans.

But no matter how many ways this old bird is cut, it seems that few of us will ever give up our passion for roast turkey at Thanksgiving. No wonder, a bronze turkey glistening on a well-appointed and food-laden table is a showstopper, and it evokes indelible memories of hearth and family and tradition.

Turkey can be a little tricky to cook and that's because these hefty birds have to remain in the oven a long time, and during the baking the breast gets done faster than the legs and thighs and ends up dry and overcooked. Many ingenious solutions have been devised for this dilemma. One food expert recommends that you bake and serve the turkey in two stages: remove the bird from the oven when the white meat is cooked, slice off the breast and then return the turkey to the oven to finish cooking the dark meat.

This may work, but it takes so much of the drama out of the dining setting, and it also forces the host to keep checking on the turkey when he or she should be enjoying the dinner, too.

Over the years I've tried many approaches, including encasing the turkey in an aluminum-foil tent, as well as baking the turkey at either 450 or 500 degrees for a shorter baking time. And after all was said and done, I was still searching for that mythical baked turkey: succulent moist breast, fully cooked legs and thighs, crisp, crackling skin.

A while back I was discussing this problem with Jerlene Sherfield, who heads the Kitchen Committee at the Cedar Grove Missionary Baptist Church in Mason, Tennessee, which is located about thirty miles from Memphis.

TURKEY STUFF

In the rush of holiday festivities, don't forget to allow plenty of time for defrosting a turkey if you use a frozen bird. Like chicken, a frozen turkey should always be defrosted inside the refrigerator—not at room temperature—and if the bird weighs more than 12 pounds or so, it generally will take more than a day to defrost.

Another point: Many turkeys today come with a button implanted in the breast, which is supposed to pop up when the bird is fully cooked. When I follow this directive I end up with dry white meat. I feel that the instant-read thermometer is more accurate than the pop-up button.

Jerlene Sherfield is a vivacious, talkative woman, in her late forties, who cares deeply about food, her church, and her family. She has been a member of Cedar Grove Baptist all of her life, and so was her mother and grandmother, and she knows all the members, and all of them know that she loves to cook. Her sister, Lillie Sherfield, lives in Rochester, New York, and the two women keep the telephone lines burning, exchanging recipes and church news and family concerns.

Jerlene doesn't have a set menu for church functions, but she says very readily and candidly that "We are Down South and we like to eat a lot," and with that proclamation she adds that a roast turkey goes a long way.

Jerlene should know. The church's Kitchen Committee plans and cooks for funeral repasts, for the homebound, and for numerous other celebrations at the church. So turkey is served often. And she has become adept at roasting the bird to perfection.

She bakes the turkey breast side down for 30 minutes, and then breast side up, protected with cheesecloth and a sheet of aluminum foil. The results is a golden, delicious, succulent but crusty bird, as welcomed in July during the church revival as at Thanksgiving.

Here's her recipe:

Perfect Roast Turkey

*b*efore you stick the turkey in the oven, know exactly how much it weighs. Allow a roasting time of 15 minutes per pound. For example, a 12-pound turkey should cook in about 180 minutes, or 3 hours. Then assemble a timer, a large square of cheesecloth, a 12-inch square of aluminum foil, an instant-read thermometer, and you are all set.

1 fresh or frozen turkey, thawed, 12 to 14 pounds
½ cup vegetable or olive oil
1 tablespoon salt
1½ teaspoon freshly ground black pepper

3 cloves garlic
6 or 7 chopped sage leaves, or 1½ teaspoons dried
1 onion
2 celery stalks
1 apple or lemon

Preheat the oven to 350 degrees.

If using a frozen turkey, defrost according to package directions (see "Turkey Stuff" on page 256). Remove the giblets and neck from the cavity and freeze to use to make broth. (Don't use the liver in the broth; it imparts an off flavor.)

Rinse the turkey under running cold water, including the cavity. Drain and then dry with paper towels.

Rub the turkey all over, outside and the cavity, with 2 to 3 tablespoons of the vegetable or olive oil. Sprinkle the bird with the salt and black pepper. Mince the garlic and finely chop the fresh sage or crush the dried herb. Rub the turkey all over, including the cavity, with the garlic and herb.

Cut the onion in quarters; the celery into chunks; the apple or lemon into quarters. Place the vegetables and fruit into the cavity of the turkey (no bread stuffing). Close the cavity with round toothpicks or skewers.

Tuck the tips of the wings under the back of the turkey. Using round toothpicks, skewer the neck skin to the back of the turkey, creating a pretty effect. Pull the legs upright toward the breast and then tie the ends together with heavy cord or with wire twist.

Oil a rack and set it into a large roasting pan. Place the bird onto the rack, breast side down, and set into the hot oven, on the middle shelf. Bake for 30 minutes.

Remove the pan from the oven. Run a thin metal spatula under the breast to make sure than it is isn't sticking to the pan. Using two clean pot holders, or slip on a pair of oven mittens, grasp the turkey at both ends, lift, and turn to its back, breast side up, and set back in the pan on the rack. Baste the turkey with a tablespoon or so of the remaining oil.

Fold the cheesecloth into a square that covers the breast, dip it into the oil until completely saturated, and lay it directly on the breast, and then lay the square of aluminum foil over the cheesecloth.

Return the turkey to the oven and bake for 2½ hours, lifting the aluminum foil and basting the bird (through the cheesecloth) every 20 minutes or so, with the pan drippings and remaining oil. During the last 20 minutes of baking remove the cheesecloth and foil so that the breast can brown evenly, and baste again.

At the end of the cooking time insert the instant-read thermometer into the fleshiest part of the thigh. If the thermometer reads 180 degrees and the juices run clear when a skewer is inserted in the leg, the turkey is done.

If the turkey isn't quite done, baste it again, place the foil back over the breast, and return the bird to the oven. Test again in 20 minutes. Watch carefully at this point, and don't overcook.

When done, remove the turkey from the oven and let it rest for 15 to 20 minutes in a warm place while you make the gravy.

Pan Gravy: Leave 3 tablespoons of the pan drippings in the pan and drain the rest. Stir in 3 tablespoons flour. Set the pan on a burner over low heat. Cook the flour, stirring, for 8 to 10 minutes or until it turns light brown. Don't allow the roux to burn. Stir in 2 cups of chicken broth or homemade chicken or turkey stock (see recipe on page 234). Bring to a gentle boil. Season with a little salt and pepper. Reduce the heat to low and cook for 10 minutes or until the gravy is thickened. Serve with the turkey.

Smoked Turkey

Serves 10 to 12

d eborah Inez Ford is the daughter of Velma Mosley, and everybody in Tyler, Texas, who knows Mrs. Mosley also knows that she is a woman who gets things done.

Deborah is no sideliner, either. She lives in Lakewood, Colorado, and either because of social engineering or genes, she is just as busy as her mother. Well, almost.

Deborah is a member of the New Hope Baptist Church in Denver, located on Colorado Boulevard, and she is actively involved in many of the church's activities. Twice monthly on Sundays she assists in a Children's Worship service, which is held for youngsters between the ages of 3 and 8. Not only is the service presented from a child's perspective, but the children are also allowed to engage in a variety of hands-on skills that build self-confidence and boost self-esteem.

During one holiday, the children constructed Santa Clauses using an assortment of materials made available. There are some twenty children in the program, and they were asked to make an ideal Santa Claus, and to the surprise of some observers, but not to Deborah, every child made a Santa Claus who either looked liked his or her mother or father.

"We thought that this was significant," says Deborah, who works for AT&T Communications, "considering that studies show that many African-American children prefer other images to their own. We really stress education here at New Hope. We have after-school tutoring and two children's choirs. I think our programs are paying off."

Deborah is also a member of the church's Grieving Committee, which provides an array of services to the family of the deceased, depending on what is needed, and this ranges from buying flowers to helping with burial arrangements. After the interment the committee also offers the family a benevolence meal, which usually consists of smoked turkey, green beans, candied sweet potatoes, macaroni and cheese, homemade rolls, and peach cobbler. However, often friends and family members supplement the menu with a variety of other dishes.

Deborah prepares the smoked turkey, and she is just as zealous about food as her mother, Velma Mosley, who isn't shy about taking the credit for her daughter's culinary expertise.

"I was a working mother with three children and they had to cook," says Mrs. Mosley. "I put Deborah on a box up to the stove. I didn't care what kind of mess she cooked, I ate it. Today she is one of the best cooks I know."

Deborah sends this recipe:

1 fresh or frozen turkey, thawed,
*   10 to 12 pounds*
¼ cup soy sauce
⅓ cup vegetable or olive oil
1 tablespoon salt
1½ teaspoons freshly ground
*   black pepper*
1 tablespoon paprika
3 cloves garlic

7 or 8 fresh sage leaves, or
*   2 teaspoons dried; or*
*   1½ tablespoons chopped*
*   rosemary, or 2 teaspoons dried*
1 onion
2 stalks of celery
1 green pepper
2 carrots
2 cups white wine or beer

Smoking requires a grill with a cover, or a commercial smoker can be used, and if so, follow the manufacturer's directions.

If using a kettle-type grill, check to make sure that when you cover the turkey the lid does not touch the bird. This is critical. If the turkey touches the hot cover during the grilling, the breast will cook too fast and is likely to end up dry and leathery.

Ideally, a turkey weighing from 12 to 20 pounds fits comfortably with plenty of air space on a grill that is at least 22 inches in diameter. However, when purchasing a turkey to be cooked on a grill with a cover, the shape of the turkey is more important than the weight. A turkey that is broad and flat will fit better on the grill and under the cover than one that protrudes high in the breast area.

Also assemble at least 70 to 80 hardwood charcoal briquettes and 4 or 5 cups of wood chips, or 5 or 6 fist-size wood chunks (see "Grilling Is Hot" on page 192). Soak the wood chunks or chips in a pot of water for at least 30 minutes, or longer if a heavier smoke flavor is desired.

If using a frozen turkey, defrost according to package directions (see "Turkey Stuff" on page 256). Remove the giblets and neck from the cavity and freeze to use to make broth or stock. (Don't use the liver in the broth; it imparts an off flavor.)

Rinse the turkey under running cold water, both inside and out. Drain and then dry with paper towels.

Rub the turkey all over, including the cavity, with the soy sauce and then with 2 to 3 tablespoons of the vegetable or olive oil. Sprinkle the bird with the salt, black pepper, and paprika.

Mince the garlic and finely chop the fresh sage or rosemary or crush the dried herb. Rub the turkey all over with the garlic and sage or rosemary.

Cut the onion into quarters; the celery into 2-inch pieces; the green pepper into strips; and the carrots into 2-inch chunks.

Place the vegetables into the cavity of the turkey (no bread stuffing). Close the cavity with toothpicks or skewers.

Tuck the tips of the wings under the back of the turkey. Using round toothpicks, skewer the neck skin to the back of the turkey to create a pretty effect. Pull the legs upright toward the breast and then tie the ends together with heavy cord or with wire twist.

Setting Up the Grill: Make a drip pan using an aluminum foil pan that is larger than the turkey so that all the drippings from the bird will go into the pan and not onto the coals. Set the pan on the shelf or grate designed to hold the charcoal. Fill the drip pan with water, or wine or beer or a mixture of the liquids. You will have to refill the pan with liquid several times during the baking.

Pile 15 to 20 briquettes on each side of the pan (see "Grilling Is Hot" on page 192). Ignite the charcoal. Leave the lid off and allow the coals to burn until they are ashy and glowing. This normally takes about 25 minutes. You'll have to add more charcoal as the turkey cooks.

Drain the wood chips or chunks. When the coals are glowing, place 1 cup of wood chips or 1 wood chunk on top of the coals on both sides of the drip pan, reserving the rest of the wood to add as the turkey bakes.

Oil the cooking grill and place in position. Place the turkey, breast side up, on the grill, directly over the drip pan. Cover the grill with its lid.

Cooking the Turkey: Brush the turkey every hour with some of the remaining oil and wine or beer as it cooks. A 10- to 12-ppound turkey should cook in 4 to 5 hours. The exact cooking time will be determined by the intensity of the fire and the shape and size of the covered grill.

However, the best way to test for doneness is with an instant-read thermometer. At the end of 3½ hours, insert the thermometer into the fleshiest part of the thigh. If the thermometer reads 180 degrees and the juices run clear when a skewer is inserted in the leg, the turkey is done.

If the turkey isn't quite done, baste and continue cooking for 30 minutes more and then test again. Watch carefully at this point, and don't overcook the turkey. Continue basting and checking for doneness every 20 minutes.

Stoking the Heat: For this type of indirect grilling, briquettes have to be added at least every hour, and the number depends on the size of the grill. For a grill that is 22-inch size, add from 5 to 8 briquettes on each side of the drip pan every hour, plus a handful of water-soaked wood chips or 1 wood chunk per side. If you want a stronger smoke flavor you can use a larger amount of wood.

Keep the Water Flowing: Be sure to keep the water pan full. It is the vapors, smoke, and spices that give smoked foods such a wonderful taste. So for a large turkey, you will have to add water to the pan several times. If you want to impart additional flavor, add wine, beer, or liqueur to the drip pan, as well as lemon peel, avocado twigs, grape vines, whole garlic cloves, and spices and herbs.

Once the turkey is golden brown, done, and smoky with flavor, and registers 180 degrees on the thermometer, remove the wire twist or twine, let the bird stand for 15 to 20 minutes, and then carve for serving.

OTHER BIRDS OF A FEATHER

When I sit down to dinner at the home of black churchfolks I know that a lot of thought, time, effort, and expense have gone into the meal, so I am not surprised if I am served stewed pheasant or Cornish hens stuffed with wild rice. These birds, along with quail, ducks, pheasants, guinea hens, capons, and geese, have also become very popular over the past two decades, and like chicken and turkey, they are available year round.

These "other birds" add an elegant and festive note to the meal, and they pretty much can be roasted like chicken or turkey, with adjustments made for size and fat content.

Specifically, ducks and geese are fatty birds and as much of this fat as possible should be removed, either before or during the roasting. To do so, slash the skin of the duck or goose all over, taking care not to pierce the flesh. Place the birds on a rack and set in a deep roasting pan so that the fat drips to the bottom of the pan as the birds bake. (It is also advisable to remove the birds from the oven and carefully drain off the oil during the baking to prevent grease splatters and fires.)

On the other hand, capons and Cornish hens, like turkey, have a low-fat content, and they need to be oiled generously and basted frequently during baking.

Similarly, I find it almost impossible to roast a pheasant even when the bird is the same size and looks almost like a chicken. Pheasants have a lot of tendons, and these birds dry out quite quickly during roasting because they are so lean. That's the reason why French chefs often insert strips of lard into pheasants to make them tender. Many Southern cooks tenderize pheasants by baking them topped with strips of salt pork or bacon. Guinea hens are easier to cook than pheasants, and in fact, have more flavor and darker meat. I cut a guinea hen into serving pieces, season with herbs and garlic, brown in a heavy skillet, and then transfer to a roasting pan, drizzle generously with olive oil plus a little white wine or beer, cover loosely with foil, and bake at 350 degrees until fork-tender. This generally takes an hour or so, and the meat doesn't dry out so much.

Quail can weigh 4 ounces or so, cook in a flash, and can be pan sautéed, broiled, baked, or smothered. And they, too, are bone-sucking delicious as are Cornish hens.

Marion Wells, who helped compile a collection of recipes at the West Hunter Street Baptist Church in Atlanta, sends this zesty and herbaceous recipe for Cornish hens.

LEMON=HERBED CORNISH HENS

Serves 4

4 small Cornish hens, about
    1½ pounds each
1½ teaspoons salt
½ teaspoon freshly ground black
    pepper
3 or 4 sprigs thyme, or ¾ teaspoon
    dried

1 teaspoon finely chopped
    rosemary, or ½ teaspoon dried
2 cloves garlic
½ cup butter or margarine
¼ cup lemon juice
1 tablespoon chopped parsley

Preheat the oven to 350 degrees.

Oil a 9 × 13-inch roasting pan and set aside. Remove the innards from the hens, rinse, and freeze to use later for a chicken broth or stock.

Rinse the hens well under cold running water. Drain and pat dry with paper towels. Tuck the wings under the breast, and if desired, pull the neck skin over the back and secure with rounded toothpicks. Sprinkle the hens inside and out with salt and black pepper. Pull the legs upright and tie with string or with a metal twist. Set aside.

Chop the fresh thyme and rosemary or crush the dried herbs. Mince the garlic.

In a small saucepan, combine the herbs, garlic, butter or margarine, lemon juice, and parsley.

Heat over low heat for 2 to 3 minutes to blend flavor. Remove the sauce immediately from heat. Brush the hens generously with the sauce.

Place the hens in the roasting pan breast side down. Set the pan on the lower shelf and bake uncovered for 15 minutes.

Turn the hens over, breast side up, and bake for 45 to 50 minutes, basting occasionally with the pan drippings and the remaining lemon sauce, or until the thighs move easily when twisted and the juices run clear when pierced with a fork.

Remove the birds from the oven and let set in a warm place for a few minutes. Remove the string or wire twist.

Serve the hens on a warm platter with the pan juices.

WELL-TRIMMED MEATS

When I was a child we used meat to boost flavor and not just as the centerpiece of our meal. Turnip, mustard, and collards greens glistened with a few slivers of ham hocks, and so did crowder peas and butter beans. A meaty ham bone was simmered with potatoes and green beans or with tomatoes,

rice, corn, and okra for delicious stews. Mama cooked neck bones laced with plenty of black pepper, onions, and rice and I thought I was eating manna from heaven. When we were treated to meatloaf and hamburgers or baked ham or pork chops, the plate also brimmed with rice or green beans mixed with white potatoes, cornbread, sautéed squash or sweet potatoes, stewed tomatoes and okra, and the serving of meat was far from deluxe in size. Sitting down to a pound-size portion of steak was unheard of for us.

At breakfast we ate a small link sausage or a slice or two of bacon or a few slivers of ham, along with biscuits or flapjacks, grits or home-fried potatoes, and then my brothers would set out for a full day of work. We ate chitterlings mostly at hog-killing time, and that was only once a year. Barbecue and open-fire grilled meats were reserved for family gatherings and special occasions.

Our inventive cooking style was shaped by necessity, and we were eating this way long before the words "cholesterol" and "saturated fat" slipped into common usage. Hypertension and heart diseases are linked with diets high in saturated fat, and salt and beef and smoked pork have been named among the main culprits. Pork also suffers the sting of the country's growing number of African-American Muslims, whose religion forbids the eating of this meat.

Truth is, both beef and pork are good sources of nutrients. Beef provides blood-building iron, while pork, which is actually a white meat and if trimmed of fat is no higher in calories than chicken, is a good source of the B-vitamin complex. Both beef and pork provide good sources of protein.

I have always felt that moderation is the key to sensible eating and drinking. If you decide to make meat a part of your diet, consider eating it every other day or no more than twice weekly, and then cut down on the amount you eat. Take a page from our forebears' history and make meat go a long way. Lillie Sherfield has been doing this for years.

Lillie lives in Rochester, New York, and is a member of the Antioch Baptist Church. Prior to a recent disability, she was a member of the

church's Mission Society and also worked on the Kitchen Committee, which cooks for funeral repasts, fellowship gatherings, and an annual gala dinner for senior citizens.

She was employed as a housekeeper for a number of years, and she is among those who care passionately about food. When we talk, our conversation almost reaches a crescendo as we exchange food techniques, how-to tips, anecdotes, food history, and recipe development, happy to be able to share such information with another enthusiast. She has a collection of more than one hundred cookbooks and innumerable recipes clipped from newspapers and magazines. So it's not unusual that during the Thanksgiving and Christmas holidays she makes twenty to thirty cakes for church friends and relatives.

"I love to cook," she says emphatically. "I love to experiment, and most of all I love to see people enjoy my food."

Lillie sends a recipe for oxtail stew that her grandmother carried out to church when she was a little girl and visited her family's hometown of Mason, Tennessee, which is near Memphis. Lillie's sister, Jerlene Sherfield, still lives in Tennessee, and she heads the Kitchen Committee at the Cedar Grove Missionary Baptist Church, the family's homechurch. The two sisters often swap recipes, especially ones that reflect family and church history.

Some years ago Jerlene sent Lillie their grandmother's recipe for oxtail and Lillie passed it on again.

"I made this recipe one day years ago during a snow storm when we didn't have much in the kitchen to cook," Lillie recalls. "I must have cooked it a hundred times since then and everybody loves it."

No wonder, this is finger-lickin' soul food.

COUNTRY OXTAIL STEW

Serves 4

4½ to 5 pounds oxtail
1 tablespoon vegetable oil
2 onions
1 tablespoon paprika
2 tablespoons flour
3 cups water or beef broth
2 cups coarsely chopped tomatoes, fresh or canned

1½ teaspoons salt
½ teaspoon freshly ground black pepper
½ teaspoon hot pepper flakes (more if desired)
½ pound fresh okra, or 1 package (10 ounce) frozen okra

Rinse the oxtail well with cold water. Dry with paper towels and cut into 2-inch pieces. Trim off any excess fat and discard.

Heat the oil in a large heavy pot. Add 2 or 3 pieces of oxtail and brown over medium-high heat for about 5 minutes, turning occasionally. Remove the meat from the pan when browned and cook the remaining meat in the same way, removing when done.

Slice the onions and add to the pot, along with the paprika and flour. Sauté over low heat for 5 minutes, stirring.

Return the beef to the pot. Add the water or beef broth, tomatoes, salt, black pepper, and hot pepper flakes. Bring to a boil and cook, covered, for 5 minutes.

Reduce the heat to very low and simmer for 4 hours or until the oxtail are tender. Stir in the okra and simmer, covered, 30 minutes longer or until the okra is tender.

Serve over hot rice or white potatoes or noodles.

BEEF DAUBE

*a*lbert Stevenson remembers that years ago there were food days in his hometown of New Orleans. On Mondays many of the African-American women simmered a pot of red beans all day while doing the laundry. Fried chicken was served on Sundays. During the week, usually on Wednesdays, many families simmered a slab of beef and sometimes pork, which was referred to as "daube."

The dish takes it name from the French word *dauber*, which means to braise, and it shows the many culinary influences of the Crescent City.

Mr. Stevenson is involved in numerous activities at the Mount Zion United Methodist Church in New Orleans, from flea markets to cooking contests, and he is just as adept at cooking beef daube as red beans and rice.

He sends this savory and delicious recipe:

1 beef brisket, about 3 to 3½ pounds	2 tablespoons flour
1 large onion	2 tablespoons vegetable oil
3 shallots	3 or 4 thyme sprigs, or ¾ teaspoon dried thyme
2 cloves garlic	1 bay leaf
½ teaspoon salt	1 cup water
¾ teaspoon black pepper	1 cup beef broth

If necessary, cut away excess fat from the beef brisket. Chop the onion and shallots. Mince the garlic. Sprinkle the meat all over with the salt and pepper, and then with the flour.

Heat the oil in a heavy pot with cover. Add the beef and over medium-high heat quickly brown all over, turning often.

Reduce the heat to low, push the beef to one side of the pan, and add the onion, shallots, and garlic. Chop the fresh thyme or crush the dried herb and add to the pot. Sauté for 5 minutes or until the onions are soft and translucent.

Add the bay leaf and the water and beef broth. Bring the pot to a boil and then reduce heat to very low.

Simmer the meat for 2½ to 3 hours or until the brisket is tender, turning the meat several times during the cooking and basting often with the pan juices so that the top of the meat stays moist. (The cooking time will vary depending on the meat, but watch carefully and don't overcook or the meat will become dry. Brisket is always chewy, not fork-tender.)

To thicken the gravy, remove the brisket and keep warm. Cook the liquid in the pan uncovered over high heat for 15 minutes, or until reduced in volume and heavier in consistency.

At serving, using a sharp knife, cut the meat into slices, place on a warm platter, and serve with the pan gravy and, of course, rice.

CURRIED BEEF STEW

*t*essa Emmanuel lives in Hackensack, New Jersey, a long way from her native Belize in Central America. Whenever she is asked to bring out a covered dish to the Mount Olive Baptist Church, located on Central Avenue, she cooks something that reminds her of home.

This savory stew is cooked in a silky curry sauce and is as delightful as a sunny Caribbean day.

4 pounds beef shanks
1 onion
2 to 3 cloves garlic
2 tablespoons vegetable oil
1 teaspoon salt
½ teaspoon freshly ground
*   black pepper*

2 tablespoons curry powder
1 cup beef broth
1 cup beer or water (more if
*   needed)*
1 medium white all-purpose potato

Cut the meat off of the shanks and into 2-inch pieces, saving the bones. Slice the onion and mince the garlic.

Heat the oil in a large pot. Add the beef, a few pieces at a time so as not to crowd, and brown over medium-high heat for 4 or 5 minutes. As each batch is finished, remove it to a platter, sprinkle with salt and pepper, and set aside.

In the meantime, reduce the heat to low and add the onion and garlic to the pan. Sauté for 3 or 4 minutes.

Stir in the curry powder. Return both the beef and bones to the pot. Add the beef broth and the beer or water. Bring to a boil, cover, reduce the heat and cook over very low heat for 1 hour.

Peel and dice the potato and stir into the pot. Cover and simmer for 1 hour longer or until the meat and potatoes are tender and the beef broth is slightly thickened. Remove the bones and discard before serving.

Serve with rice.

Saturday-Evening Beef Stew

Serves 4 to 5

arion Wells sends this recipe from the cache she collected from members of the West Hunter Street Baptist Church in Atlanta, Georgia. Mrs. Wells says it's the favorite recipe of church member Mary Wyche.

It's also a delightful hearty stew:

3 pounds beef short ribs

2 onions

1 green or red pepper

1½ teaspoon dried rosemary

1½ teaspoons salt

½ teaspoon freshly ground
   black pepper

2 to 3 teaspoons paprika

2 to 3 tablespoons flour

2 tablespoons bacon drippings
   or vegetable oil

1 cup beef broth

2 cups water

4 small potatoes

3 carrots

Select lean short ribs and cut them or ask the butcher to cut into 2½-inch pieces. Trim any excess fat from the beef ribs and discard.

Set aside.

Chop the onions; core and dice the green or red pepper; crush the rosemary.

Sprinkle the meat with the salt, black pepper, and paprika. Dust the meat lightly with the flour, shaking off any excess.

In a large heavy saucepan or pot, heat the bacon drippings or oil.

Add a few pieces of ribs at a time to the pot and brown the meat on all sides. Remove the meat from the pan when browned and add the remaining pieces, browning in the same way.

Pour off all of the oil in the pot. Return the beef back to the pot. Add the onions, green or red pepper, and rosemary and sauté, stirring, over medium heat for 4 to 5 minutes.

Add the beef broth and water. Cover and bring to a boil. Reduce the heat to low and simmer for 2 hours, or until the ribs are just tender.

THE TENDER AND TOUGH SIDE OF MEAT

Both beef and pork can be braised, broiled, sautéed, fried, baked, grilled, or barbecued, and to a large extent, the cut of meat determines the most suitable cooking method. Generally speaking, the part of the animal that gets the most exercise has the most muscles and therefore yields a tougher cut of meat.

For example, meat cut from the legs, shoulder, rump, neck, and flank has a lot of gristle, tendons, and muscles, and that's the reason our grandmothers simmered ham hocks, beef shanks, short ribs, and neck bones for half the day. These are the less-expensive cuts of meat, and they are delicious in stews and soups and for seasoning peas and beans and greens.

On the other hand, meat from the loin section, which is near the back, can be almost buttery tender, and you pay premium price for this quick-cooking meat. A tenderloin of beef or pork loin can be baked or roasted, or cut into chops or filets, and then sautéed, broiled, or grilled in a matter of minutes.

However, there are dozens of cuts of meat, and the key to cooking one right is to find a good supermarket or butcher, and always know how you plan to cook the meat before you buy it.

Meanwhile, peel the potatoes and cut into eighths. Scrape the carrots and cut into ½-inch chunks.

Add the potatoes and carrots to the pot and simmer for 1 hour longer or until the vegetables are done and the meat is fork-tender.

Serve the stew over hot, fluffy rice or noodles.

Neat Meatloaf

*b*arbara Boller is the organist at the Our Lady Queen of Peace Catholic Church in Arlington, Virginia, and she sends a very harmonious recipe for good old-fashioned meatloaf.

Our Lady Queen of Peace is a vibrant church, and every Sunday families from far and near gather there for a breakfast that consists of scrambled eggs, pancakes, bacon, juice, and coffee or tea, and the tab is two dollars, plus 25 cents for the coffee.

Eileen Melia, who handles correspondence for the church, sends a recipe that Barbara often brings out to the church's many social events, along with these words:

"Many of the families who come here for service and breakfast on Sundays no longer live in the community," writes Eileen. "Some of the families come from Washington; others from way down in Virginia. Although we have an international congregation now, we try to retain our black history."

This is Barbara's recipe:

1 large onion
2 stalks celery
1½ pounds lean ground beef
½ pound ground pork or veal
1 egg, beaten
1 tablespoon Worcestershire sauce
1 teaspoon salt
¼ teaspoon freshly ground
   black pepper

1 cup soft bread crumbs (from
   leftover bread)
2 tablespoons spicy mustard
4 tablespoons dark molasses (more
   if desired)
1 cup ketchup

Preheat the oven to 325 degrees.

Oil a shallow roasting pan or casserole and set aside.

Chop the onion and the celery. Combine in a large bowl with the ground beef, ground pork or veal, egg, Worcestershire sauce, salt, and pepper.

Stir in the bread crumbs and mix until the mixture is well blended. Form the mixture into a loaf, patting firmly so that the loaf keeps its shape. Place the loaf in the oiled pan.

Mix together in a small bowl the mustard, molasses, and ketchup. Beat until blended. Pour about half of the sauce over the meatloaf. Bake the meatloaf in the hot oven for 1 hour and 15 minutes or until set and the juices run clear, basting occasionally with the remaining sauce.

Let the meatloaf set for a few minutes in a warm place, and then transfer to a warm platter. If the meatloaf is to be served later, reheat in a microwave or in a hot oven set at 300 degrees for 15 to 20 minutes.

The Men's Club Chili

Serves 4 to 6

On the second Saturday in February, William Graham makes the chili, cooks the rice, and bakes a pound cake for the monthly meeting of the Metropolitan Men's Club, which was formed by his church some twenty-five years ago. His assigned cooking partner prepares a salad, buys the bread, orders the beer and soda, and by 6 P.M. most of the twenty-two club members are huddled around a table at the Runyon Heights Community Center in Yonkers, New York.

This soiree is something of a respite for Mr. Graham, who is the treasurer at the Metropolitan African Methodist Episcopal Zion Church, and keeps a busy calendar of community and church concerns. He is also on the Board of Stewards of the Hudson River District Lay Council, which oversees twenty-two churches, and he is the treasurer of the Runyon Heights Club, a civic group.

"I treasure my volunteer work," says Mr. Graham. "It is an integral part of my life. I stress it, and so does my wife, Gloria, and my daughter, Tiffany.".

Mr. Graham also likes to cook, and whenever it is his turn to prepare the meal for the Men's Club meeting, he stirs, fusses over, and simmers his chili for the best part of the day. Then he packs up his offering and heads for the community center. Shortly after arriving at the center, the men discuss community and church issues and then open up their wallets and take up a collection for two beneficiaries: From September to June, the club donates one hundred dollars monthly to the Metropolitan A.M.E. Zion Church, located on Belnap Avenue in Yonkers, to help pay for heating fuel; at the end of the year the group also awards a five-hundred-dollar college scholarship to a needy local student.

After the business matters are resolved, the men, who range in age from twenty-five to sixty-five, sit back and enjoy their fine meal and one anothers' company.

"Runyon Heights is one of the safest neighborhoods in Westchester County," says Mr. Graham, who is a supervisor for the New York City

Department of Juvenile Justice. "We have the lowest incidence of juvenile crime and the lowest incidence of dope crime in the county. And our church is the center of this community; supported by families who have been members for generations. People don't usually leave Runyon Heights, they die here."

Mr. Graham sends this warming recipe for wintertime chili:

1 onion
1 green pepper
3 cloves garlic
1 or 2 hot chili peppers
3 or 4 sprigs oregano, or 1 teaspoon dried oregano
2 tablespoons vegetable oil
2 pounds lean ground chuck
2 teaspoons ground cumin
2 to 3 tablespoons chili powder

½ teaspoon freshly ground black pepper
1½ teaspoons salt
2 tablespoons soy sauce
1 cup water or beer (more if needed)
1 can (28 ounces) plum tomatoes, undrained
2 cups cooked red beans (see "Counting Peas and Beans" on page 95)

Chop the onion; core and dice the green pepper; mince the garlic and the chilies. Chop the oregano or crush the dried herb and set aside.

Heat the oil in a large heavy pot. Add the ground beef and brown quickly over high heat, stirring to brown evenly.

Using a slotted spoon, remove the meat from the pan, leaving the juices in the pan. Reduce the heat to low, and stir in the onion, green pepper, garlic, chilies, and oregano. Sauté 4 or 5 minutes or until the onions are translucent.

Stir in the cumin, chili powder, black pepper, and salt. Sauté the spices over low heat for 2 minutes, stirring well.

Add the soy sauce, water or beer, and the undrained tomatoes. Bring to a boil and cook briskly for 5 minutes, using a fork to break the tomatoes into small pieces.

Reduce the heat to very low and stir in the beef. Cover and simmer for 1½ to 2 hours. (If the chili sauce becomes too thick, stir in a little more water or beer.)

Add the cooked beans and simmer for 1 hour longer, stirring occasionally. Let the chili sit at least 30 minutes, or preferably overnight, before serving.

At serving, reheat if necessary and serve over white or brown steamed rice.

The recipe can easily be doubled or tripled for a crowd.

Variation: One pound of ground turkey or chicken can be substituted for 1 pound of the beef. And Mr. Graham says that he often cooks the chili in a crock and lets it simmer for 5 or 6 hours, especially if he has to go out on church business.

Members of the Sons of Allen Club barbecue and sell spareribs on Super Bowl Saturday to raise funds for the Mount Moriah African Methodist Episcopal Church in Annapolis, Maryland. At the grill, left to right: Nathaniel Williams, Vance Wallace and John Harris, Jr.

HOG-KILLING TIME

By 10 A.M. there were far more hands available to help than were actually needed to slaughter the hogs, but this was usually near Christmas in the dead of winter and families wanted to have plenty of food in the house during the holidays. So Daddy put everybody to work who came out, and they went home late that evening with a bundle of fresh meat. In those days most of the black families in our town were seasonal workers, and there was little for the loggers, lumberjacks, sharecroppers, farmers, cotton millers. or ice makers to do in freezing-cold weather but help one another, and they were paid in goods in return for their services. But even with plenty of hands available, hog killing was still a lot of work, considering that a pig easily weighed 350 to 400 pounds.

Daddy said that it was too much trouble to slaughter a hog more than once a year, so he almost always killed two at a time. The hogs were slaughtered, hung on a scaffold or from a tree limb to drain, then washed, scrubbed, singed, gutted, and washed again. A roaring fire was set, and while the men waited to work they warmed themselves by the fire, pulling up their collars against the piercing cold, which was needed to keep the pork from spoiling. Plus, Daddy said that the cold set the meat and made it easier to cut.

I used to watch, spellbound by the rituals, which had the seriousness of surgery yet the animation of a festival. I realize now that the meat for our family for the next twelve months was on the line. Now and then a serious look would cross Daddy's jovial face as he hurried the men to get the pork cut up and into the salt boxes as quickly as possible.

With practiced skill, Mr. Shine, Mr. Pete, Mr. Oscar, and Daddy would slash the slab of fat from across the hog's back. The skin was removed and the fat was thrown into two big cast-iron pots that had been set on the fire. The white fat soon rendered under the intense heat, and when it was bubbling hot and liquid, Mama would cut up the skin into pieces and drop it into the hot oil to make crisp cracklings. The oil was cooled and poured into large cans for lard. The cracklings were passed out to the workers, along with a couple pans of hot cornbread, roasted sweet

Well-Trimmed Meats

potatoes, and a can of molasses that Daddy had earned from helping Mr. Ras, who owned the sugarcane mill.

The tempo of the work picked up. Spareribs were cut from under the rib cage, hams from the rear rump, roasts and chops from the section between the ribs and back, meat for sausages and butts for roasting from the shoulder, bacon from the underbelly. Once this prime meat was cut, it was washed and drained and laid out to air dry, and the men seemed to relax a little bit. They told stories and cracked jokes and then turned their attention to every remaining inch and ounce of the pig: feet, snout, jowls, head, tongue, tail, liver, ears, kidneys, brains, and the intestines. This meat was not smoked but was eaten by the family over the next several days and shared with neighbors and the men who helped out.

The rest of the meat was smoked. Mama had already washed and scalded the hickory boxes that were used to salt the meat before it was smoked. I loved the feel of salt sinking through my fingers, and I was allowed to scatter handfuls of the coarse grains into the boxes, and I made sure that I completely covered the bottom of the boxes as Daddy had instructed. The men then placed the meat into the boxes, sprinkled on more salt, added another layer of meat, and continued that way until the box was full. The boxes of salted meat were hauled into our smokehouse and kept in the salt for the next two to three weeks.

Once Daddy decided that the "salt had took" and the pork was preserved, the meat was taken out of the boxes, soaked in cold water to remove some of the excess salt, and hung up for smoking. Daddy used hickory and pecan wood for smoking; some other families used oak. The meat was smoked for four or five days, but a herbaceous, woody aroma wafted across our backyard long after the pork picked up a reddish brown patina and a glistening sheen.

Memories of my family's hog killing came to mind the other day when a recipe for roast pork arrived from James Powell, who grew up in hog-raising Henderson County, Kentucky, which is near the Indiana border, separated by the Ohio River.

When I talked to Jim we had so many similar anecdotes to exchange

and share that I thought for a moment that he had mixed up his geography and actually had grown up in Choctaw County in Alabama. We talked about all the little arcane minutia of hog killing: types of wood used for smoking and for the salt boxes, the best way to hoist the pig for draining, how long the hog was smoked, the name and position of various cuts of pork.

As we crisscrossed into each others' thoughts, we were both struck by the similarities that existed years ago in the two far-apart counties: the black community was isolated in those days, and we looked to each other for our support system and services.

"Our world was smaller back then," recalls Mr. Powell. "The black church and school was the center of our lives and everything radiated from that. We helped at hog-killing time, we helped in the tobacco fields, we helped each other when we were sick, and everybody returned the same favor. Our world was limited to each other. In those days we didn't have a television in every household to show us how the rest of the world lived."

Jim grew up a member of the Saint Paul's Missionary Baptist Church, which was in Henderson County, Kentucky, went off to college to Xavier University in New Orleans, and in 1958 converted to Catholicism. Today he lives with his wife, Lucy, in Arlington, Virginia, and is a member of the Our Lady Queen of Peace Catholic Church, which was founded in 1945 by a group of black parishioners. The church is known for its spirited services and social gatherings, attended by the increasing number of immigrants who come primarily from Africa, the West Indies, and Latin America.

Jim wears many hats at Our Lady Queen of Peace Church and all of his work is volunteer. He is the church's official photographer and plant supervisor, and in the later position he oversees church landscaping and contracts for everything from roof to boiler repairs, and in many cases, Jim steps in and helps to do the work himself.

"I see my work with the church as giving something back to the community," says Jim, who retired a few years ago as a high school

Well-Trimmed Meats

teacher and administrator for the Fairfax County public school system. "I've been blessed."

Jim sends this recipe for roast pork, which is his favorite offering at the church's numerous potluck dinners:

ROAST PORK

Serves 6

1 pork rib roast, about 4 pounds
1 teaspoon dried sage
1 cayenne pepper, or ¼ to ½
   teaspoon cayenne
1 teaspoon salt
½ teaspoon freshly ground
   black pepper

½ cup cider vinegar
2 bay leaves
6 cloves
1 teaspoon dry mustard, or
   1 tablespoon prepared mustard
2 to 4 tablespoons brown sugar

Preheat the oven to 325 degrees.

If necessary, trim off excess fat but leave an ⅛-inch layer of exterior fat on the roast so that the meat doesn't dry out during the baking. Lightly score the meat with a sharp knife, making shallow slashes about 2 inches apart.

Crush the sage and if using the fresh cayenne, finely mince the pod. Rub the pork all over with the sage, cayenne, salt, and black pepper.

Place the pork into a shallow roasting pan and bake in the hot oven for 20 minutes.

Meanwhile, in a small pan, combine the vinegar, bay leaves, cloves, mustard, and brown sugar. Heat over a low flame for 2 or 3 minutes, stirring to combine and to melt the sugar.

Remove the sauce immediately from the heat.

Pour some of the sauce over the pork and roast for 1½ hours, basting every 20 minutes or so with a little of the sauce.

At the end of the cooking period, remove the pan from the oven. Insert an instant-read meat thermometer into the roast and check to see if the temperature reads 170. If so, the pork is done.

If not, continue cooking for another 20 minutes. When fully cooked and the pork is golden brown and its juices run clear, removed the roast from the oven.

Let stand in a warm place for 15 minutes and then cut into ribs for serving. Serve with the pan juices.

John Harris, Jr., keeping a keen eye on the ribs during Super Bowl Saturday at Mount Moriah African Methodist Episcopal Church, Annapolis, Maryland.

Well-Trimmed Meats

Rum-Glazed Spareribs

Serves 4

renda Brooks has been taking cooking classes and entering cooking contests since junior high school, so she likes her food to make a visual statement. On a recent Christmas morning she fussed with the frosting on a chocolate cake and went rummaging through her home in Washington, D.C., searching for the pretty floral napkins that she thought she had bought the week before. She then got out six serving trays and a half dozen nice boxes and packed up the food she had cooked: fried chicken, spareribs, macaroni and cheese, hash brown potatoes, green beans, and biscuits. She then gingerly placed the chocolate cake, pound cake, and brownies into the boxes, and got ready to make her rounds.

By midday, her boxes in hand, she was visiting the homes of six homebound senior citizens, who were treated to a Christmas dinner, courtesy of Ms. Brooks and her church, the Incarnation Catholic Church on Eastern Avenue.

"I give them enough food for two meals," Brenda says. "This is something I enjoy doing. Whenever the church asks for volunteers, I always sign up. I love to cook; at age five I was making yeast bread from scratch. And it is a treat for me to help these senior citizens have a nice holiday."

She sends this heady recipe for spareribs that are basted with dark rum, pineapple juice, and spices:

1 slab of meaty pork spareribs,
  3 ½ to 4 pounds
1½ teaspoons salt
1 teaspoon freshly ground
  black pepper
2 to 3 cloves garlic

1 teaspoon allspice
1 teaspoon dry mustard
¼ cup lemon juice
2 cups pineapple juice
¾ cup dark brown sugar
1 cup dark rum

Preheat the oven to 325 degrees.

Trim off all visible fat from the spareribs and discard. Sprinkle the ribs with the salt and black pepper.

Mince the garlic. Rub the ribs all over with the garlic, allspice, and mustard.

Combine in a small saucepan the lemon juice, 1 cup of the pineapple juice, ½ cup of the brown sugar, and the rum. Heat over low flame for 1 to 2 minutes, stirring until the mixture is well blended.

Lay the ribs flat in a large roasting pan. Pour over the rum sauce. Cover the pan with a lid or with a layer of heavy-duty aluminum foil, sealing the edges. Bake for 1 hour, turning once or twice, basting with the pan juices.

Remove the foil or lid. Bake the spareribs, uncovered, for 30 to 40 minutes, turning occasionally, or until the ribs are browned and tender.

When done, remove the pan from the oven. Place the ribs on a serving platter and keep warm.

Set the roasting pan on the burner. Stir in the remaining ¼ cup sugar and 1 cup pineapple juice. Bring to a boil, scraping bits in the pan. Reduce the heat to low, add the ribs to pan, and ladle the sauce all over. Heat for 4 or 5 minutes, completely covering the ribs with the sauce.

Place the ribs back on the serving platter and pour over the sauce.

Pot luck for the Feast of the Epiphany at Our Lady Queen of Peace Catholic Church in Arlington, Virginia.

Well-Trimmed Meats

Love-Glazed Ham

Serves 10 to 12

f necessity is the mother of invention, then let us all give due praise to Brenda Jones, whose inventiveness created the love feasts that have become a way of life at the Bronx Christian Charismatic Prayer Fellowship, a church located in New York's South Bronx.

The church, which occupies two storefronts on Third Avenue, is headed by the Reverend Jerome Alexander Greene, and his wife, Assemblywoman Aureila Greene, both longtime community activists. The Reverend and Mrs. Greene started the church in the early 1980s in their living room, and today it has more than 120 members, including Brenda Jones and four grandchildren she is raising.

Mrs. Jones says that a few years ago she realized that by the evening service on Sundays, her children were always hungry, even when she thought she had packed enough food to last all day. Services at the church on Sunday run from early morning to after 8 P.M.

"I didn't have money to go out and buy fast food for the children's dinner," recalls Mrs. Jones, "so I started fixing a bit for them in the church kitchen. Then somebody noticed me cooking and brought in a little food and asked me to cook it. Eventually during services on Friday nights some of the members began chipping in five dollars each to buy food for me to cook for the Sunday dinner. That was how we got started.

"I usually cook the food at home and heat it up at the church. We have a big stove, microwave, and refrigerator. I make fried chicken, baked ham, meatloaf, greens, pepper steak, mashed potatoes, rice, yams, string beans, cornbread, roast turkey, whatever. The church picks up the food from my apartment, which is in Harlem. I am physically unable to work, don't have much money, but this is a way I give back to the church in tithing.

"We have a wonderful time here. Sometimes other people pitch in and bring a dish from home. Another church member, Sister Ceciley Bland, does the baking. She loves to make cakes and pies. Another church member has a catering business and helps out. We started calling our dinners our 'love feasts.' I love them and I love my church."

Mrs. Jones send this lovely recipe for baked ham:

1 half smoked ham (6 to 8
pounds), butt or shank
Whole cloves
2 cups water

2 cups pineapple juice
½ cup brown sugar (more if
desired)

Preheat the oven to 350 degrees.

Trim off excess fat from the ham but leave a thin layer of fat, about ⅛-inch thick, so that the meat doesn't dry out during baking. Stud the ham with about 1 dozen cloves.

Place the ham, fat side up, in a large roasting pan, preferably one with a cover. Pour in the water. Cover the pan with the lid or with heavy-duty aluminum foil, sealing the edges well.

Place in the hot oven on the lower shelf and bake for 45 minutes. Turn the ham over, reseal, and bake 45 minutes longer or until the ham is tender.

Remove the ham from the oven and drain off the water in the pan. Pour ½ cup pineapple juice over the ham. Place the ham back in the oven and bake, uncovered for 20 minutes.

Meanwhile, prepare the glaze: Combine in a medium saucepan the remaining 1½ cup pineapple juice and the sugar. Bring to a boil, stirring, and then reduce the heat to low and simmer for 10 minutes.

Pour the glaze over the ham and bake for 40 to 45 minutes, basting occasionally with the sauce in the pan, or until the ham is golden and glazed.

The ham is done when an instant-read thermometer inserted in the thickest part of the meat registers 170 degrees.

Allow the ham to rest for 15 or so minutes, and slice thinly.

Well-Trimmed Meats

SMOTHERED PORK CHOPS

Serves 6

*t*he fact that LaVinia Hairston lives in Buffalo, New York, and her church, the Grace Presbyterian Church, is located in Martinsville, Virginia, doesn't faze her the least. She has worked out the logistics of this long-distance problem quite nicely, thank you.

LaVinia is a lawyer, and she keeps in contact with the church by writing a bimonthly book review for the church's newsletter, "Grace's Good News." During the summer she spends at least a month in Martinsville and attends numerous church services and functions. And during the rest of the year she is likely to visit Martinsville again, and of course, attend church. The church is located on Fayette Street.

"My family goes way back with that church," says LaVinia, thirty-nine, who was born and raised in Buffalo but spent summers in Martinsville. "My maternal great-grandfather, Jobie Kinley Sr., joined the church in the early 1880s, shortly after it was founded.

"My mother and father were married in the church. One of my aunts, Annie Bell King, has been a deaconess for more than twenty years. I just can't bring myself to join another church, although I do attend services at a local church here in Buffalo."

A few months ago LaVinia began creating a living memorial to her family and her church, which is historically all black. She gathered a cache of family photographs, some dating back to 1914, most of them depicting suppers, breakfasts, outings, weddings, receptions, and other celebrations at Grace Presbyterian. She had the photos imprinted on fabric squares, and then sat down and stitched them together for a quilt, just as women quilted years ago.

Other family members decided to donate to this project. Deaconess Annie Bell King sent her an original square from a quilt that had been made by her great-grandmother. Her mother, Mae King Hairston, gave her a crocheted doily that she had made years ago. "This quilt represents three generations of handiwork by the women in my family," says LaVinia. "Even though we are a very small family, the faith and spirit of the past generations live on through us. Over the last one hundred years, five generations of my family have worshipped at Grace Presbyterian. I have my quilt hanging on a wall in my home. It connects me to my family, my church, and my faith."

LaVinia sends this recipe for smothered pork chops that was passed on to her by Deaconess Annie Bell King, who says that the dish has been in the family so long she can't remember who was the first to take it out to Grace Presbyterian Church.

6 shoulder pork chops
1½ teaspoons salt
1½ teaspoons freshly ground
  black pepper
2 teaspoons paprika
1 cup milk
1 egg
1 cup flour
1 small green pepper
1 medium onion
½ stalk celery

1 clove garlic
¼ cup oil or bacon drippings
2 tablespoons cider vinegar
½ cup water or chicken broth
  or Homemade Chicken Stock
  (see recipe on page 234)
1 cup tomato sauce, either
  commercial or homemade
1 tablespoon mustard
1 tablespoon brown sugar

Trim any excess fat from the pork chops. Rub with the salt, black pepper, and paprika.

In a medium bowl, beat together the milk and eggs until well blended. Pour the flour into a plastic or brown bag.

Dip one pork chop at a time into the egg-milk mixture and coat all over with the batter. Then drop into the bag and shake the bag to coat the pork chop with the flour. Remove from the bag and dust off any excess flour. Coat the remaining pork chops the same way and set aside.

Core and dice the green pepper; chop the onion and celery; mince the garlic. Set aside.

Heat the oil or bacon drippings in a large heavy skillet that has a lid. Add two or three chops at a time and brown on both sides.

Remove from the skillet and brown the remaining chops in the same way, and then remove from the skillet.

Well-Trimmed Meats

Drain off all of the oil in the skillet except 2 tablespoons. Set the skillet back on the burner. Stir into the skillet the green pepper, onion, celery, and garlic. Sauté over medium-low heat for 5 minutes, stirring occasionally.

Add the cider vinegar, water or chicken broth, tomato sauce, mustard, and brown sugar. Bring to a boil, stirring.

Reduce heat to low and add the pork chops, scattering the vegetables on top of the meat. Cover and cook 35 to 40 minutes or until the pork chops are done and tender.

Serve with rice or mashed potatoes.

Chitterlings Deluxe

Serves 6

he coming Christmas holidays quickly eclipsed the excitement of the hog killing, and my family moved about with anticipation. Mama would bake at least four cakes and an equal number of pies. Daddy would buy several bags of nuts and fresh coconuts and we would sit around and shell the nuts, crack the coconuts, and eat the morsels and listen to his stories from the past. He could either make us shiver with tales of brutal lynchings or fire our imaginations for world travel as he talked about the days he had worked on the construction of the Golden Gate Bridge in some place named San Francisco. It was a strange place, he said, some white folks would even go up and jump off the bridge.

For Christmas dinner Mama roasted fresh pork and made cornbread dressing, potato salad, and greens. She'd pull out several jars of canned peas and beans and filled the house with the warming aroma of Chicken 'n' Dumplings, which was made with a big hen, since we seldom had turkey. She often would simmer the hen whole and then bake it in the oven with the cornbread, and that was our "turkey."

Whoever stopped by our house was greeted with the offerings from our table. We decorated the dimestore Christmas tree with ribbons, red and green crepe paper, shiny baubles, and silver icicles. We didn't have much money to buy presents, but for once during the year the ceaseless work of our household was put on hold and we thought of our own enjoyment, and that was our gift to ourselves and to one another.

Our holiday lasted until the New Year. In those days a midnight supper was often held at Shiloh Baptist Church after the night watch service to wish good fortune for the coming year. Since we had just slaughtered a hog, Mama carried out the chitterlings.

This was her recipe, which I have modified over the years:

10 pounds chitterlings
1¼ cup cider vinegar
2 onions
2 stalks celery
1 green pepper
3 cloves garlic
1 teaspoon dried oregano or thyme
½ teaspoon hot pepper flakes

2 bay leaves
2 teaspoons salt
¾ teaspoon freshly ground
   black pepper
1 cup apple juice or apple cider
1 to 2 cups water
1 unpeeled white potato

If using frozen chitterlings, defrost in the refrigerator overnight. If using fresh, empty by turning inside out.

Wash the chitterlings with warm water and then, using a small knife, scrape away as much of the lining and fat as possible and all of the feed left on the intestines. This is an arduous task and will take an hour or more to do. Rinse the chitterlings 4 or 5 more times with cold water.

When thoroughly cleaned and free of all debris, place the chitterlings in a pan and cover with cold water. Stir in 1 cup of the cider vinegar, mixing well. Let soak for at least 1 hour.

At the end of the soaking, drain the chitterlings and rinse again before cooking.

Slice the onions; chop the celery; core and dice the green pepper; and mince the garlic. Crush the oregano or thyme.

Place the chitterlings into a large pot. Add the onion, celery, green pepper, garlic, herb, hot pepper flakes, bay leaves, salt, black pepper, apple juice or apple cider, and 1 cup of the water.

Scrub the potato and add to the pot. (The potato will absorb the chitterlings' intense aroma.)

Bring to a boil. Cover and reduce the heat to very low. Simmer for 3 hours or until the chitterlings are tender, stirring occasionally, adding the remaining cup of water if needed.

Remove the potato and discard. Stir in the remaining ¼ cup vinegar and simmer for 20 to 30 minutes more.

Variation: To make deep-fried chitterlings, cook as directed above. Drain and dry well. Cut the chitterlings into 3-inch strips. Heat about

3 cups of oil in a deep heavy pot until a deep-frying thermometer reaches 375 degrees.

Meanwhile, pour 1 cup cornmeal (or flour) into a brown bag or plastic bag. Add the chitterling strips, shaking to coat with the cornmeal or flour.

Drop a handful of the strips into the hot oil and fry for 2 to 3 minutes, turning over with a large spoon or long-handled tongs. Remove from the oil, drain on paper towels, and continue frying the remaining chitterlings in the same way. Serve with lemon wedges, if desired.

Well-Trimmed Meats

SWEET TEMPTATIONS

Years ago in the South black families celebrated the Christmas holidays with fragrant cakes, succulent pies, and luscious puddings. Our other savory soul food was pushed to the corner, so to speak, as our inimitable way with sweet things took center stage. And our culinary creations were as rustic

Christmas dinner at St. Luke's Episcopal Church in Williamsbridge, Bronx, New York, circa 1950.

as blues and as improvisational as jazz.

Sweet potatoes were mashed and flavored and sweetened and turned into luscious pies. Peaches and berries canned during the summer harvest sparkled under flaky, golden crusts. Bananas were mixed with custard and vanilla wafers and baked into a pudding. Somebody always had on hand a jar of homebrewed fruit brandy and would give you a cup to sprinkle over the fruit cake or bread puddings.

Frosting and fillings and icings were made with homemade jams and jellies, as well as with nuts and fruits from trees growing in the backyard. Freshly made molasses was mixed with spices for gingerbread cake. Pecans and peanuts went into velvety fudge, shiny brittle, and too-rich pies. Not even the coldest day was too cold for homemade ice cream and a devil's food cake, especially if relatives were home for Christmas from "Up North," where they said Negroes invited you to their homes and gave you too much liquor, not enough food, and never a slice of cake or pie!

To this day, I can't think of anything I would rather do in the kitchen than bake a cake. I love the pastiche of fruits, nuts, butter, and flour;

the feel of the silky flour and of the voluptuous butter; the whipping and stirring; the suspenseful rising of the cake layers; the endless creations; and the fine-tune precision required for baking perfect cakes.

You can say a prayer, adjust the season, turn the heat either up or down, and a pot of greens or peas will more than likely end up all right. Cake making isn't quite so simple. Unlike a stew or soup, once a cake is in the oven baking, you can't take it out, place back into the bowl, and stir something else into the batter.

A baked cake that is light, tender, and even-grained—the signature of a fine cake, requires accurate measuring, correct mixing, and fresh, top-notch ingredients.

The eggs should be fresh, no more than three days old; the milk should be no more than a day old; and if the double-acting baking powder has been in the kitchen cabinet for more than three months, it should be thrown out and a fresh can bought.

For best results, assemble all the ingredients at least an hour before turning on the oven. This allows the butter or other shortening to soften and the eggs to warm to room temperature. If you are beating egg whites, allow at least two hours for the eggs to warm to room temperature. Set out the milk from the refrigerator when you begin mixing the cake.

Cakes can be made with either cake flour, all-purpose flour, or unbleached flour (see "Flour Types" on page 15) but each type of flour produces a cake with a different texture. For example, cakes made with cake flour are more finely grained and delicate than cakes made with unbleached flour, which are more crumbly.

Since all-purpose and unbleached flour absorb more liquid than cake flour, it is best to use the flour type specified in the recipe. And always sift the flour just before measuring.

When assembling the utensils, have available the cake pans specified in the recipe; standard measuring cups and spoons; a sifter; mixing bowls; mixer; long-handled wooden spoons; a rubber spatula; and a wire rack for cooling baked cakes.

Sweet Temptations

Butter and flour the cake pans as directed in the recipe, preheat the oven, and fill the cake pans no more than two-thirds full.

You are now ready to bake my sister's chocolate cake, which every member of Shiloh Baptist in Choctaw County in Alabama has eaten more than once over the years.

My sister is a devout and spirited churchwoman, and she was one of the founding members of Shiloh's Home Mission Club. Years ago I loved going to her house when the choir members came over to rehearse for Sunday service. She would think nothing of coming home from work—she was the cook at a local café—and, as she would say in her off-handed way, "throw together a cake."

Here is one of her recipes:

Judith Price, controller and president of its community enrichment center, sets the dessert table at Canaan Baptist Church in Harlem during a Black History Month celebration.

CHOCOLATE ICING CAKE

Makes one 3-layer cake; serves 8 to 10

3 cups cake flour
2½ teaspoons baking powder
⅛ teaspoon salt
½ teaspoon baking soda
½ pound (2 sticks) butter or
  margarine, softened

2 cups sugar
4 eggs
2 teaspoons vanilla extract
1 cup buttermilk

Preheat the oven to 350 degrees.

Butter three 8-inch cake pans and dust lightly with flour, shaking out excess flour. Set aside.

Sift the flour before measuring and then sift again with the baking powder, salt, and baking soda.

Place the butter or margarine in a large bowl and beat with a wooden spoon until just soft. Using an electric beater set on medium or creaming speed, gradually add the sugar and continue creaming until it is light and fluffy. This should take from 3 to 5 minutes (see "All Stirred Up" on page 304).

Beat in the eggs one at a time, mixing well after each addition. Stir in the vanilla extract.

Set the mixer on low speed. Add about ¾ cup of the flour at a time, alternating with ⅓ cup buttermilk, beating just until blended after each addition, beginning and ending with the flour. Scrape down the sides of the bowl after each addition.

When all the flour and buttermilk have been added, beat the batter on medium speed for 1½ to 2 minutes or until it is smooth and satiny and looks like ice cream. Don't overbeat the batter.

Pour the batter into the prepared cake pans, dividing evenly between the pans. Shake the pans gently to level the batter.

Place the cake pans in a triangular pattern on the middle shelf in the hot oven. Make sure that the cake pans are not touching.

Bake for 30 minutes or until the cake layers are brown and puffy and a

Sweet Temptations

knife inserted in the centers comes out clean, or until the cake pulls away from the sides of the pan.

Remove the cake layers from the oven, place on a wire rack, and allow to cool in the pans for 10 minutes.

Run a knife or metal spatula around the edges of the cake pans, tap gently, and carefully turn out the cake layers onto the wire rack to cool completely. This is a very delicate cake; don't attempt to move the layers until they are completely cooled.

When thoroughly cooled, frost with Chocolate Icing (see recipe on page 303).

To assemble, place four strips of wax paper on the edge of a cake platter to catch dripping frosting and filling. Place one of the layers on the cake platter top side down so that a level surface is obtained.

Spread the top of that layer with about ½ cup icing. Place the next cake layer bottom side down, which should result in an even "fit." Spread the top of that layer with about ½ cup of the icing.

Place the third layer, bottom side down, on the second layer. Beginning with the sides, spread the cake all over with the icing, moving from the bottom to the top of the cake.

When the cake is frosted, remove the wax paper strips and discard. This techniques leaves the cake plate spotless.

Allow the icing to set before serving, but don't refrigerate the cake. Store the cake in a cool place under a domed cake cover.

CHOCOLATE ICING

Makes about 3 cups

1½ cups sugar
⅓ cup unsweetened cocoa
⅛ teaspoon salt
1½ cups evaporated milk, undiluted

1 teaspoon vanilla extract
2 tablespoons butter or margarine

Combine the sugar, cocoa, and salt in a heavy saucepan. Gradually stir in the evaporated milk. Place the pan on the heat and bring the mixture to a rolling boil, and then immediately reduce the heat to medium. Cook, stirring occasionally with a wooden spoon, until the icing thickens, for about 25 minutes. Watch carefully and don't allow the icing to scorch. The icing should resemble thick honey.

Remove the icing from the heat and stir in the vanilla extract and butter or margarine. Pour the icing into a bowl and allow it to cool completely before using, stirring occasionally.

To hasten the thickening, set the bowl into a large pan of ice water and let it remain until the icing is as thick as applesauce.

ALL STIRRED UP

When Mama and the church sisters baked cakes, they would spend half the day in the kitchen beating the batter by hand, striving for, as they said, "cakes light as a feather." Beating incorporates air into a cake batter so that the layers can rise in volume during the baking, and although I am not gadget-happy, I give due praise to the electric mixer.

The first step in mixing a cake is called creaming, since the mixture is beaten until it looks like grainy ice cream. To do this, first place the butter or margarine or shortening in a large bowl and stir with a spoon until it is soft and creamy. (Don't use the mixer for this; the fat only sticks to the beaters.)

Now set the mixer on medium, or on "creaming" speed, and gradually add the sugar. Don't rush this process; the mixture should end up light and fluffy, but still somewhat grainy. This normally requires about 5 minutes of beating. Scrape down the sides of the bowl every once in a while during the creaming.

Add the eggs one at a time, beating for 40 seconds or so after each addition.

Mixing in the flour and milk can get a little tricky, because the two ingredients should be added alternately, beginning and ending with the flour and beating after each addition. This means that the flour should be added in four additions and the milk in three.

Pay strict attention to the beating at this point. If the batter is beaten too much the cake ends up heavy and dry; if it isn't beaten enough the cake can be coarse and grainy.

Here's a good procedure: With the mixer on low speed, beat the batter for about 20 seconds after each addition of flour and milk, scraping down the sides of the bowl after each addition. When all the flour and milk are added, increase the speed to medium and beat the batter for about 1½ to 2 minutes or until it is satiny and smooth and looks like thick, soft ice cream.

CAKES BAKED WITH LOVE

Lovie Williams is the mother of eight boys and seven girls, and she remembers that years ago the family would start getting ready for Sunday church service on Saturday afternoon. Dresses, shirts, and pants that had been laundered and starched earlier in the week were sprinkled with water, allowed to soak, and ironed with a smoothing iron that was stuck in the hot coals and heated. The girls' hair was combed and plaited, and as soon as that was done, they searched in dresser drawers for ribbons and barrettes to tie in their braids the next day. White ankle socks were gathered, and the girls old enough to wear red fox stockings with the black seams, made sure they had garters to keep them up. Lovie's husband, John Williams, always had to remind the boys to polish their shoes.

When everyone's clothes were ready, Mrs. Williams would start thinking about Sunday dinner. She was living then on a farm in Belonzi, in the hauntingly beautiful Mississippi Delta near Greenwood, Mississippi, and from an early age she had learned to pull together a meal from whatever was on hand.

"The Lord just blessed us when it came to feeding our family," says Mrs. Williams, who is seventy-two. "We always did."

Green beans were mixed with white potatoes and simmered until tender. A couple handfuls of okra were added to the collard greens. The crowder or purple-hull peas were cooked with ham hocks. Sweet potatoes were baked. Fresh eggs were boiled and added to potato salad. In the dead of winter dried peas and beans replaced the summer butterbeans and crowder peas. Chicken was fried; pork was roasted. Dumplings were added to a pot of stewing chicken, which was generally a hen. Cornbread was baked. Trees bore fruits that were turned into jellies and jams. The local watermelons and cantaloupes were so sweet that the children thought they were eating dessert, even though something sweet—tea cakes, jelly cake; blackberry, peach, apple, or sweet potato pie-was cooked every day.

On Sunday mornings Mrs. Williams listened for the ringing of the

Sweet Temptations

bell at the Mount Olive Missionary Baptist Church, which was within walking distance of her house. The church was large by country standards, and she remembers that a table in the pulpit held a lovely crystal pitcher and several drinking glasses that sparkled in the sunlight every time the preacher lifted the vessels and poured water during service. A baptismal pool was located right in the sanctuary, covered by a removable polished wooden floor when it wasn't in use. The deacons used to lift up the floor and pump water—by hand—into the pool for the ceremony. It was here that her children were baptized.

At the sound of the 9:30 A.M. church bell, Mrs. Williams says she would mentally note that she had no more than a good hour and fifteen minutes to make it to church on time for the morning service. She would hasten her pace a bit, and then think to herself about what else had to be done. Breakfast had long been cooked, all the children fed, and she had finished cooking the rest of the meal for the dinner after church service. The children had been bathed, and most of them were already dressed in their Sunday clothes. Sometimes the older children went on ahead of the family and attended Sunday school.

Then, as she remembers, despite their best-laid plans, one or another of their children would get a headache, stomachache, couldn't find something to wear, and had to stay home from church that day.

"I regret to this day that I never got all my fifteen children to church at one time," says Mrs. Williams wistfully, who today is a mother of the church at the Mount Calvary Christian Center in Jackson, Mississippi. "Seems like no matter how I tried, something would happen and somebody had to stay home. But they all grew up in the church and they all turned out all right. Some go to church more than the others. I got one preacher, two deacons, and nobody is in jail. I told my husband the other day that God blessed up with our children."

Mrs. Williams sends this recipe for a cake made with homemade jelly that she says every one of her fifteen children loved when they were growing up:

Coconut-Jelly Cake

Makes one 2-layer cake; serves 8

2 cups cake flour
2 teaspoons baking powder
Pinch of salt
8 tablespoons (1 stick) butter or
    margarine, softened
1¼ cups sugar
3 eggs
1 cup milk

1 teaspoon vanilla extract
1 teaspoon lemon extract
1½ cups Old-Fashioned Fruit
    Jelly (recipe follows)
2 cups freshly grated coconut
    (from 2 coconuts), or packaged,
    unsweetened coconut

Preheat the oven to 350 degrees.

Butter two 8-inch cake pans and dust lightly with flour, shaking out the excess. Set aside.

Sift the flour, measure, and sift again with the baking powder and salt. Set aside.

Place the butter or margarine in a large bowl and beat with a large spoon until soft and creamy. Using an electric beater set on medium or creaming speed, gradually add the sugar and beat until light and fluffy (see "All Stirred Up" on page 304). This should take from 3 to 5 minutes.

Add the eggs, one at a time, beating only until blended after each addition.

Set the mixer on low speed. Add the flour and milk alternately to the batter, beginning

A baptism at Guilford Baptist Church, Columbia, Maryland.

Sweet Temptations

and ending with the flour, beating only until blended after each addition.

When all the flour is added, set the mixer on medium speed and beat the batter for about 1½ minutes or until it is creamy and smooth. Stir in the vanilla and lemon extract, mixing well.

Pour the batter into the prepared cake pans, dividing evenly between the two. Shake the pans gently to level the batter. Place the filled cake pans on the middle oven shelf, diagonally across from each other.

Bake in the hot oven for 25 to 30 minutes or until the cake layers are puffy and golden brown and a knife inserted in the centers comes out clean, or the cake pulls away from the sides of the pan.

Remove the cake from the oven and cool in the pans on a wire rack for 10 minutes. Run a metal spatula or knife around the edges of the cake to loosen. Carefully turn out the cake layers onto the rack and cool completely.

To assemble the cake, place four strip of wax paper on a cake platter to catch any dripping jelly. Brush off any cake crumbs and place one of the layers on the cake platter, top side down. Spread the top of the layer with about ½ cup of the fruit jelly. Sprinkle on ½ to ¾ cup of the grated coconut.

Add the second cake layer, bottom side down. Spread the top and sides of the cake with the remaining jelly and then sprinkle the cake all over with the remaining coconut.

Old-Fashioned Fruit Jelly

Makes about 4 half pints

Lovie Williams grew up on a large farm in the Mississippi Delta near the Tennessee border. The family raised everything they ate, and sold the rest. There was a profusion of fruit trees and bushes, and on summer days their bearings were turned into jellies, jams, and preserves.

Mrs. Williams says that jellies and jams made in small batches jell better.

She sends this recipe:

*4 to 5 pounds fresh plums or
  peaches*
1 cup water
*Sugar, 1 cup per 1 cup of
  fruit juice*
*1 box (1.75 ounce) powdered
  fruit pectin*

*2 large squares of cheesecloth or
  other white cloth*
*4 sterilized pint jars (see
  "Getting Canned" on
  page 148)*

Scrub a large stainless steel or enamel pot with baking soda, rinse well, and then scald with boiling water. This procedure removes any food aromas from the pan.

Rinse the fruit well. Cut away any blemishes. Remove stems and discard. Don't peel the fruit. Cut in half and remove the pits and then cut into chunks or chop coarsely.

Place the fruit in the pot. Add just enough water to cover; about 1 cup, but not much more than that.

Place the pot on the heat and bring the mixture to a full boil. Reduce the heat to medium and cook, stirring occasionally with a wooden spoon, for 10 to 15 minutes or until the fruit bursts open and loses it color.

Remove the cooked fruit from the stove and cool completely. (This can remain in the refrigerator overnight once it is cooled.)

When the fruit is cooled, skim off any foam that has risen to the top of the mixture. Have ready a large square (at least 30 inches) of triple-thickness cheesecloth or sheeting, or a clean white cloth or kitchen towel. (Some specialty stores sell jelly bags; my mother used a flour sack.)

Drape the cloth over a large clean bowl or pan. Strain the fruit juice through the cloth. Grab up the edges of the cloth and form a ball. Squeeze the ball well to extract as much fruit juice as possible. Discard the fruit pulp.

Using another piece of cloth or cheesecloth, strain the juice again—without squeezing—to make sure that juice remains sparkling clear.

Sweet Temptations

Measure the extracted fruit juice and pour back into the large pot. For every cup of juice, add 1 cup of sugar. Place the pot on the stove and bring to a full boil.

Immediately reduce the heat to medium and cook the sugar-fruit mixture for 10 minutes, stirring occasionally.

Stir in the powdered pectin, bring to a rolling boil, and boil for exactly 1 minute. Watch carefully; the jelly burns easily at high temperature.

Remove the jelly immediately from the heat and pour into the hot sterilized canning jars, leaving a ¼-inch headspace at the top of each jar.

Seal at once. Cool the jelly and store in a dark place. Refrigerate after opening.

BAKING TOOLS

Cakes are baked as layers, loaves, sheets, tubes, or cups, but that doesn't mean that the pound cake recipe will work in the muffin tins. Most recipes are not interchangeable so it's best to use the type and size of cake pan specified in a recipe.

Aluminum or stainless cake pans are best for cake baking, and they should be bright and shiny so that the layers brown evenly. Dull, dark pans cause the cake layers to brown too fast and too unevenly. Cake layers baked in ovenproof glass pans brown faster than in metal pans, so the oven temperature has to be reduced by 25 degrees to prevent overbrowning.

But even as important as the type of pan is the amount of cake batter that you put into the pan. Ideally, pans are filled until about two-thirds full. If the pan is too big the cake will not rise properly and evenly and will end up dry and crusty. If the pan is too small the cake texture will be coarse and the batter stands the chance of overflowing.

As for pies, ovenproof glass allows you to look at the crust and determine when it is brown enough. Glass pans also hold heat better than aluminum, resulting in a crisper crust.

An accurate oven temperature is also important. From time to time check the temperature with an oven thermometer, and if you determine that the oven is "off," have the thermostat checked by a professional. The investment is worth the reward: a tender and moist and light-as-a-feather cake that is rich in flavor.

Sweet Temptations

Tea Cakes

Makes about 3 dozen cakes

*t*he telephone answering machine at Emily and Robert Morris's home rings out with the greeting "Praise the Lord," and before you even talk to this couple you know that church is a special part of their daily lives. Emily and Robert are members of the Mount Olive Baptist Church in McLoud, Oklahoma, where Emily volunteers as church clerk.

Emily and Robert have three children, all of whom are on the cusp of adulthood, and like many other parents in their midforties, they now look at their children and see both the past and the future.

"Our food and our church are so much a part of our history," says Emily forcefully. "I just want my children to keep it up."

Emily sends this recipe from her childhood, which she has already taught her daughter, Dava Albert, how to make. Dava works with a youth group at Mount Olive Baptist Church.

Emily writes: "I grew up in rural Oklahoma in the 1950s in the country town of Stonewall. My family's house was at one end of the road, and my Aunt Lucy's house was at the other end. The black church, Angel Wing Baptist Church, was in the middle of the road, right between the two houses.

"We spent many days in that church, and I also spent many summer days playing baseball under Uncle Jim's huge pecan tree. Upon completing a few innings of ball with my cousins and other neighborhood children, we would walk down to my Aunt Lucy and cousin Regina's house.

"Aunt Lucy would have a fresh batch of homemade tea cakes. We loved the large, round golden cakes that were neither too sweet nor too soft, but just right. The hint of the vanilla flavoring left the taste buds wanting more.

"My brother, William, who is six years younger than me, always received the largest one. After much thought, we decided that the smaller the hand, the larger the tea cake seemed.

"Many family members have tried to duplicate Aunt Lucy's tea cakes, but without complete success. As I have time to reflect on those days, I now realize that the secret of Aunt Lucy's tea cakes was the way she served

them. She always served them with a smile, a hug, kind words, and with love."

½ pound (2 sticks) butter or margarine, softened
1½ cups sugar
2 medium eggs
2 tablespoons milk or cream

2 teaspoons vanilla extract
4 to 4½ cups all-purpose flour
4 teaspoons baking powder
1/8 teaspoon salt

Preheat the oven to 375 degrees.

Lightly grease a large cookie or baking sheet. Set aside.

In a mixing bowl cream the butter or margarine and sugar until light and fluffy. Add the eggs, milk or cream, and vanilla extract and continue beating until smooth.

Sift the flour, measure, and sift again with the baking powder and salt.

Stir 4 cups of the flour into the creamed mixture and mix together to make a stiff dough. Add a little more flour if the batter is still sticky.

Sprinkle a pastry board or cloth lightly with sugar. Place the dough onto the board or cloth and roll out lightly to about ½ inch thick.

Using a 2- or 3-inch biscuit or cookie cutter, cut dough into biscuit shapes. Place the rounds about 1 inch apart, on the greased cookie or baking sheet. (You'll have to bake two batches.)

Set on the middle shelf of the hot oven. Bake for 12 to 15 minutes, or until the tea cakes are golden brown and puffed.

Remove the pan from the oven and set on a wire rack. Let cool in the pan for 10 minutes, and then remove from the pan and finish cooling on the rack.

Variation: For spiced tea cakes, sift with the flour ½ teaspoon cinnamon and ¼ teaspoon nutmeg.

FOUR WOMEN AND A POUND OF CAKE

We weren't the least bit surprised that Lillian Hayes's pound cake took top honors at the cook off at her church, the Saint Mark African Methodist Episcopal Church in Corona, Queens. Lillian made the cake with a recipe that had been passed on to her by her late mother, Annie Thomas, who was known back home in Waycross, Georgia as a superb baker.

Her mother was a member of the Mount Pleasant Baptist Church in Waycross, located on State Street, and during church revivals she would dress up Lillian's daughter and her granddaughter, Ann Pratt Hairston, in a ruffled, starched, and crisply ironed dress, pin a ribbon on her long braids, and carry out a box of food to the church, which usually held a cake or two.

Ann now lives in the Bronx, in New York City, and she sends a recipe for the pound cake that her grandmother passed on to her and Lillian years ago. Ann says that she keeps her recipes packed away in a box, just like her grandmother used to do.

The cake is a classic pound cake: 1 pound each of flour, butter, sugar, and eggs, but no milk or baking powder. This translates to 4 cups flour, 2 cups or 4 sticks butter, 2 cups sugar, and 8 to 10 eggs.

Ann sends this recipe:

SPICED POUND CAKE

Makes two 9-inch loaf cakes; serves 10 to 12

4 cups cake flour
$\frac{1}{8}$ teaspoon salt
1$\frac{1}{2}$ to 2 teaspoons ground nutmeg
or mace
1 pound (4 sticks) butter or
margarine, softened

2 cups sugar
1 pound eggs, about 8 to 10
2 teaspoons vanilla extract
Confectioners' sugar

Preheat the oven to 325 degrees.

Butter 2 loaf pans (9 × 5 × 3 inch), dust with flour and then shake out excess flour. Set aside.

Sift the flour before measuring, and then sift again with the salt and nutmeg or mace. Set aside.

Place the butter or margarine in a large bowl and beat with a large spoon until soft and mushy. Using an electric mixer on medium or creaming speed, gradually add the sugar and continue creaming the mixture until it is light and fluffy. This should take 10 to 12 minutes (see "All Stirred Up" on page 304).

Weigh the eggs to make sure you have 1 pound. Add the eggs, one at a time, beating on medium speed for about 1 minute after each addition, scraping down the sides of the bowl now and then. Stir in the vanilla.

Set the beater on low speed. Add about one third of the flour at a time to the creamed mixture, beating well after each addition. This should take about 3 or 4 minutes.

After all of the flour is added, set the mixer on medium speed and beat the batter for 2 minutes longer, occasionally scraping down the sides of the bowl. The batter should be shiny, satiny, and fluffy.

Spoon the batter into the prepared cake pans, dividing evenly between the two. Shake the pans gently to settle the batter.

Place the pans in the hot oven on the middle shelf, diagonally across from each other, not touching.

Bake for 1 hour and 15 minutes or until golden brown and a knife inserted in the centers comes out clean.

Remove the cakes from the oven and cool on a wire rack for 10 minutes. Run a metal spatula or knife around the edge of the pans to loosen the cakes and then tap the pans gently.

Carefully turn out the cakes onto a wire rack. Sprinkle with the confectioners' sugar, if desired, and cool completely.

Sweet Temptations

Holiday Pound Cake

Makes 2 loaf cakes; serves 10 to 12

*a*nn Pratt Hairston often laughs to herself remembering the fierce independence and individualism of her grandmother Annie Thomas, and of her sister, Sarah Clark, who was Ann's great-aunt.

Annie Thomas was a stalwart member of Mount Pleasant Baptist Church in Waycross, while her sister was a devout member of the Church of God in Christ, a Pentecostal church located on Daniel Street. And both of the women had their way with cakes.

Ann sends this recipe and memories:

"When I was growing up in Waycross, Georgia, the Christmas holiday was a special time. Everyone looked forward to my aunt Sarah Clark's pound cake, which was completely different from my grandmother's spiced pound cake. She made her pound cake with candied fruits and pecans, and it was as fancy as a fruitcake.

"Aunt Sarah was a mother of the church at the Church of God in Christ in Waycross. She was an outstanding member; never missed a Sunday.

"Like Grandma Annie, she always had treats for the children, which was usually some of her home cooking. In those days we used to go to church for Christmas Eve service. When we ate Aunt Sarah's cake we used to wish that Christmas came more than once a year."

This is a rich and delectable cake that you are certain to enjoy anytime of the year. It too is made the old-fashioned way, with a pound of flour, sugar, butter, and eggs.

½ cup candied cherries
½ cup candied pineapple
1 cup pecans
1 tablespoon all-purpose or cake flour
4 cups cake flour
⅛ teaspoon salt

1 pound (4 sticks) butter or margarine, softened
1 cup firmly packed light brown sugar
1 cup granulated sugar
1 pound eggs, about 8 to 10
2 teaspoons vanilla extract

Preheat the oven to 325 degrees. Butter and lightly flour 2 loaf pans (9 × 5 × 3 inch), shaking to knock out excess flour. Set aside.

Chop the candied cherries, pineapple, and pecans. Place in a bowl and sprinkle over the tablespoon of flour, tossing to coat well. This keeps the fruit and nuts suspended in the batter. Set aside.

Sift the cake flour before measuring and then sift again with the salt. Set aside.

Place the butter or margarine in a large bowl and beat with a large spoon until soft and creamy.

Using an electric mixer on medium or creaming speed, gradually add both the light brown and granulated sugar and continue creaming the mixture until it is light and fluffy. This should take 10 to 12 minutes (see "All Stirred Up" on page 304).

Weigh the eggs to make sure you have 1 pound. Add them, one at a time, beating for about 1 minute after each addition, scraping down the sides of the bowl now and then. Stir in the vanilla.

Set the beater on low speed. Add about one third of the flour at a time to the egg mixture, beating well after each addition. This should take about 3 or 4 minutes.

Set the beater on medium speed and beat the batter for about 2 minutes longer, or until it is shiny and satiny and fluffy, occasionally scraping down the sides of the bowl.

```
╲╱╲╱╲╱╲╱╲
```

Stir the candied fruit-nut mixture into the batter, mixing well, but don't beat again.

Pour the batter into the prepared pans, dividing evenly. Shake the pans gently to level the batter. Smooth the top with a metal spatula.

Set the pans on the middle shelf in the hot oven. Don't allow the pans to touch.

Bake for 1 hour and 15 minutes or until golden brown and a knife inserted in the centers comes out clean.

Remove the cake from the oven and let cool in the pan on a wire rack for 10 minutes. Loosen edges of the cake with a metal spatula or knife and turn out onto a wire rack and cool completely.

Variation: Ann Hairston often bakes this cake a few weeks before Christmas and during that period she dips two squares of cheesecloth into brandy or dark rum, wraps one square around each cake, and then encloses it in aluminum foil and stores the cakes in a cool, dark place. Whenever she thinks about it, Ann says she unwraps the cakes and adds a little more brandy or rum.

On Christmas Day she is rewarded with a delectable, buttery cake that is pretty and heady.

Ann laughs and says that her Aunt Sarah was a teetotaler and probably wouldn't approve of her embellishments, but the cakes always leave her holiday guests swooning.

A SLICE OF PIE

I can't remember the number of times I have walked into a black family's house in the South and after a few minutes of greeting came the offer, "Would you care for a slice of pie, a piece of cake?"

Not only were cakes and pies the hallmark of our hospitality, they allowed us the opportunity to show off our artistry in the kitchen, and it was a challenge that we welcomed.

Actually, baking a pie is much easier than baking a cake. The signature of a good pie is a crisp, tender, and flaky crust, and once this technique is learned, a pie can be put together in a matter of minutes.

A pie crust is made with flour, water, and shortening or fat, and this can either be lard, vegetable shortening, butter, or margarine. However, the ingredients must be put together with a quick, "light" hand, for if the pastry is handled slowly or roughly, or if the shortening is allowed to melt, the pastry will end up tough and hard after baking. The key is to have all the ingredients as cold as possible. Ice water is essential.

The goal in pastry making is to distribute the fat evenly throughout the flour, and this can be done with a pastry blender, with two knives, or with your fingers. This should be done as quickly as possible, because you don't want the fat to melt from the heat of your fingers or from the action of the utensils. Once the shortening or fat is "cut in," the mixture should resemble coarse cornmeal.

The greatest care is required when adding the ice water. Only an approximate amount of water can be given, since the amount required varies with the type of flour and shortening used. Usually 3 to 4 tablespoons of ice water are required for 1 cup of flour.

For best results, sprinkle the water a tablespoon at a time over the flour mixture while tossing it with a fork. Push the moistened portions to one side before adding more water so that a dry portion can be sprinkled each time.

When the flour mixture is moist enough to hold together and is slightly sticky, quickly form into a ball. If too little water has been added there is not much that can be done at this point except profit from experience. If too much water has been added you can work in a little more flour, although your dough will be streaky and not as flaky.

Wrap the dough in plastic wrap or foil and place in the refrigerator for about 20 minutes. This allows the gluten in the flour to relax and the dough rolls out easier.

To roll out the dough, sprinkle the work surface with a little flour and spread it evenly over the surface. Cover the rolling pin with a cloth "stocking," which prevents sticking and reduces the amount of additional flour needed during the rolling-out process. A fine pie crust is made up of layers of crisp dough with air spaces in between. Excess flour causes the pastry to resemble cardboard.

The rolling should be quick but light, since heavy pressure causes the pastry to stick and breaks the surface. Start each stroke at the center of the dough and roll toward the edges, keeping pastry in as circular a shape as possible. Lift and turn the pastry occasionally to make sure it is not sticking, and rub a little extra flour on the board if necessary.

Don't allow a filled pie crust to linger in a warm room. Either pop it into the hot oven immediately or refrigerate until ready to bake.

The following recipe uses a mixture of equal parts butter and vegetable shortening. Many bakers prefer lard, while others prefer vegetable shortening, and some prefer all butter. Pie crusts made with vegetable shortening or lard are thought to be a little bit flakier than all-butter pie crusts, even though this too is debatable.

Basic Two-Crust Pie Shell

2 cups all-purpose flour
¼ teaspoon salt
5⅓ tablespoons butter

5⅓ tablespoons (⅓ cup) shortening
6 to 8 tablespoons ice water
1 egg white, lightly beaten

Sift the flour and salt into a medium bowl. Add the butter and vegetable shortening and using either a pastry blender, two knives, or your fingers, cut or crumble the flour, butter, and shortening until the mixture is the texture of coarse cornmeal.

Sprinkle the ice water over the dough and quickly stir it together with a fork. Form the dough into a ball and turn onto a lightly floured board or pastry cloth. Dust the ball lightly with flour if it sticks.

Wrap the dough in plastic wrap or aluminum foil and chill for 20 minutes.

To make the pie crust, remove the dough from the refrigerator and place on a lightly floured board or cloth. Divide the dough into two parts, one slightly larger than the other. Use the larger piece for the bottom crust and the smaller part for the top crust.

For a 9-inch pie crust, roll out the larger piece of dough into at least a 10-inch circle and as thin as possible, less than ⅛ inch thick.

Carefully slide the rolling pin under the center of the dough, lift up the dough, and place it in the pie pan. Do not stretch the dough. Use your fingers to fit the dough loosely into the pie pan.

Trim the pastry edges evenly with a knife or kitchen scissors, leaving about ½ inch of dough extending over the rim of the pan all around.

Prick the bottom of the pie crust with a fork and then brush all over with the beaten egg white. This keeps the pie shell from becoming soggy during baking.

Fill the pie crust with a generous amount of filling.

Roll out the remaining half of dough in the same way as done for the bottom crust. Carefully lift up the dough and place it over the filling.

Trim the pastry edges evenly. Press the bottom and top pastry edges firmly together, and then crimp with your fingers or with the tines of a fork for a pretty border design. Or stand the pastry edge on the rim of the pie pan and pinch with your fingers into a flute design.

Prick the top crust all over with a fork or cut several slits or a fancy design near the center to release steam during the baking. Bake according to recipe directions.

Variation: For a one-crust pie, use one half of the above recipe and proceed as directed, brushing the pastry shell with egg white before placing in the filling.

Sweet Temptations

LEMON CHESS PIE

Makes 1 pie; serves 6

My father was a born storyteller, and I remember him saying that this pie was created by a slave, who when asked by the approving plantation owner what was it called, responded "Jes pie." Eventually, so the story goes, this description evolved into the name "Chess Pie."

As for history, I wish I could turn back time and tell my sister or brother that this is not "just pie." It is a culinary masterpiece of tantalizing sweet-and-sour flavors that is dearly loved to this day in the South.

The following recipe comes from John Wesley Reed Jr., the music coordinator at the Macedonia Baptist Church, which is located on 22nd Street in Arlington, Virginia. John is a church-dedicated young black professional, and his commitment and humor bode well for the church of tomorrow. And for the Lemon Chess Pie.

John says that this rather self-effacing story is really true. He writes:

"Aunt Annie Mae and Uncle Joe had insisted 'Don't make this pie with a mixer. Use a fork for stirring.'

"Of course I didn't listen, knowing that they still make cakes from scratch and mix by hand rather than use an electric mixer.

"Aunt Annie Mae and Uncle Joe live in Winston-Salem, North Carolina, and the recipe they were giving me for Chess Pie has been in the family for sixty years. It's been carried out to numerous church functions.

"But there I was, for the sixth time in two days, dumping an entire pie into the trash. Six times I had carefully made a flaky pie crust from scratch, six times I had beaten together the filling with my electric beater. Each time I put my mixer in overdrive and beat it a little longer. Once I even went over to the CD player and let the mixer run for a full minute. 'Maybe I am not combining it well enough' I told myself.

"And six times I watched through the glass door of my high-tech oven as the pie refused to set like my trusted Aunt Annie Mae's pies. By that time I had lost my religion and was glad no one was around to hear my new vocabulary.

"Finally I made a Chess Pie. I did it by hand, stirring the ingredients quickly. The reward was a sweet, solid, lemony filling. I ate three slices in celebration!

"Aunt Annie Mae and Uncle Joe were right. Those electric beaters incorporate too much air and cause the filling to separate. I learned from that experience: This pie must be made by hand in the same way it was made when that was the only way to do it."

1 unbaked 9-inch pie crust
   (see recipe on page 320)
4 eggs
1¼ to 1½ cups sugar
Pinch of salt
1 tablespoon flour or cornstarch
1 tablespoon fine-grain cornmeal

¼ cup buttermilk
4 tablespoons butter or margarine,
   melted
1 tablespoon finely grated lemon
   peel
¼ cup freshly squeezed lemon juice

Preheat the oven to 400 degrees.

Prepare the pie shell. Prick generously and brush lightly with beaten egg white.

Place on the lower shelf of the hot oven and bake for 5 minutes. Remove the pie shell from the oven and set on a wire rack to cool.

In the meantime, break the eggs into a large bowl and beat lightly with a fork or wire whisk.

Add the sugar and beat until just blended. Stir in the salt, flour or cornstarch, and cornmeal and mix well.

Pour in the buttermilk and butter or margarine in a steady stream, beating until smooth. Stir in the lemon peel and lemon juice, mixing only until they are blended in.

Pour the filling into the pie shell.

Set the pie on the middle shelf of the hot oven and bake at 400 degrees for 10 minutes.

Reduce the oven temperature to 325 degrees and bake for 30 minutes longer or until the custard is set and a knife inserted in the center comes out clean.

Remove from the oven and cool on a wire rack. Chill, if desired.

SOUTHERN PECAN PIE

Makes 1 pie; serves 6

few years ago Dr. Rubye Taylor-Drake found among her late mother's belongings at least 150 recipes, some of which were clipped from newspapers and magazines; others were written on the back of envelopes and sheets of paper that seemed hurriedly torn from notebooks. A few of the recipes were yellowed from age.

The late Sara Taylor was a home economics teacher, and since she was a superb cook, she was a lightning rod for food ideas and service at the New Canaan Baptist Church in Aliceville, Alabama.

Today her daughter is a member of the board of trustees and the chairwoman of the Budget Committee at the Metropolitan Missionary Baptist Church in Chicago. She is also a college professor.

Dr. Taylor sends her mother's recipe for pecan pie:

1 unbaked 9-inch pie crust
  (see recipe on page 320)
3 eggs
½ cup sugar
1½ cups dark corn syrup

½ teaspoon vanilla extract
2 tablespoons melted butter
  or margarine
1 heaping cup shelled pecan halves

Preheat the oven to 350 degrees.

Prepare the pie crust. Prick the pastry shell all over with a fork and brush lightly with beaten egg white. Set aside.

Place the eggs in a large bowl and beat lightly, just until they are foamy. Add the sugar, corn syrup, vanilla extract and the butter or margarine. Mix well.

Coarsely chop or break the pecans and stir into the egg mixture.

Pour the filling into the pie shell.

Place the pie pan on the lower shelf of the hot oven and bake for 45 to 50 or until the pie is golden brown and puffed, and a knife comes out clean when inserted into the center. (Watch the pie carefully. If it overcooks it can become gummy.)

Cool on a wire rack and serve.

BUTTERMILK PIE

Makes 1 pie; serves 6

*U*ntil she retired a few years ago, Sarah Irby was involved in so many church and community activities that her husband used to jokingly refer to her as the neighborhood's social director.

Mrs. Irby lives in East Harlem, New York, and much of her church work is on behalf of the Memorial Baptist Church, which is located across town on 115th Street. She is a member of the church's W. W. Monroe Guild, a service and fund-raising club.

The Guild holds a bake sale several times during the year, and when Mrs. Irby doesn't bake her famed lemon cake, she takes out two or three of her buttermilk pies, which are made by an old family recipe that was passed on to her by her mother.

Mrs. Irby migrated to New York City in 1943 from Fredericksburg, Virginia, where the family ran a small restaurant and were members of the Shiloh Baptist Church (New Sight), located on Princess Anne Street.

She sends this wonderful recipe:

1 unbaked 9-inch pie crust (see recipe on page 320)	2 eggs
	4 tablespoons butter or margarine
2/3 cup sugar	1/2 teaspoon vanilla extract
3 tablespoons flour	1/2 teaspoon lemon extract
1 cup buttermilk	1/2 cup grated or shredded coconut

Preheat the oven to 425 degrees.

Prepare the pie crust. Prick the pie crust all over and brush lightly with beaten egg white.

Set on the lower shelf of the hot oven and bake for 5 minutes. Remove from the oven and cool on a wire rack.

Meanwhile, in a large bowl combine the sugar, flour, and ½ cup of the buttermilk. Mix well.

Beat the eggs and melt the butter or margarine. Add the eggs, the remaining buttermilk, the butter or margarine, and the vanilla and lemon extracts to the bowl. Mix until well blended.

325

Sweet Temptations

Pour the filling into the cooled pie shell. Sprinkle the top with the coconut. Set the pan in the hot oven on the middle shelf.

Bake at 425 for 10 minutes and then reduce the heat to 350 degrees.

Bake 30 to 35 minutes, or until the pie is fluffy and a knife inserted into the center comes out clean.

Cool on a wire rack.

Sweet Potato Pie

Makes 1 pie; serves 6

r ecently during Old-Fashion Day at the New Shiloh Missionary Baptist Church in Miami, Eva Mae Grace put on a white bonnet, a floor length skirt, and cotton stockings—just like some black women wore to church years ago.

Mrs. Grace is a deaconess at New Shiloh, and her husband, David, is a deacon. They cooked and carried out several boxes of food to the event, which is held annually on the second Sunday in December.

Everybody loved the Grace's family satiny sweet potato pies. Their recipe follows:

4 medium sweet potatoes (enough to yield 2 cups mashed)
1 unbaked 9-inch pie crust (see recipe on page 320)
8 tablespoons (1 stick) butter or margarine, softened

1¼ cups sugar
2 eggs
¼ cup milk
1 teaspoon vanilla extract
2 teaspoons ground allspice

Scrub and rinse the sweet potatoes. Cut away eyes or sprouts and discard. Place the unpeeled sweet potatoes in a large pot. Cover with water and bring to a boil. Cook over medium-high heat for 25 minutes or until the potatoes are tender when pierced with a fork. (The potatoes can also be steamed over boiling water for about 30 minutes or until tender.)

Preheat the oven to 350 degrees.

Prepare the pie crust. Prick generously all over with a fork and brush lightly with beaten egg white. Set aside.

Remove the cooked potatoes from the hot water and drain. Peel while still warm and transfer to a large bowl.

Using an electric mixture set on low speed, beat the potatoes until they are light and fluffy.

Add to the bowl the butter or margarine, sugar, eggs, milk, vanilla extract, and allspice. Beat again for 2 to 3 minutes or until the filling is smooth and creamy and well blended.

Pour the filling into the pie shell. Use a knife or metal spatula to spread the filling evenly.

Place the pie on the bottom shelf of the hot oven and bake for 1 hour or until the pie is lightly browned and a knife inserted into the center comes out clean.

Cool on a wire rack before serving.

Old-Fashioned Apple Pie

Makes 1 pie; serves 6

izzie Brooks heads the Kitchen Committee at the Broomfield Christian Methodist Episcopal Church in Richmond, Virginia, and she laughs and says that when it comes time to work, some of the committee volunteers don't work out. But the job always get done. Every fourth Sunday the committee prepares a dinner for forty to fifty senior citizens. Twice a year the committee cooks for the pastor's Appreciation Day activities, which draw close to 150 guests. And throughout the years there are funeral dinners for bereaved families, as well as food for a variety of other social activities at the church, which is located on Jefferson Davis Highway.

Mrs. Brooks remembers that her days were just as busy years ago down on the farm in Robeson County in North Carolina, where her family lived and worked and worshipped. Her family, she says, grew and raised virtually everything they ate, except a few staples such as coffee, rice, sugar, and chocolate, which were bought from the general store. It was a large extended family of a dozen or more members, and everybody was expected to work and go to church.

They were members of the Mack Chapel African Methodist Episcopal Church and during revivals and homecomings, her mother and grandmother would pack a blue-enamel dish pan or scrubbed wooden box with food, and the family would set out for church, walking in groups along the country roads.

Mrs. Brooks remembers blackberry pie, strawberry shortcake, peach cobbler, tea cakes, lemon chess pie, hand-churned ice cream, chocolate cream pie, apple pie, pear tart, sweet potato pie, and during the holidays, more than enough cookies and cakes. And since offering something sweet was the quintessential badge of hospitality, a cake or pie was kept on hand to offer to the unexpected but welcomed guests.

"We didn't think a thing about getting up anytime of night and cooking if somebody came by," she remembers.

And Mrs. Brooks doesn't think a thing about rolling up her sleeves in

the Broomfield Church kitchen. Whenever she bakes and serves her delicious apple pie, not one morsel is left.

She sends this recipe:

1 unbaked 2-crust pie shell
   (see recipe on page 320)
4 or 5 large tart cooking apples,
   such as greening, Cortland,
   Rome beauty, or a mixture
   of the three
½ to 1 cup sugar, depending on
   sweetness of the apples

¼ teaspoon ground cloves
1 teaspoon ground cinnamon
2 tablespoons all-purpose flour
½ teaspoon vanilla extract
½ teaspoon lemon extract
4 tablespoons butter or margarine
1 egg white
1 tablespoon sugar

Prepare the pie crust. Roll out slightly more than half of the dough for the bottom crust and lift carefully into the pie pan. Save the remaining pastry for the top crust. Wrap in plastic wrap and place in the refrigerator.

Prick the bottom crust all over and brush lightly with beaten egg white. Set the crust in the refrigerator. Preheat the oven to 400 degrees.

Rinse and dry the apples. Peel, core, and cut into quarters and then into ⅛-inch-thick slices. Place slices in a large bowl. Add the sugar, cloves, cinnamon, flour, and extracts. Mix gently but well.

Spoon the apples into the pastry shell. Cut the butter or margarine into little pieces and scatter over the apples.

Roll out the remaining pastry into a 10-inch circle. Fold lightly in half, lift carefully, and unfold over the apples in the pie pan.

Using a sharp knife or kitchen scissors, trim the edges of the pastry, leaving about ½ inch extending over the rim of the pie pan all around.

Stand the pastry edge on the rim of the pie pan. Crumple with your fingers to make a pretty border, or crimp edge with the tines of a fork. Prick the top all over with a fork, or cut slits in the top so that steam can escape during the baking. Set aside. Lightly beat the egg white and brush on the top of the pie. Sprinkle on the sugar for a nice glaze.

Place the pie on the lower shelf of the hot oven and bake for 45 to 50 minutes or until it is golden brown and crusty.

Sweet Temptations

BLACKBERRY PIE

Makes 1 pie; serves 6

*i*t never bothered me in the least that when we returned home from picking blackberries, my hands were tinted a rosy blue and that my arms always had a welt or two, despite the fact that I had taken Mama's advice and worn a long-sleeve shirt.

The berries reached their majestic beauty and flavor in mid–June and we knew that we would be rewarded for braving the prickly patches. By midafternoon Mama's pies or cobblers would be sitting on the kitchen table, oozing syrupy sauce and redolent with aroma. Then we would nudge ourselves, glad that we hadn't eaten up all the juicy and sweet berries that morning right off the bramble.

The recipe that brought back those memories came from Mary Godfrey, who lives in Choctaw County in Alabama, and is a member of the Shiloh Baptist Church.

1 unbaked 2-crust pie crust (see recipe on page 320)	½ teaspoon lemon or orange peel
4 cups fresh blackberries	3 tablespoons flour or cornstarch
1 cup sugar, or more if desired	4 tablespoons butter
1 teaspoon ground cinnamon	1 egg white
1 teaspoon vanilla extract	1 tablespoon sugar

Prepare the pie crust. Roll out slightly more than half of the dough for the bottom crust and lift carefully into the pie pan. Save the remaining pastry for the top crust. Wrap in plastic wrap or aluminum foil and refrigerate.

Prick the bottom crust all over and brush lightly with beaten egg white. Set the pie crust in the refrigerator.

Preheat the oven to 400 degrees.

Meanwhile, combine in a bowl the blackberries, sugar, cinnamon, vanilla extract, lemon or orange peel, and flour or cornstarch. Mix gently and carefully; spoon into the pie shell.

Cut the butter into small pieces and scatter over the berries.

Roll out the remaining pastry dough into a 10-inch circle. Fold lightly in half, lift carefully, and unfold over the blackberry filling. Using kitchen scissors or a knife, trim the pastry extending over the rim of the pie pan, leaving a ½-inch overhang so as to make a pretty border.

Pinch or crimp the pastry on the rim of the pie plate, using your fingers or a fork. Pierce the top pastry layer all over with a fork or cut in several slashes with a knife so that the steam can escape during baking. This help keeps the pastry from becoming soggy.

Brush the top pastry layer with a little egg white and then sprinkle on the sugar.

Bake in the hot oven for 45 to 50 minutes or until the pastry is golden brown and the pie is hot and bubbly and the filling has thickened.

Cook on a wire rack before serving.

MORE SWEET THINGS

This old-fashioned pone, which is made without a crust, was almost as popular as sweet potato pie when I was growing up in the South. Food lore says that the name is derived from the French world for bread, *pain,* which we African-Americans borrowed from Southern Cajuns and turned into "pone."

Lillian Hayes, a member of the Saint Mark African Methodist Episcopal Church in Corona, Queens, remembers this dish from her childhood in Waycross, Georgia. Her recipe uses molasses, ginger, sweet potatoes, and buttermilk for a winning combination of flavors. And, as I remember, we did eat this pone as if it were bread.

Serves 6 to 8

4 cups finely grated uncooked sweet
    potato, about 2½ pounds
5⅓ tablespoons butter or
    margarine, softened
1 cup sugar
¾ teaspoon powdered ginger,
    cinnamon or allspice

3 eggs
½ cup dark molasses, mild flavor
1 cup buttermilk
3 tablespoons all-purpose flour
½ teaspoon baking soda
⅛ teaspoon salt

Preheat the oven to 325 degrees.

Butter a shallow 2-quart baking pan. Set aside.

Rinse the sweet potatoes well. Peel and cut away any blemishes. Using either a grater or food processor, grate finely. Set aside.

In a large bowl combine the butter or margarine and sugar and beat until light and fluffy. Stir in the grated sweet potatoes and spice. Set aside.

In a small bowl, beat the eggs and molasses until thick. Stir into the sweet potato mixture. Stir in the buttermilk, flour, baking soda, and salt.

Pour the mixture into the buttered baking dish. Set the dish in the hot oven on the middle shelf. Bake for 1 hour and 15 minutes or until the pone is crusty and a knife inserted in the center comes out clean.

Remove from the oven and cool on wire rack for 10 minutes. Serve warmed or cool completely and chill.

SKILLET PINEAPPLE UPSIDE-DOWN CAKE

Makes one 8- or 9-inch cake; serves 6 to 8

a few years ago Mabel Kinzer was rummaging through her belongings and came across one of her mother's favorite recipes. Her mother was the late Mabel James, who was a member of the Philathea Club at the Providence Baptist Church in Greensboro, North Carolina.

This was a women's club, and Mabel remembers that her mother spared no efforts when the club met at their home.

Her daughter is a fine hostess, too, and a devout and active member of the Little Union Baptist Church in Dumfries, Virginia.

Mabel sends this recipe for an upside-down cake, which is an old favorite in the South. Mabel's recipe calls for a cast-iron skillet but you can also use a 9-inch-square cake pan.

This is her very memorable recipe:

8 tablespoons (1 stick) butter
  or margarine
1 cup firmly packed dark brown
  sugar
½ cup chopped pecans (optional)
1 can (20-ounce) pineapple slices,
  undrained
6 or 7 maraschino or candied
  cherries

1 cup all-purpose flour
1 teaspoon baking powder
⅛ teaspoon salt
3 eggs, at room temperature
5⅓ tablespoons butter or
  margarine, softened
½ cup sugar

Preheat the oven to 375 degrees.

Place the butter or margarine in an 8- or 9-inch straight side cast-iron skillet. Set over low heat to melt. Stir in the brown sugar and nuts and mix well. Remove from the heat and set aside.

Drain the pineapple slices, reserving ⅓ cup of the juice.

Arrange the pineapple slices in the skillet in a single layer. Insert a cherry into the center of each ring. Set aside while preparing the cake batter.

Sweet Temptations

Sift together the flour, baking powder, and salt and set aside.

Separate the eggs, placing the white in a spotlessly clean medium bowl and the yolks in a large bowl.

Beat the eggs whites on high speed until stiff peaks form. Set aside.

Beat the eggs yolks on medium speed until they are thick and smooth. Add the softened butter or margarine and beat again until well blended.

Gradually add the sugar to the egg and butter mixture and beat on medium or creaming speed until the mixture is light and fluffy, for about 3 minutes. Stir in the reserved pineapple juice and mix well.

Add the flour and beat the batter on low speed for about 1 minute or until it is shiny and satiny.

Carefully fold in the beaten egg whites, mixing well.

Spoon the batter over the brown sugar and pineapple slices, using a spatula to spread evenly. Shake the pan gently to settle the batter.

Place the cake in the hot oven on the middle shelf. Bake for 30 to 35 minutes or until the cake is golden brown and puffed and a knife inserted in the center comes out clean.

Remove the cake from the oven and set on a wire rack. Let cool for 5 minutes; no longer.

Loosen the edges of the cake with a metal spatula or knife. Put a serving platter or cake plate over the cake pan and invert the cake onto the plate or platter, fruit side up.

Serve warm or cool.

PARTY LEMONADE

*Makes about 1½ quarts or 4 to 6 servings;
double or triple the recipe for a crowd*

*d*uring the summer months churchfolks are in and out of Mattie Hodges's house all the time, especially when she cooks in her backyard.

Mrs. Hodges is a member of the Ebenezer Baptist Church in Atlanta, and she says nothing quenches Southern summer thirst like this sappy, sweet, delicious lemonade:

4 to 6 large lemons
½ cup sugar (more if desired)
2 cups boiling water

3 cups cold water
1 tray (12) ice cubes

Rinse the lemons, discard the stems, and roll on a table until soft. Place on a cutting board, and slice crosswise as thinly as possible.

Place the lemon slices in a glass bowl and sprinkle over the sugar. Pour over the boiling water and let the lemons set at least 30 minutes, occasionally pressing the slices against the sides of the bowl to extract as much flavor as possible. When the mixture is thoroughly cool, stir in the cold water.

At serving, pour the lemon mixture into a chilled pitcher, add the ice cubes, and serve immediately.

Sweet Temptations

Homemade Vanilla Ice Cream

Makes about 3½ quarts

Years ago "Down South," church events shaped our lives just like the seasons. Early winter brought the hectic pace of the Christmas holiday church services, plus visiting friends and relatives. The attendance during the dead of winter was always sparse at both the Shiloh Baptist and Allen Temple churches, for the old wood-burning heaters just never seemed to emit enough heat.

By Easter Sunday the weather was usually sunny and balmy, and since I was particularly eager to wear the new dress that Mrs. Edressa had made for me, I could hardly wait to get to church. Shiloh Baptist was always crowded for this service, for in addition to showing off our Easter finery, we schoolchildren put on a recital and were treated to an Easter egg hunt after the service. Sometimes a few of the sisters brought out food.

A large crowd gathered in May for the Mother's Day church service, and by the middle of June when the Alabama weather began to reach its feverish pitch, churches throughout Choctaw County and the adjoining Washington County were crowded every Sunday with throngs of people who came out for revivals, homecomings, and singing conventions.

I loved attending the singing conventions. Back in those days every church had a choir and most churches had one or two gospel choral groups. Throughout the summer, from June to October, various churches took turns hosting the conventions, which brought in choir members and gospel singers from far and near. Some of the singing groups were considered local celebrities, and when word passed on Saturday afternoon that the Causey Sisters or the Phillips or some other gospel group was singing at such and such church on Sunday, we would start arranging to catch a ride to that church with whomever was fortunate enough to own a car.

The singing seemed to hit its stride in late afternoon after the morning service. The preaching was over, the shouting had ceased. Church sisters passed out food in the churchyard from boxes brought from home. Others sold fish sandwiches, ice cream, snowballs, and soft drinks. Boyfriends and girlfriends held hands. Old friends greeted one another. People filed in and out of the church, attracted by whatever choir or gospel group was singing.

The singing was ceaseless and fine-tuned; vibrant and hopeful. Voices as harmonious as honey spread through the churches and rekindled our faith with the intensity of the hot Alabama sun. In early evening as the daylight was finally dimming, we would catch a ride home, so content, no longer thinking of our bittersweet existence.

I thought of these memories recently when my beloved sister, Helen, sent a recipe for homemade ice cream, which she considered no more trouble to churn and take out to Shiloh Baptist than a couple of her chocolate cakes.

3 cups milk	*1 quart chilled light or heavy*
6 large egg yolks	*cream, or equal parts of each*
1½ cups sugar	*20 pounds crushed ice, about*
⅛ teaspoon salt	*3 pounds coarse rock salt*
1½ to 2 tablespoons vanilla extract	

Heat the milk in the top of a double boiler over simmering water until hot and bubbly. This should take about 10 minutes. Don't allow the milk to boil.

Meanwhile, place the egg yolks in a medium bowl and using an electric mixer, beat until they are frothy. Add the sugar, salt, and 1½ tablespoons of the vanilla extract and beat on high speed until well blended.

Add 2 or 3 tablespoons of the warm milk to the egg yolk mixture and beat again. Stir in ¼ cup of the milk to the egg yolks and mix well. Now add the egg mixture to the milk in the double boiler and mix well.

Raise the heat a bit. Cook the custard, stirring frequently, for 12 to 15 minutes or until it thickens and coats a spoon.

Remove the custard from the heat and pour immediately into a large clean bowl. Let the custard cool completely, stirring occasionally to release steam.

When the custard is completely cooled, cover the surface with plastic

Sweet Temptations

wrap or wax paper to prevent a skin from forming. Place the custard in the refrigerator and chill for at least 1 hour or longer. Chill the light or heavy cream and the ice cream freezer container.

To freeze the ice cream: Pour the custard and the chilled cream into the freezer container, filling about ⅔ full. Using a long-handled spoon, stir to mix well. Taste and add more vanilla extract if you wish.

Insert the dasher into the container and close with the lid. Set the filled container in the freezer bucket. Fit on the crank. Place the freezer in a large tub or shallow basin so as to catch the brine as it forms.

To pack the freezer with salt and ice: Use 1 cup coarse rock salt to every 8 cups (2 quarts) of crushed ice, layering the salt and ice to the top of the freezer. Don't cover the lid with salt.

To churn: Follow the manufacturer's direction for an electric unit. If using a hand-churned freezer, let the packed freezer stand for 3 or 4 minutes, and then crank slowly for about 5 minutes or until you feel a slight resistance and the mixture begins to freeze. The ice should start melting and turning to brine. Remember to check the freezer's water hole as you turn to make sure that the brine is flowing out of the freezer and into the tub or basin.

Now turn the crank rapidly for 5 or 6 minutes or until you feel a definite resistance. This rapid action beats up the cream and causes it to swell.

Once the ice cream starts freezing, reduce the crank speed and turn slowly and evenly for 20 to 30 minutes or until the crank is difficult to turn, adding more ice and salt as needed.

The ice cream is ready for packing when it has a dull appearance, adheres to a spoon, and retains its shape. By thermometer test it should read 27 degrees. It should be firm and mellow, velvety and free from grains. If it is grainy, then too much salt was used or the turning was too rapid.

To pack the ice cream: Drain off as much brine as possible from the freezer bucket, tilting to do so. Remove the crank unit and carefully clean off the lid of the freezer container, making sure no water or salt gets into the container. Remove the dasher and scrape off the ice cream from

it back into the container. Scrape down the ice cream from the sides of the container and pack the ice cream. Cover the top of the container with a sheet of aluminum foil and replace the lid. The ice cream will become harder during the ripening.

To ripen the ice cream: Repack the freezer bucket with ice and coarse salt, using 4 cups of ice to 1 cup of salt, layering the salt and ice until the bucket is full. Cover the top of the freezer with several thicknesses of newspapers or with burlap bags or some other heavy cloth or canvas. Set the freezer in a cool place and allow the ice cream to ripen for about 2 hours and then serve in your prettiest bowls.

Variation: Nuts, candy, fruits, coffee, chocolate, and spices can be added to homemade vanilla ice cream and the only key concern is determining when to make the additions.

Revival in progress at Soul Saving Holy Church in Detroit, Michigan.

Sweet Temptations

Flavoring and spices, such as peppermint, cinnamon, or almond can replace the vanilla extract and should be added to the scalded milk, as can a square or two of unsweetened chocolate. A cup of strong brewed coffee can replace a cup of milk.

Before ripening the ice cream, you can also stir in 2 cups of crushed fruit or berries, or a few handfuls of crushed peppermint sticks, peanut or pecan brittle, or chocolate chips and delight both children and grownups alike.

PHOTO CREDITS

Chapter 1: *p. 7, top; p. 9:* Milbert Orlando Brown; *p. 7, bottom; p. 33:* Angela Peterson; *p. 7, center; p. 23:* Schomburg Center for Research in Black Culture, Austin Hansen Collection; *p. 19, p. 42:* Hayden Roger Celestin; *p. 27:* Gloria Johnson.

Chapter 2: *p. 53, bottom; p. 62:* Jewell Rutledge; *p. 53, top; p. 64:* J. Henson; *p. 55:* James Powell; *p. 80:* Milbert Orlando Brown; *p. 85:* Gloria Johnson.

Chapter 3: *p. 89, left; p. 107:* Jewell Rutledge; *p. 89, right; p. 104:* William Ransom; *p. 91:* James Powell; *p. 108:* Hayden Roger Celestin; *p. 122:* Robert Rawls.

Chapter 4: *p. 127, top; p. 132:* David Grace; *p. 127, bottom; p. 128:* Schomburg Center for Research in Black Culture, Austin Hansen Collection; *p. 141; p. 172:* Jewell Rutledge; *p. 145:* William Ransom; *p. 150; p. 165:* Hayden Roger Celestin.

Chapter 5: *p. 177, top; p. 182:* J. Henson; *p. 177, bottom; p. 204:* Gloria Richardson; *p. 191:* Milbert Orlando Brown; *p. 204:* Jacob Terrell; *p. 213:* Gloria Johnson.

Chapter 6: *p. 217, top:* Hayden Roger Celestin; *p. 217, bottom; p. 218; p. 222; p. 243; p. 246:* Milbert Orlando Brown; *p. 225:* Gloria Richardson; *p. 237:* Jewell Rutledge.

Chapter 7: *p. 267; p. 280; p. 285:* Cherie Whyms; *p. 287:* James Powell.

Chapter 8: *p. 297, top:* Milbert Orlando Brown; *p. 297, bottom; p. 300; p. 307; p. 339:* Hayden Roger Celestin; *p. 298:* Schomburg Center for Research in Black Culture, Austin Hansen Collection.

INDEX

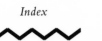

Index

Index

Index

Thermometer:
  oven, 311
  for testing, 256, 289
Thomas, Annie, 316
Thomas, Clifford, 144–46
Thomas, Florence, 219–20
Thomas, Irene, 144–46, 160
Tillman, Thurmond, Reverend, *107*
Tomato:
  sauce, 101
  soup, lentil and, 116–17
Tubbs, Letha, *218*
Turkey:
  defrosting guidelines, 256, 261
  memories of, 255–56, 293
  recipes:
    Men's Club chili, 280
    roast turkey, 257–58
    smoked turkey, 260–62
    thermometer for, 256
Turmeric, 55
Turnips:
  mixed greens recipe, 130
  primer on, 142

Unbleached all-purpose flour, 15, 299

Vegetables, *see specific types*
  hot pepper, 153–54
  okra, green, 151–52
  potatoes:
    sweet, 160–63
    white, 165–70
  recipes:
    batter-fried, 149–50
    salad, squash, 159
    soup, rice-, 73
    summer squash, 155–58
Vinson, Darryl and Shelda, 133

Waffles, Saturday, 27–29
Wallace, Vance, *280*

Waxwood, Susie B., 171–72
Wehani rice, 58
Wells, Jazzmin, *27*
Wells, Marion, 30, 55–56, 159, 264, 274
Wells, Ruth, Dr., 84, *85*
Wells Restaurant (Harlem), 26
West Hunter Street Baptist Church (Atlanta),
  30, 55, 159, 264, 274
Westminster Presbyterian Church (Los
  Angeles), 5, 248–49, 252
Wheat flour, 50
Whigham, Mary Lee, 13
White, Helen, 33, 73
White, John, 208, 215
White, Levord, Laura, and Lee, 151
White, Roy, 162, 245
White, Victoria, 208
White potatoes:
  memories of, 164
  potato salad, 165–67
White rice, 58
White roux, 214–15
Whole wheat:
  bread, 48–49
  flour, 15–16
Whyms, Cherie, 60
Wild rice:
  characteristics of, 58, 71
  history of, 71
  pecan, 58
  pilaf recipe, 70
Williams, Celestine, 19–20
Williams, John, 305
Williams, Lovie, 96, 305, 308
Williams, Nathaniel, *280*
Witherspoon Street Presbyterian Church
  (Princeton, NJ), 171
Wood:
  in grilling process, 192, 260–62
  for smoking meats, 282–83

Yeast:
  breads, *see* Yeast breads
  guidelines for, 37, 43

Index